By Still Waters

ANITA HIGMAN & MARIAN LESLIE

By Still Waters

365 Devotions to Quiet & Refresh Your Soul

BARBOUR BOOKS
An Imprint of Barbour Publishing, Inc.

Published by Barbour Books, an imprint of Barbour Publishing, Inc., 1810 Barbour Drive, Uhrichsville, Ohio 44683, www.barbourbooks.com

Our mission is to inspire the world with the life-changing message of the Bible.

Member of the
Evangelical Christian
Publishers Association

Dedication

To Shannon Perry

Thank you for the inspiration, the music,
the friendship, and the laughter.
You are an amazing gift to this world!

ANITA HIGMAN

To Joanna

You are the picture of grace under fire—
and that example is a blessing to many,
including me. Love, joy, and much,
much peace to you, my friend.

MARIAN LESLIE

Introduction

By *Still Waters* is a collection of 365 devotions that will remind you daily that God is not only there, but He wants you to come away with Him to rest by still waters—to capture your heart with His winsome love—to restore you, quiet you, woo you, inspire you, stroll with you, and beautify you all the way to your soul. May you delight in this journey. . . .

Joy Comes in the Morning

Weeping may stay for the night,
but rejoicing comes in the morning.
PSALM 30:5 NIV

*I*mpossible. Sometimes that one word describes the day perfectly. Right? Other words that might come to mind are *dreadful*, *unredeemable*, *unbearable*—with a little of the ridiculous thrown in.

Some days feel like all that can go wrong has indeed gone wrong. The world has done its worst.

How do you overcome traumas and disappointments? How can you rise above chronic illness and loss? With the heart knowledge of a real friendship with a real God. When all the pretty words of the world crumble away like fool's gold, the promises of God remain as solid as granite.

Even when circumstances appear hopeless, He really is working things for our good. God Almighty can—in His supernatural power—wash away the terrors of the night. He alone can bring peace and joy in the morning. If you don't feel like singing, that's okay. If you weep, He weeps with you. If you doubt, He's still there.

Reach out to Him. See what good things the Lord has for you.

Lord, help me to know that You are powerful—the whole earth
is under Your authority—and yet You are attentive and gentle
enough to cradle me in Your steadfast love. Amen. —AH

Dust Dwellers

Let those who dwell in the dust wake up and shout for joy.
ISAIAH 26:19 NIV

When the sun's rays stream in through the window, children like to pound the couch cushions. Thousands of particles turn and fly and tumble in the sun-warmed air.

It's so much nicer to think of it as a dust-fairy celebration than a sign of household neglect.

We are dust dwellers. It does not matter if you dust once a year or once a day, every time that light shines into your home, dust will appear. Most of us have no idea how many layers of dust we're living with at all until that light reveals it.

Isaiah 26 speaks of "those who dwell in the dust." They are those who dwell in the dust of nations leveled to the ground by the Lord for their disregard of the oppressed. And they are those who choose to live in a dust cloud instead of following the clear path God makes for us.

The truth is, if you are a dust dweller, chances are you miss a lot. But when the light of God's glory starts to shine in your life, you can't help but see that He is the way to perfect peace. He is the Rock eternal. He is the one who can accomplish all that we cannot—even dusting. And that's something to wake up and shout for joy about!

Lord, establish peace in my life today. Shine Your glory in my life and help me see beyond the dust. Amen. —ML

Traveling Light

"Take my yoke upon you and learn from me, for I am gentle and humble in heart, and you will find rest for your souls. For my yoke is easy and my burden is light."
MATTHEW 11:29–30 NIV

As tourists, we tend to put *waaay* too much stuff in our suitcases, and then we drag that luggage around until we think our arms will fall off. That's when we ask ourselves, "Did I really need that fifth pair of strappy sandals or that pile of potentially useless gizmos like that battery-powered de-nubber for my sweaters?" No, probably not, but we are determined to carry it all. Just in case. Right?

And so it goes with life. We tend to lug around too much stuff—burdens we were never meant to carry—until we think our spirits might collapse from the weight of it all. But when we hand our baggage over to the Lord—all that doubt and sin and regret and fear and bitterness and failure and sorrow—well, we can suddenly move our focus to the beautiful world God has given us on this earthly journey. All the blessings. All the beauties. All the love. Traveling light never felt so good.

Lord, show me how to give You all my heavy burdens and leave them at Your feet. Amen. —AH

The Real Deal

*"I no longer call you servants, because a servant
does not know his master's business. Instead, I have
called you friends, for everything that I learned from
my Father I have made known to you."*

JOHN 15:15 NIV

*A*ll our lives we search for at least one good and true and
loyal friend. Don't we? One who loves us lavishly, without
reservation. One who doesn't pretend to love us because we
have something to offer in return—fame, money, prestige, fa-
vors, or business prospects. One who knows us truly all the way
through—even those sorry, sinful parts—and loves us anyway.
One who's in the relationship for the long haul. No. Matter. What.

In case you haven't known that truest, dearest friend, it is
Jesus of Nazareth. He's the real deal. He is the most intimate
friend you'll ever find, the most trusted confidante you'll ever tell
your secrets to, and the most cherishing of lovers—right down to
your very soul. And Jesus not only wants to be with you for the
here and now, but for all time. Now that's true love!

So, seek the friendship. Embrace the love, the mercy, and
the grace of Christ. It's right here waiting for you.

*Oh Lord, thank You for loving me and for
calling me friend! Amen.* —AH

When We Think Praying Matters Not

*When the wine was gone, Jesus' mother said to him,
"They have no more wine." "Woman, why do you involve
me?" Jesus replied. "My hour has not yet come." His mother
said to the servants, "Do whatever he tells you."*

JOHN 2:3–5 NIV

We pray and pray and pray some more. Sometimes we're
caught murmuring, "If in the end God is going to do
what He wants, then what is the point of praying?" A perfectly
honest question.

In the book of John, we see that Jesus wasn't planning on
creating more wine at the wedding at Cana when they ran out,
and yet His mother had faith that He would. And later in this
passage we discover that Jesus did indeed make the wine after
all. Not just any wine, but the best. Perhaps we can glean from
these verses that we can turn the heart of God when we pray.
He won't always give us exactly what we want when we want
it, but He is swayed by our prayers and petitions.

Jesus set the example for us by praying to the Father while
He was on earth, and His prayers were answered in a mighty
way. That should encourage us. When we talk to our Lord, He is
not only listening, but He will be faithful to move on our behalf!

*Lord, thank You for hearing my prayers and for
supplying my every need. Amen. —AH*

For the Beauty of It

*When God began creating the heavens and the earth,
the earth was a shapeless, chaotic mass, with the
Spirit of God brooding over the dark vapors.*
GENESIS 1:1–2 TLB

Have you ever created something so excellent, so beautiful, that it made your heart ache with joy? That it made you sigh in your spirit and know there is a God? Perhaps a watercolor painting that captures an orchid so flawlessly, it's as if you could reach out and pluck it. Or a strain of music on the cello that sounds so sweetly melancholic, it makes your heart smile. Or an arrangement of words that so elegantly expresses your love for someone that your hand naturally comes to rest over your heart.

Do you think God felt these emotions when He created the heavens and the earth? All the vast array of splendor and mysteries and breathtaking wonder? Perhaps He did. We are, after all, made in His image, so we would inherit some of the same emotions.

Creating is yet one more way to connect with the One who created all things—including you. Why don't you create something today for the beauty of it and then offer it to the Lord as a gift? It will be one of those "by still waters" kinds of moments you will want to experience over and over and over.

*Lord, show me what we can create together today. I am
excited about the possibilities! Amen. —AH*

He Wants You Back

For I am convinced that neither death nor life,
neither angels nor demons, neither the present nor the
future, nor any powers, neither height nor depth, nor
anything else in all creation, will be able to separate us
from the love of God that is in Christ Jesus our Lord.
ROMANS 8:38–39 NIV

You might think you've sinned too much. Gone too far. Hated too much and loved too little. Cheated and caroused, judged and gossiped. And then lied and denied it all with abandon. Maybe there was a season when you even thought that you could live life without God. Now you realize that without God, nothing good exists. Truly nothing but a hopeless, barren wasteland. Please don't let the enemy of your soul keep you from those clean, cooling waters of repentance and the exquisite joy of coming home.

Nothing can separate you from the love of God. You can run back into His arms. Right now. He will forgive you for all your sins. All. And He will remember them no more. Let His redemptive power flow through you, restoring your soul. Drink it in. Smile again. Sing songs of splendor. Yes, God loves you. He wants you back. For now. For always.

Lord, thank You that when I go astray and
become the worst prodigal daughter, You always
welcome me home. Amen. —AH

May We Gasp at the Wonder!

*Whoever conceals their sins does not prosper, but the
one who confesses and renounces them finds mercy.*

PROVERBS 28:13 NIV

Imagine you're at a banquet, and you can't quite see the
people seated on your side of the table because the person
next to you is blocking your view. When your seatmate finally
leans back in his chair, and you can see your table companions
clearly, you gasp in wonder. Little did you know, all the while
you were eating and chatting away, you had been dining with
someone you truly love.

All our lives we have been in the midst of the most exalted
company of all—the King of kings and the Lord of lords! But
our view gets hindered with sin. The good news is that when
we confess our transgressions, the Lord offers us mercy. He will
forgive us and cleanse us from all unrighteousness.

May we gasp in wonder that the Lord is always in our midst!
He is here, ready to listen, to guide, to forgive and restore, to sup
with us in intimate communion, and to love us like we've never
been loved before. Now that's a dinner guest like none other!

*Lord Jesus, thank You for forgiving my sins.
Please help me to resist the temptations of this world
and to follow You more closely. Amen. —AH*

It All Has Meaning

Then, following him, Simon Peter also came. He entered the tomb and saw the linen cloths lying there. The wrapping that had been on his head was not lying with the linen cloths but was folded up in a separate place by itself.
JOHN 20:6–7 CSB

In this dark, war-torn, sin-stained world we live in, watching the news almost requires depression meds. Let's face it, these are anything but peaceful times on our earth. So, what is the one thing that can calm our worries and soothe our feverish brow?

Knowing the promise of Jesus.

It's interesting to note that in some upscale restaurants, the waiter will drop by to fold your napkin after you excuse yourself to go to the restroom. Why do they do that? Because the staff knows you are coming back. That is surely why Jesus folded the grave cloth that wrapped His head. He not only told us over and over in His Word that He will return, but even in that gesture of folding His burial cloth, He wanted to leave us a clear and hope-filled message. "Yes, I am coming back."

When we sweat world events, let us ever be reminded of this promise of Christ. It's a vow that changes everything—the way we live in this world, the way we hope for the future, and even the way we deal with the evening news.

Jesus, I am grateful for Your pledge to return, and I am filled with joyous expectation! Come, Lord Jesus, come! Amen. —AH

One Who Will Never Disappoint

Because he turned his ear to me,
I will call on him as long as I live.
PSALM 116:2 NIV

People try to listen to us. They really do. But husbands will eventually glaze over after a while. Maybe even frown in exasperation or nod off right in the middle of one of our "stories from our crazy day." Sometimes friends are too busy to listen, too exhausted from their long day at work, or they are so weighted down with their own burdens they can't seem to focus on us. Bottom line? When it comes to human beings truly listening to you and really understanding you, well, everyone will eventually disappoint you. Everyone—even the most faithful spouse, the most trusted pastor, the most beloved friend.

But there is one friend who will never disappoint us, and that is Christ our Lord. He will turn His ear to you and He will listen. No exasperated frowns, no glazing over, and no nodding off. Are we fully embracing this wonderful blessing? This kind of warm attention, this tender affection, this lavish love?

The time is now to call on Him. To be heard. To be understood. To be loved.

Oh Lord, how happy You make me, knowing
that You are always there, hearing me, loving me.
May we always stay in close communion. Amen. —AH

The Elephant in the Room

*For all have sinned and fall short of the glory of God,
and all are justified freely by his grace through
the redemption that came by Christ Jesus.*
ROMANS 3:23–24 NIV

The elephant in the room.

It's called sin. No one wants to look at it, let alone acknowledge it and repent from it. Why? One spiritually deadly word—*pride*. Humans hate admitting they've done anything wrong, so we listen to the whispers that tell us that if we ignore sin, the problem will go away.

Beware of a popular movement that promotes self-compassion, which does not acknowledge sin but promises emotional wellness by simply letting yourself off the hook. This thinking is opposite from what the Bible teaches. This practice is like putting a bandage over a filthy wound. There can be no healing. Only more pain.

We need to say, "Hey, I see this sin in my life. It's real, and it's destroying me. Jesus, I recognize You as the only way, the truth, and the life. Please forgive me. Set me free from the clutches of sin. I want to live with You, now and for all eternity."

Then comes real freedom. Real healing. Real peace—as gentle and inviting as the waters lapping up on the shores of an irresistibly beautiful pond. May every one of us find that place, that peace.

*Oh Lord, I confess my sins to You. Thank You
for Your mercy and forgiveness. Amen.* —AH

Let Us Live Free

Get rid of all bitterness, rage and anger, brawling and slander, along with every form of malice. Be kind and compassionate to one another, forgiving each other, just as in Christ God forgave you.
EPHESIANS 4:31–32 NIV

They say that revenge is sweet, but whoever came up with that adage was not considering the toll on the human heart. We may convince ourselves that retaliation is a jewel that can be polished with pride, but we soon discover it is really a burdensome stone around our souls, dragging us into the depths. Justice in a court of law is not the same thing as taking vengeance on a fellow sojourner, and the latter should be left to God alone, who knows how to administer the perfect combination of righteous judgment and mercy.

Let us live free from these vengeful tendencies as well as other offenses such as rage and slander and bitterness. With the Lord's help, we can walk free of hate and live a life that focuses on His pure and perfect love.

Lord, please don't let me give in to the temptation of thinking it's my right to settle the score with people, but instead help me to be kind and compassionate in all my dealings, forgiving others as You've forgiven me. Amen. —AH

Nearer to Each Other

*"I led them with cords of human kindness, with ties of love.
To them I was like one who lifts a little child to the cheek,
and I bent down to feed them."*

HOSEA 11:4 NIV

God has many attributes, but one facet of His character is love. Hosea 11:4 gives us a glimpse into His tender care for us when God speaks of leading His people with the cords of human kindness and His ties of love. This verse doesn't just refer to people in Bible times, but to us in our modern world.

The Lord is reminding us that He is so completely in love with us and cares for us so dearly, that He refers to Himself as a parent lifting us up to His cheek, so we can be nearer to Him. Then He feeds us tenderly with His strong and loving hand.

When life appears to be spinning out of control, our hearts long to know such comforting words—that God still loves us, in spite of our sin, rebellion, and denial. Our spirits call out in welcoming laughter and joy to hear this good news! How can anyone turn away from such love?

Lord, I am awed, humbled, and profoundly grateful that You loved me enough to send Your Son to die for me. I love You, Lord, with all my heart. Amen. —AH

The Best Night's Sleep

*"Peace I leave with you; my peace I give you.
I do not give to you as the world gives. Do not
let your hearts be troubled and do not be afraid."*

JOHN 14:27 NIV

As Christians, our spirits should feel as calm as palm fronds gently swaying in a warm tropical breeze. After all, we are trusting in the Lord for all our needs, right? But many times, the jittery anxiousness in our inner being more closely resembles a palm tree bent low, as if battered and frayed in hurricane-force winds. Big difference in those two visuals. Even when we are at rest we are not always at peace. Can you relate?

As Christians, we are promised real peace from our Lord. Not the counterfeit serenity the world promotes and peddles. But a lasting, supernatural, quiet joy that settles deep in the soul. The kind that gives us a refreshing night's sleep. The warmest laughter. And the most genuine smiles.

"Don't let your heart be troubled," our Lord reminds us. Trust in Him. Accept the peace Christ offers freely, and share it with all those who cross your path.

*Lord, I trust in You for all my needs, and I accept
the peace You speak of in Your Word—the peace
that passes all understanding. Amen. —AH*

Getting Ahead of God

*But do not forget this one thing, dear friends:
With the Lord a day is like a thousand years,
and a thousand years are like a day.*

2 PETER 3:8 NIV

When it comes to God, His timing is everything. But does mankind usually wait patiently on God? In the Bible we read how Abraham and Sarah got ahead of God by making a baby "their" way, which delivered disastrous results. And we see many similar "human fixes" today in our own lives, with equally destructive effects.

Why then do we still cling to this mode of operation? Perhaps we secretly harbor the thought, *God is too busy to take care of all our needs, so we'll help Him take care of things.* Many times in the Bible when people prayed to God, they didn't receive what they wanted at that moment. Since God is all-knowing, only He knows the perfect timing for everything. He has a vantage point that is far different from ours—it is not a finite perspective, but eternal. After all, it says in 2 Peter, "With the Lord a day is like a thousand years, and a thousand years are like a day."

In our fast-paced world, we want everything. Right. This. Minute. But there is much virtue in patience. It's yet another way to live a "by still waters" kind of life in the Lord.

*Lord Jesus, please help me to wait on
You with faith and patience. Amen.* —AH

If Not for Love?

The Word became flesh and made his dwelling among us.
We have seen his glory, the glory of the one and only Son,
who came from the Father, full of grace and truth.
JOHN 1:14 NIV

Why, Lord, did You come to be with us? All that magnificent glory—enough to fill the universe—and yet You willingly humbled Yourself to the confines of a mother's womb. All that growing up with brothers and sisters and laughter and tears and noise and bother. All that education in the woodworking profession to help Your earthly father in the family business. All that training up in scripture and gaining of wisdom so You could begin Your miraculous mission. And then finally, taking on the betrayal of friends and the unfathomable suffering we know You endured. Why?

Lord, I know why You came to be with us—it was all for love. You loved us enough to save us from ourselves. To offer Your hand of friendship and redemption. To bring us the truth that would set us free. All we need to do is say yes!

Oh Lord, my answer is yes! My heart is overflowing
with gratitude that You in all Your majesty felt the
desire to come down to live among us and offer us life
eternal. May I always follow Your grace and truth.
I look forward to being with You in heaven and
knowing that kind of love for all eternity. Amen. —AH

Are You That Lost Sheep?

Then Jesus told them this parable: "Suppose one of you has a hundred sheep and loses one of them. Doesn't he leave the ninety-nine in the open country and go after the lost sheep until he finds it? And when he finds it, he joyfully puts it on his shoulders and goes home."

LUKE 15:3–6 NIV

Being utterly lost in the middle of a big bustling city can be truly scary. Why? Because of all the unknowns out there. Maybe the strangers we meet will wish us harm. What if darkness falls before we can discover which way we went wrong? In our frantic state of mind, we begin to search for a friendly face, someone in authority who might guide us where we need to be.

That is so much like our spiritual lives here on earth. We are all lost and in desperate need of someone to save us. Maybe we don't know all the missteps we made, but we know something is very wrong. We have a mighty rescuer in Jesus. He is more than a friendly face in the bustling crowd of strangers. He is the only one who can guide us safely home. He is hoping you will always call out to Him whenever you have need.

Lord, some days I find myself so lost and alone. Please place me on Your sturdy shoulders and carry me back home. Amen. —AH

Embrace That Promise!

*"My Father's house has many rooms; if that were not so, would
I have told you that I am going there to prepare a place for
you? And if I go and prepare a place for you, I will come back
and take you to be with me that you also may be where I am."*
JOHN 14:2–3 NIV

Tears flow easily on this side of eternity, especially when it
comes to saying goodbye. As a baby, Mom leaves you in
someone else's arms, and that tiny "letting go" feels scary and
unnatural. When the school bus driver rumbles down the road
with your precious cargo for the very first time, teardrops trail
down your cheeks. Then there are the empty-nest send-offs, the
friends who move away, and worst of all, that dreadful loss when
your beloved is taken away in death. You ache so deeply, you
feel you may never recover.

But as Christians, we are promised to one day reside with
the Lord—in a special place that He's prepared for us—where
there will be no more heart-wrenching farewells or tears or
loss. To have that daily assurance from God's Word can give
us peace that will sustain us through the most grueling days
and through those nights that threaten to keep us sleepless and
sorrow filled. Embrace that promise. He is coming back!

*Thank You, Lord, for heaven—the land
of no more sad goodbyes, but instead a
place of Your joyful presence! Amen. —AH*

A Longing Deep Within

*He has made everything beautiful in its time. He has
also set eternity in the human heart; yet no one can
fathom what God has done from beginning to end.*
ECCLESIASTES 3:11 NIV

As humans, we chose our own way—a way that led away
from the light and the beauty and the wholeness and the
love. Away from God.

But we have a living legacy—that mankind was made
in God's image. Even after our epic fall into sin, that sublime
rendering is still imprinted deep in our hearts.

Every one of us comes to a time in our lives when we
know that there is more to life than just making do, day after
day after day. That this transient world can't be all there is to
our existence. We ache for a paradise lost—for that exquisite beauty and wonder beyond our brokenness, for that intimate
relationship with our Maker. We long for the time when we
could walk with Him in the cool of the evening.

Jesus came to fulfill that deep longing in our hearts. To
offer us mercy and forgiveness. To bring us back to a place of
beauty in our souls. To restore us to a place of fellowship with
the Father. To offer us paradise!

*Lord, thank You for setting eternity in my heart.
May I never be parted from You! Amen.* —AH

Shrinking Violets

For the Spirit God gave us does not make us timid,
but gives us power, love and self-discipline.
2 TIMOTHY 1:7 NIV

We are not always bright, bold, and beautiful in our faith. Sometimes we can be half-hearted in our walk, ineffectual in our interactions and relationships in the world, and maybe even cower a bit when dealing with Satan and all his temptations and influences on our lives.

But 2 Timothy reminds us that the Spirit of God gives us something far from a "shrinking violet" mind-set and lifestyle. As Christians, we have every reason to display true grit as we walk in God's glory. We can march forward confidently with conviction and poise, and with the Lord's help, we can courageously stand against the attacks of the enemy. The Lord gives us power and self-discipline to accomplish all that He has called us to do, and because of our great hope in the Lord's promises, we can find joy and laughter and love!

So, if you find yourself being a shrinking violet, ask God to turn you into a sunflower—bright, bold, and beautiful—in the Son!

Thank You, Lord, that You have given me not only the desire to live a triumphant Christian life, but You have given me all the supernatural power to make it happen! Amen. —AH

Oh How Dearly You Love Me!

See what great love the Father has lavished on us, that we should be called children of God! And that is what we are!
1 JOHN 3:1 NIV

Have you ever smothered your child in kisses? Those moments usually come when your heart is merrily and utterly besieged with emotion for your child—feelings of delight and devotion and pure affection for your beloved wee one.

John tells us that God has called us His children, and He has lavished love on us. That word *lavished* is intriguing, since it means heaping and smothering and showering. There is no holding back or skimping with that word. It's all-out love.

In the Bible, the Lord makes it clear that He loves us ardently, in words and in action. The most significant deed was creating a perfect plan of redemption with His only Son, Jesus. He didn't do it out of some distant and disconnected duty to His creation, but because we are His sons and daughters. And as we find delight and joy in our children, the Lord finds joy in us.

How have you responded to such sweet and boundless love?

I am so humbled and happy, knowing how greatly You love me, Lord. I love You too! May I always bring You delight in all I do. Amen. —AH

The Darkest Valley

Even though I walk through the darkest valley,
I will fear no evil, for you are with me;
your rod and your staff, they comfort me.
PSALM 23:4 NIV

Some days we face such brutal news that it feels as though death is knocking at our door. Maybe not a literal death. But boy, oh boy, when too many things go wrong with too many of the people we care about, well, it can feel like a kind of death.

What can we do in times when we walk through those darkest valleys? When all seems lost? And maybe even when it feels that a physical death would be welcome over the torment of this life?

The Bible does not promise us rosy days all our earthly lives. In fact, Jesus told us there would be trouble in this life. But Jesus overcame the world. And the Bible does give us promises—that the Lord will not leave us when we're in those dreadful valleys. With Christ by our side we have no reason to fear evil or dark valleys or even death.

Take comfort in knowing the Lord is with you. Not just in a faraway place. He's right here with you. Now. Always. Know this. Believe it. Speak it out loud until it makes it from your lips down to your heart.

Oh Lord, I am walking that darkest valley now.
Please sustain me. Be ever near me. And let
me rise up again in joy! Amen. —AH

The Perils of the Journey

*Because you are my help, I sing in the shadow of
your wings. I cling to you; your right hand upholds me.*
PSALM 63:7–8 NIV

If you've ever been a hiker for long, you know there are perils with this rigorous pastime. You might discover slippery steps next to a rock face and a cliff below that plummets to the ocean. Or a boardwalk that seems way too narrow as it passes over a wild terrain. Or a bridge that swings precariously over a canyon.

When your heart beats like a bongo, your palms go clammy, and you think you're not going to make it, you tend to cling to something, right? A railing on the boardwalk or bridge. A rope along the bluff. Or we drop down and latch on to the very ground itself.

Sounds good when discussing hiking, but when it comes to this perilous life, we tend to cling to what can't even steady us, let alone keep us upright. The list of things humans latch on to when they are filled with fear is as long and creative as it is useless. The only One worth cleaving to is Christ. Psalms says He will uphold us as we cling to Him—and that because of His help we can actually sing in the shadow of His wings. Clinging was never so real and never felt so good!

*Praise You, God, for Your promises as we press
forward on this perilous journey! Amen. —AH*

Come Away with Me

He makes me lie down in green pastures,
he leads me beside quiet waters.
PSALM 23:2 NIV

Another day has tanked, and you're a heartbeat away from giving up. You look up and wonder, "Is there more?"

Then you hear the voice of the Good Shepherd. If you let Him, He will lead you to quiet pastures of green, green grass. Yes, give yourself a moment of repose on that soft patch of meadow. You finally release a breath of air that feels as though it's been held tightly for a lifetime. Then the breeze sighs through a nearby willow tree. Sheep graze and bumblebees whirl. Water from a pond glistens diamond-like as it laps against the shore. You rest. You listen. And after some soul sharing with the Lord, your heart begins to unfold like the petals of a rose.

In that deep rest, you come to know that your spirit was made for so much more than what you see in this finite and fallen world. You were meant for joy, full and overflowing. You were meant for creative pleasures beyond human imaginings. You were meant for a divine dance with the One who knows you and loves you best. You were meant not only for a few days of heaven but an eternity of it!

Can you hear the voice of the Good Shepherd? "Come away with Me."

Lord Jesus, please lead me daily to those green
pastures and by those still waters. Amen. —AH

You Are Mine

*There is no fear in love. But perfect love drives
out fear, because fear has to do with punishment.
The one who fears is not made perfect in love.*
1 JOHN 4:18 NIV

It usually happens like this. It's about three a.m., and you wake up with a start. Maybe from a stomach cramp. A dog's bark. A bad dream. The room is still dark, and you need to get back to sleep. The problem is, your brain is now working overtime and fear comes calling with a thousand dreadful possibilities. A layoff at work. The same cancer your father had. A sin revisited. A friend's betrayal. The sudden death of a beloved relative. It's all just too much.

At the height of your terror, you cry out to Jesus. In one supernatural moment—you remember whom you belong to. You can hear that heavenly whisper, "You are mine." Yes, you are in a relationship with the one who knows unspeakable suffering. He understands all the things that terrorize you in the darkest of nights. And He is the only one capable of cooling your feverish brow.

And so the night lightens with love—Christ's love for you— and that love is brighter and warmer than a thousand stars and more than enough to extinguish those night terrors. Yes, He is right there, embracing you with His perfect love.

*Lord, thank You for helping me back to sleep when
my spirit becomes riddled with fears. Amen.* —AH

The God of Open Doors

"Ask and it will be given to you; seek and you will find;
knock and the door will be opened to you."
MATTHEW 7:7 NIV

Boy, oh boy, this old world sure can be a friendless kind of place at times. Kids grow up feeling left out of various social circles—in sports, in clubs, on the bus, in the cafeteria as well as in the classroom, and unfortunately sometimes even in the church youth group. You name it, and kids can and will be left behind, sometimes unintentionally, other times intentionally. And grown-ups aren't suddenly immune to this problem when they get out of school. They visit social media sites in hopes of staying happily involved and connected with others, only to discover that at times they feel truly disenchanted and more lonesome than ever.

But where mankind fails us—and people *will* fail us—God does not. We are reminded in Matthew 7:7 that He is a God of open doors. If you seek Him, you will indeed find Him. If you knock, He will open the door for you. No closed heart or locked doors or social snubs there. Doesn't that sound lovely? Doesn't that sound warm, right down to your soul?

Imagine being invited into the company of the living Savior. Right here, right now.

Thank You, Lord, that I serve a God of
invitations and open doors! Amen. —AH

The Mother of All Hugs

"But the Helper (Comforter, Advocate, Intercessor—Counselor, Strengthener, Standby), the Holy Spirit, whom the Father will send in My name [in My place, to represent Me and act on My behalf], He will teach you all things. And He will help you remember everything that I have told you."

JOHN 14:26 AMP

When life goes awry and your eye has begun that twitching thing, how do you comfort yourself? Maybe a hug, a scoop of gelato with chocolate sauce, a bouquet of fresh-cut roses, a walk in the sunshine, some good belly laughs over a favorite comedy movie, a lavender-scented bubble bath, chicken and dumplings, a latte with a dear friend, reading a page-turning novel, or even diving into a batch of warm clothes straight out of the dryer? *Ahhh*, yes. Comfy comforts.

But sometimes even all those delight-filled goodies won't be enough to calm us and sustain us. When it comes to serious comfort, we need the mother of all hugs. We need the Holy Spirit—Comforter, Advocate, Intercessor, Counselor, Strengthener, Standby. We need all of the above. When Jesus left this earth, He promised to not leave us as orphans, but to send the Holy Spirit. We can rely on His help. Always remember and take heart—in this lonesome world, we are never ever alone.

Holy Spirit, please comfort me, strengthen me, encourage me, teach me, and guide me in all I do. Amen. —AH

Such Plenty, Such Pleasure

"Yet he has not left himself without testimony: He has shown kindness by giving you rain from heaven and crops in their seasons; he provides you with plenty of food and fills your hearts with joy."

ACTS 14:17 NIV

Oh, those roly-poly pumpkins with curly, piglet-tail vines. We pick them, create carved masterpieces with them, eat them in a hundred different culinary ways, or we just roll them down the hill for fun. Yay!

Hard not to wonder what God's purpose was when He created a pumpkin. Was it to enchant the taste buds? For the beauty of it? For the sheer delight in its shape and color? Or maybe too, it was for the love of us, knowing someday He would see our faces light up over those golden fields—season after season, generation after generation—with smiles.

The pumpkin patch is only one wonder in the many harvest fields that we enjoy. As it says in Acts 14:17, rain from heaven brings us crops in their season. He gives us food and fills our hearts with joy. Praise God for such peaceful scenes, such plenty, and such pleasure!

Wonderful creator God, thank You for all Your kindness in creating the bounty of this earth and all its beauty. I am slain with joy! Amen. —AH

All the Bright Stars

They will have no fear of bad news;
their hearts are steadfast, trusting in the LORD.
PSALM 112:7 NIV

When we gaze up at a clear night sky, we can ponder two very singular features—the celestial lights, such as the moon and stars, or we can focus on the blackness and the daunting unknown of all that surrounds the many brilliant points of light.

So much like our spiritual lives. We can concentrate on the darkness—the evil tidings that come. Or we can choose to focus on the goodness of our God, the miracle of our existence, and the wonder of His unfailing love. We can use our free will to choose to trust, knowing that the Lord has been our help and strength in the past, and He will continue to be in the future.

The dark night of trouble will come in this life. Yes, from time to time, there will be bad news. We can't always trust people or circumstances or even ourselves, but we can count on the Lord. We can put our faith in the many bright stars of God's good nature, the promises in His Word, and His forever love.

Lord, when bad news comes, remind me of Your consistent
help, Your goodness, and Your love for me. Amen. —AH

The Book of Love

Your unfailing love, O LORD, is as vast as the heavens;
your faithfulness reaches beyond the clouds.
PSALM 36:5 NLT

As parents we long to love our children tenderly, unconditionally, sacrificially, and well beyond measure. Sometimes in a moment of joy and affection, we throw our arms open wide and say, "I love you, oh-so big. Well, no, even bigger!"

When we read the Bible, it's easy to get bogged down in theological debates and cultural differences we see in ancient times, but we shouldn't forget that the whole of the Bible can be seen as a book of love—God's profound devotion to His children. The Bible is a record of the creation of mankind, our collapse into sin, and the epic stories that led up to the greatest story of them all—the birth and death and resurrection of Jesus Christ—which offers us redemption from sin and restoration into the kingdom of God. This kind of sacrificial, unfailing love is as vast as the heavens, and it reaches beyond the clouds!

It is as if the Creator of the universe reached down with tender feelings of joy and affection for us, opened wide His arms, and said, "I love you oh-so big. Well, no, even bigger!"

I am so grateful, Lord God, that You have shown
us in Your Word how much You love us all—
love me—so very big. Amen. —AH

Where Peace Is Found

*"Peace I leave with you; my peace I give you.
I do not give to you as the world gives. Do not let
your hearts be troubled and do not be afraid."*
JOHN 14:27 NIV

At some point in our lives, we all gaze into the mirror to take one of those serious looks at our reflection. The kind of penetrating stare that goes so deeply we must be searching for signs of tumult or disquiet in the soul. We are hoping we find peace there, aren't we? That is what everybody wants—every last one of us.

In fact, mankind is in a frantic search for a stillness in one's soul. We will do anything for it. We try various religions, meditations, Eastern practices, medications—legal and some illegal—and we try to deify various people, objects, or even try to worship a variety of elements in nature. The Bible offers us clear wisdom and power on all matters of peace.

Jesus told us that He will give us peace. It is that simple, that profound, and that beautiful. The Lord is the only one capable of offering us a supernatural peace that passes all understanding. Accept the gift! Embrace the Giver!

*Lord, I thank You for real peace—that I don't have
to be afraid or troubled in this world! Amen. —AH*

A Wonky Mess

*Jesus replied, "No one who puts a hand to the plow
and looks back is fit for service in the kingdom of God."*
LUKE 9:62 NIV

Humans are notorious. We sweat the big stuff. We sweat the small stuff. We just sweat a lot.

We cannot seem to let go of the past. We fret over the future. We wring our hands over all the minutiae in our present lives. When we do that as Christians, Jesus says we aren't fit for service in His kingdom. That makes a lot of sense.

Jesus' plow illustration is effective in that when a farmer looks back while he is trying to plow, the rows will get crooked, and the field will become a wonky mess. When we keep doing that looking-back thing over our failures, regrets, confessed sins, and fears, we can't be fully fit for service. We will invariably stumble, lose our focus, our way. Maybe even lose our sleep and our health. We will be useless.

Because every minute we spend looking back, we can't give our full attention to praising, celebrating, caring, harvesting, serving, laughing, growing, communing, glorifying, creating, giving, delighting, sharing the Good News, fellowshipping, and loving!

It comes down to one word—*trust*. Where does your trust lie?

*Lord, I give You my past, my present, and my future.
Help me not to look back but to look forward
with anticipation and joy. Amen. —AH*

We Did It Our Way!

*We all, like sheep, have gone astray, each of
us has turned to our own way; and the Lord
has laid on him the iniquity of us all.*
Isaiah 53:6 niv

O ver the centuries, mankind hasn't changed much. Not really.
Sure we may have a double shot of espresso instead of a
double shot of goat's milk. We might zoom across the freeway
in a sports car rather than lumber across a desert on a camel.
And we might wear stilettos instead of leather and wooden
sandals. But every one of us has gone our own way in this life.
Like tottering sheep along a sheer cliff, we have gone astray
from our Master and we're close to peril at every turn. In modern
times, we might even say it with a smug little smile, "Yes, we're
doing it our way!"

But "our way" never works. How many centuries will it take
for us to learn this vital truth? "Our way" is an exercise in futility
without God's help. And that celestial navigation starts with an
acknowledgment of sin. We are sinners. We can say it. But if
we confess our sins, we can move forward to a repentant heart,
forgiveness, and freedom. Then comes the peace that is sung
about in the hymns of old. Then comes the victory that brings a
heart full of joy. Then comes the spiritual growth and the beauty
of a life well lived!

Lord, please help me to do life Your way! Amen. —AH

The Bible according to Me

*All Scripture is God-breathed and is useful for teaching,
rebuking, correcting and training in righteousness,
so that the servant of God may be thoroughly
equipped for every good work.*
2 TIMOTHY 3:16–17 NIV

Living without the truth is like skipping through a building just as someone shuts off all the lights. Most likely, we will either slam into a wall full-force or fall headlong down a flight of stairs. In other words, there's going to be significant pain if we keep marching stubbornly into that darkness.

Since God created the world, it's only right that He should be the one who guides us with the light of His Word. But many people don't think the Lord's precepts are important, and many no longer even know what the Word of God says.

Today people are simply making the choice to believe whatever they want. That the Bible isn't God-breathed, but merely a general book of guidelines. They may feel they can twist the scripture to their own way of thinking—the Bible according to me—or simply leave out the verses that offend them. But this mind-set can only lead to more chaos and destruction, while following Christ and the Bible will bring us to a place of peace, refreshment, and renewal—a place where we can find all the deepest longings of our soul.

*Lord, may I read Your Word daily and follow
Your lead in every area of my life. Amen.* —AH

My Heavenly To-Do List

*The Spirit you received does not make you slaves,
so that you live in fear again; rather, the Spirit you
received brought about your adoption to sonship.
And by him we cry, "Abba, Father."*
ROMANS 8:15 NIV

Bake a cheesy casserole for my new neighbor. Check. Listen patiently to Aunt Zelda talk about her throbbing gout. Check. Whisk the kids off to school with a Bible verse and a kiss. Check. Look toward the heavens with a grateful heart. Check. Pray for my boss instead of threaten to quit. Check.

Okay. Another day done. Next!

See how simple life would be if God would give us a written to-do list on our mirrors every morning? Then, during the night, that list would miraculously renew itself, and we'd know each and every day exactly what we were to do. We could mark off our days and our lives as efficiently as a robot.

But we're not machines. We are unique creatures made in God's image, and what we have been offered from God through Christ is not at all like an impersonal daily to-do list. Romans 8:15 makes it obvious that we are adopted sons and daughters! We've been offered loving conversation, intimate closeness, and an eternal relationship with the Most High God!

Let us remember daily, it's not about the list—it's about the love.

Oh Lord, how glad I am that You and I are friends! Amen. —AH

The Father of Lights

*Every good gift and every perfect gift is from above,
and comes down from the Father of lights,
with whom there is no variation or shadow of turning.*
JAMES 1:17 NKJV

When we think of light, all sorts of delight-filled images come to mind, such as the peaceful glimmer of moonlight on water, fireflies that wink their way through the woods, cascades of sunlight spilling down from a cloud, the soft luminosity of fox fire, the glitter-spray of starlight, and the dazzling strikes of lightning. Even man-made lights of all kinds come from resources that our creator God made—who is also referred to as the Father of lights in James 1:17. Yes, He is the true source of all light, and these are His gifts to us.

But God's most beautiful gift of light will always be His Son, Jesus—who is called the Light of the world. With one look into His eyes, one touch of His hand, and one moment in the presence of His light, how can we ever be the same? Yes, the Father of lights has given us the greatest gift of all—redemption and eternity with Him. What ultimate peace and joy! Have you taken the time to open this radiant gift of light?

*Creator God, thank You that You have created such
beauty and light in this world. And thank You for
sending the greatest Light, Jesus Christ. Amen.* —AH

The Firstfruits of the Day

*"Be still before the LORD, all mankind, because he
has roused himself from his holy dwelling."*
ZECHARIAH 2:13 NIV

Absorbed. Swamped. Whirling. Harried. Good description of our modern workdays. So, when are we ever truly still? Do we give God back a kind of firstfruits of the day with our time? That is, the freshest part of the day before we drop from exhaustion? Do we make time for Bible reading, prayer, and being still before Him? Do we do it begrudgingly or out of love?

When we do spend time with the Lord, we should approach His throne with great anticipation. Expect good things as the Lord rises from His holy dwelling. To hear you. To answer you. To commune with you. To change you. To love you.

Yes, bask in His presence. The experience will alter all things. The way you see your day, your life, and eternity. The way you greet your neighbor. The way you work and play and eat and worship. The way you deal with hardships, raise your kids, use your talents, love yourself, and love all the rest of humanity. Time spent with God is never wasted—it is time given back to the One who created time in the first place, and the One who so graciously gave it to you as a gift.

*Lord, help me to always give You the loving
devotion You deserve! Amen. —AH*

The Master of Distraction

*"Martha, Martha," the Lord answered, "you are worried
and upset about many things, but few things are needed—
or indeed only one. Mary has chosen what is better,
and it will not be taken away from her."*

LUKE 10:41–42 NIV

Satan—the enemy of our souls—wants to distract us in any
way he can from what is truly important in our lives. He
keeps us chasing around, becoming downright fusspots over
minutia when what is vital is right before our eyes! Sometimes
our diversions can even be good deeds.

In the book of Luke, a woman named Martha was busy
preparing a large meal for her houseguests while her sister,
Mary, listened to Jesus' teaching. Martha was in the midst of a
courteous act, yes, but her sister had chosen more wisely. Mary
let the mundane things wait for a moment while she became still,
focusing on what was miraculous before her—Jesus.

What is the master of distraction tempting you with? What
keeps you from spending time in the Lord's presence, to bask
in His love, to grow in His grace, and to become the beautiful
woman He created you to be?

*Jesus, I don't want to be a workaholic. Please show
me how to find a balance between being industrious
and remembering to let You lead me to still waters
so that I might hear from You. Amen.* —AH

That Divine Design

"For I know the plans I have for you," declares the LORD, "plans to prosper you and not to harm you, plans to give you hope and a future."

JEREMIAH 29:11 NIV

Random.

Isn't that the word that sometimes slithers its way into our thinking when times get rough? Days when nothing makes sense and order and purpose don't seem to be any part of our universe?

And yet, even on those days, if we look—truly look with our souls—we can see design all around us. In the spectacular lacework of a spider's web. The elaborate and intricate patterns of a snowflake. In a million other handmade pieces of nature and in the very things we are moved to create. Yes, patterns and purpose are everywhere, and you are a part of that beautiful creative plan.

Design equals hope! So, believe not in the random, but in the real. Open your heart to the truth and the promise in Jeremiah 29:11. There is a God who loves you, who has a hope and a future for you, and He wants your story to have a most happy and heavenly ending!

Please show me the plans You have for me, Lord Jesus. I want to follow Your blueprint completely so that I may know Your purpose and experience Your joy. Amen. —AH

DAY 40

The End of Yourself

*They were at their wits' end. Then they cried out to the LORD
in their trouble, and he brought them out of their distress.*
PSALM 107:27–28 NIV

You're headed to bed, but you know you're just going through the motions. You already know there will be no sleep tonight—just like the other nights. Why? Your career has unraveled. Your friends aren't returning your calls. And your robust health is just a memory. It's as if life has strapped you into one of those medieval catapults and flung you into an abyss where no one can hear your weeping and wailing. Yes, you've officially come to the end of yourself.

The book of Psalms contains a great deal of these same kinds of lamentations of the heart. David had a lot of angst, and he felt close enough to God to come before Him to express a wide range of emotions. David did trust God to meet him in his distress and come to his rescue.

When you're troubled or you've come to the end of yourself, you too can cry out to the Almighty, who is the same God of power and faithfulness who heard and rescued David!

*Thank You, Lord, that I can bring all my worries
and needs to You. In Jesus' name I pray. Amen.* —AH

Soul Spa

If we confess our sins, he is faithful and just and will forgive us our sins and purify us from all unrighteousness.
1 JOHN 1:9 NIV

Okay, here's the spa experience in one word—*aah*. What a treat, right? To rest there on a warm massage table, letting your muscles relax and the tensions drain right out of you. Some types of therapeutic massages are even thought to be a detox for the body. How cool.

This concept of detoxification is big business, but what about a cleansing of the soul too? Wouldn't that be marvelous? "Okay, where can I get it done, and how much will it cost me?"

This soul spa procedure is free, and you don't have to drive anywhere! Sin is the spiritual toxin, and confession to Christ is like a detox for the soul. Yes, you can have this cleansing experience anytime, anywhere, and the price has already been paid up-front by the most loving, giving person to have ever walked this earth—Jesus of Nazareth. Why not accept the soul spa experience gift card (from Him) and come to know the warm and relaxing and restorative effects of forgiveness. It will change your life both now and in eternity.

Lord Jesus, I am so grateful for Your gift of salvation and the ability to confess my sins to You, knowing You will forgive me of all unrighteousness. Amen. —AH

Ready to Receive

*"Come to me, all you who are weary and burdened, and I
will give you rest. Take my yoke upon you and learn from me,
for I am gentle and humble in heart, and you will find rest for
your souls. For my yoke is easy and my burden is light."*
MATTHEW 11:28–30 NIV

Life is proficient at giving us some pretty brutal whammies.
Unexpectedly. Sharply. Memorably. And those worldly blows
have a way of staying with us, don't they? Whether they come
from other people, our own sin, this fallen world, or the attacks
of the enemy, those harsh life events keep our spirits in flinching
mode. It's almost as if we're locked that way, frozen in time,
until something—Someone—can set us free.

But God offers us the gentlest of words in Matthew 11:28–
30. Read them every time you have need. It is a passage that
makes us want to gently unwind on a hammock. Perhaps under
a cluster of willows where the sun is warm but the breeze is
cooling. And there, with our Lord by our side, we let all our
burdens go to Him.

Then when we finally unclench our spirits, we will be
freer—no longer to flinch and cower but to praise and receive!

*Lord, I thank You, that when I am weary and
burdened, You will give me rest. Amen. —AH*

Spiritual Grunge

*Bear with each other and forgive one another if
any of you has a grievance against someone.
Forgive as the Lord forgave you.*
COLOSSIANS 3:13 NIV

*G*rudge. What a word. It sounds and looks a lot like the word *grunge*. You know, like the black slimy stuff you have to clean out of your shower stall. I guess one could say that a grudge has some similar properties as grunge. They are both grimy things that become harder to get rid of the longer they hang around.

We fool ourselves with grudges, thinking that they are a good thing. We convince ourselves that those little resentments, envies, and bitter thoughts will balance the scales of injustice in our favor. They may make us feel like we are in control again, but that's only an illusion. Grudges are indeed as nasty and slimy as black mold. They won't bring us a smile—not a lasting one anyway. In the end, grudges will only make us sick.

The only way to a free, healthy, and happy life is to forgive. Easy? Never. Necessary? Absolutely. After all, when we've sinned and fallen short of the glory of God—over and over and over—the good Lord has been gracious and giving and compassionate enough to forgive us.

*Forgive me, Lord, for the grudges I hold against people.
Let me forgive them as You have forgiven me. Amen. —AH*

A New Kind of Refreshment

*"Now change your mind and attitude to God and turn to him
so he can cleanse away your sins and send you wonderful
times of refreshment from the presence of the Lord."*
ACTS 3:19 TLB

Aah, nothing like sipping on a flute of cold lemonade on a hot summer day. Or swaying to and fro on a porch swing as cooling breezes tickle your cheek. Or perhaps strolling hand in hand along a forest path as you discover the hidden beauties of nature. Sweet times of refreshment. Who doesn't want to sign up for that?

But God's Word takes refreshment to a whole new level. The Lord's love for us is so passionate that He doesn't want us to stay in our sin, but He desires to cleanse us from all those wrongdoings—all the offenses that weigh us down and keep us from doing life in the big and beautiful way He intended.

How do we begin? Simply confess your sins before God, let the Lord Jesus wash you clean, and bask in His healing presence. It will be like drinking a spiritual tonic laced with supernatural power!

*Lord, help me to change my attitude toward You. Cleanse
me from all my sins. I'm looking forward to wonderful
times of refreshment in Your presence! Amen. —AH*

These Present Sufferings

*Yet what we suffer now is nothing compared
to the glory he will give us later.*
ROMANS 8:18 TLB

What do you do when hardship falls so hard on your life that it takes your breath away? This time you won't be able to sigh that deep sigh of relief, knowing that the pain didn't fall on you. Because it did—the suffering came to you this time around. And the first question is always "Why?"

Sometimes even when we think the question is important, God doesn't always give us the answer. We will indeed encounter troubles, but as Christians, we will never face them alone. And the peaceful assurance of Romans 8:18 can be a soothing balm to the soul. Just like a mom with a cooling washcloth on a fevered brow, or a dad's encouraging whispers that all will be well. As Christians, our current sufferings will only last a moment compared to eternity. The miseries we experience now will be forgotten in the splendor and beauty and wonder that await us in heaven. Praise to You, Lord God, that we have hope!

*Thank You, Jesus, that I can look forward to a
place with You, where there will be no more earthly
tragedies and sufferings. No more weeping in the
night, but joy, sweet joy, for all time. Amen.* —AH

Oh, to Be Blessed by You

*This makes for harmony among the members,
so that all the members care for each other.*
1 CORINTHIANS 12:25 NLT

*A*re you one of those women who *love* to do for others? You're the person out-baking, out-loving, out-volunteering, out-mothering, out-counseling, out-giving, out-shining everyone in sight.

You are a modern-day, superhuman star of the Bible! Get out of the way, world. You are coming through to save and protect the universe!

Until you collapse in a little sighing heap, of course, and your face dons a weak smile of relief.

No human can do everything—not even a woman. Sometimes you need to let others do for you. Let others be the blessing. That's why the verse in 1 Corinthians 12:25 tells us we are to care for *each other*—not one person or a handful of folks who think they can do it all. Otherwise our good deeds might slip into a prideful kind of offering. Let someone serve you, counsel you, love you. Let someone else take the reins for a while. Then you can rest and rejuvenate and have some of that "by still waters" time you've always wanted—always needed.

*I'm exhausted, Lord. Please show me how to let others
be a blessing in my life. And show me how to find those
precious "by still waters" moments with You. Amen.* —AH

That Smile on Someone's Face

Do not let any unwholesome talk come out of your mouths,
but only what is helpful for building others up according
to their needs, that it may benefit those who listen.
EPHESIANS 4:29 NIV

A string of ugly words can taint the air faster than a blast of blue smoke backfiring out of an old beater pickup truck. Yep, that's a good analogy for an unwholesome tongue wagging out of control. You've listened to it. You've endured it. Maybe some of that nasty, belching backfire has even spewed out of *your* mouth!

But that kind of noxious chatter is berating, not beneficial. It won't bring us peace or joy. It will only bring us, and everyone in hearing distance, a curdled stomach and a sour spirit.

Instead, let us all uplift one another. Let us sweeten the air with our speech, not with reckless flattery—which is worth less than nothing—but with genuine encouragement. Let us offer support that will build others up according to their needs.

Yes. There's nothing quite like that smile on someone's face that you personally put there. Feels so great you want to do it again and again. And again.

Lord, teach me how to use my words wisely and
how to be an encouragement to others. Amen. —AH

Tears Are like Rain

When Jesus saw her weeping, and the Jews who had come along with her also weeping, he was deeply moved in spirit and troubled. "Where have you laid him?" he asked. "Come and see, Lord," they replied. Jesus wept. Then the Jews said, "See how he loved him!"
JOHN 11:33–36 NIV

The scent of rain—what a pure and earthy aroma. Then there is the cleansing silky feel of rain as it showers down on us and bathes the earth. Nothing else quite like it.

Tears can be like rain for the spirit, washing us clean from sorrow. Humans come equipped with tear ducts, and they are necessary in this fallen world. Even Jesus—who was fully God and fully man—was born with the ability to shed tears. When Jesus' friend Lazarus died, and He saw Martha crying and those around her weeping along with her, He was deeply moved in spirit and troubled. But then the scriptures go on to say, "Jesus wept."

What a comfort to know that our Lord understands our grief and sorrow in a very profound and personal way—since He too experienced the heartache of these emotions as well as the splash of salty tears on His cheek.

Holy Spirit, comfort me with tears when I have need of them. Like a gentle rain, let them wash away the sadness and sorrow. Amen. —AH

Not a Pipe Dream!

The steadfast love of the LORD never ceases;
his mercies never come to an end; they are
new every morning; great is your faithfulness.
LAMENTATIONS 3:22–23 ESV

For some people, birthdays are anything but exciting, since they force us to notice the ever-growing assembly of gray hairs, the wobbling of our turkey gobblers, and the carnival of not-so-merry crinkles around our eyes!

However, birthdays are also a time for babies to be born and a time to thank God for gifting us with another year to live and laugh and love. Birthdays are also for eating a bit of cake, opening some pretty presents, and for those fresh beginnings. That last part—fresh beginnings—becomes more important as the years go by. As one accumulates not only pleasant memories, but remembrances of misfortune and sin and regret—these events can drag behind us and clog up our present as well as our future.

Fresh beginnings may sound like a pipe dream, but it's a promise in God's Word. Yes, the steadfast love of the Lord never ceases. His tender mercies never end but are new every morning. So, thank God, every dawn we can experience a new fresh start!

I'm so happy, Lord, that in this ever-changing
world Your love is steadfast and Your mercies
never come to an end. Amen. —AH

Some Down Time

*The apostles gathered around Jesus and reported to him
all they had done and taught. Then, because so many
people were coming and going that they did not even
have a chance to eat, he said to them, "Come with me by
yourselves to a quiet place and get some rest." So they
went away by themselves in a boat to a solitary place.*
MARK 6:30–32 NIV

We are not androids. We are not meant to work continuously
as if made of metal and wheels and motors. But sometimes
we act that way. We push and push and push until we are ill
with an autoimmune disease or a heart attack or worse.

Jesus showed us while He was here on earth how to shut
down for a while. The book of Mark tells us clearly that the
apostles were going so strong in their ministry with Christ that
they didn't even have time to eat. Jesus simply took them away
from the crowds to a place where they could rest, eat, and refresh their spirits. Jesus knew well what they needed. Jesus still
knows what we need today.

Is the Lord whispering to you right now? "Come with Me
by yourself to a quiet place and get some rest."

*Lord, I don't want to make myself sick with too much
stress and work. Teach me how to balance work and
play and rest. In Jesus' name I pray. Amen. —AH*

A Life of Love

Anyone who claims to be in the light but hates a brother
or sister is still in the darkness. Anyone who loves
their brother and sister lives in the light, and there is
nothing in them to make them stumble.
1 JOHN 2:9–10 NIV

Hate is a wily beast. It will sneak up on you in the darkness. Then it will lunge at you, latch on to your spirit, and never want to let go. Hate comes with a never-healing wound that festers and oozes ugliness until we either learn to live with it or we make the Christlike choice to denounce this vile creature of hate.

Hard to do, right? You might shout, "But you don't understand what that other person did to me. She ruined my life! How can I forgive her?" But even though hate may morph into what looks like justice, it is only another smoke-and-mirrors trick from the enemy of your soul. Hate accomplishes nothing but despair for everyone involved, including you. Only forgiveness can wash away that wretched emotion that threatens every part of your being.

Hate destroys, but love heals. God wants us to be well in body, mind, and spirit.

Lord, are there some people I need to forgive right now?
Please show me who they are; help me to forgive them
and to make things right. Amen. —AH

What May Seem Impossible

The LORD makes firm the steps of the one who delights
in him; though he may stumble, he will not fall,
for the LORD upholds him with his hand.
PSALM 37:23–24 NIV

Many of God's creatures have astonishing climbing abilities, such as the alpine ibex. These mountain goats can climb what appear to be impossibly vertical cliffs. From the looks of it, one wrong move—this way or that—and they would plummet to their deaths. But they don't seem the least bit concerned about the peril. God equipped them for this kind of a climb, and they can pull it off.

We live in a fallen and perilous world, and if we miss the path or lose our spiritual footing, things could go badly for us. But with Christ's help, we can do what seems impossible. With the Lord by our side, we can indeed navigate the many perils of our climb. God has a grip on us. Hold tightly to Him, no matter what!

Holy Spirit, please blaze my path with Your holy light and guide me so that every foothold is sure. And if I do stumble, help me not to fall. Please give me the strength and courage to get back up and keep on going! Amen. —AH

A Good and Great God

"For the LORD your God is living among you.
He is a mighty savior. He will take delight in you
with gladness. With his love, he will calm all your
fears. He will rejoice over you with joyful songs."
ZEPHANIAH 3:17 NLT

With the way the world is spinning out of control these days, well, the natural response is to be frightened. Evil no longer bothers to slither under one's door as if filled with shame. Evil now pounds down your door and brazenly strolls in uninvited. It's easy to see why fear can rule us and make our hearts pound as if we're running from something. We are.

Then we think of this reassuring verse, and God's loving and calming presence comes to mind. Cooling our feverish brow. Drying our tears. Reassuring us with soothing and compassionate whispers. Beyond such intimate care, the Lord is also our mighty Savior who lives among us. We need not fear anything or anyone.

So, take heart. The world may on occasion bring darkness and calamity to our doors, but when the Lord lives with us, we can stand up to it. We can face anything when God is by our side.

Thank You, Jesus, that You are with me every
hour of every day. To guide me, protect me,
and calm my many fears. Amen. —AH

Delighting Our Hearts

Ointment and perfume delight the heart.
PROVERBS 27:9 NKJV

The Bible has so many references to spices, oils, incense, and perfumes; we get the idea that God delights in wonderful fragrances.

We discover in the book of John that while Jesus was here among us, He too welcomed the comforting beauty of scent. "Then Mary took about a pint of pure nard, an expensive perfume; she poured it on Jesus' feet and wiped his feet with her hair. And the house was filled with the fragrance of the perfume" (John 12:3 NIV). Later we read that Jesus was pleased that Mary had created such a worshipful and compassionate moment with this special perfume of the day.

Yes, there are so many healing and pleasurable scents that God has gifted us with. We can relax with lavender. Be invigorated with peppermint. Swoon over the essence of roses. Thrill over the fragrances of cinnamon, orange, and eucalyptus, just to name a few! What is your favorite aroma? There is a world of scents, which the Lord has given us as gifts. May our lives be richer and more enjoyable as we use them, and may we grow closer to the Giver.

Lord, thank You for all the glorious fragrances of this earth.
May they bring delight to my heart! Amen. —AH

On Wings like Eagles

*But those who hope in the LORD will renew their strength.
They will soar on wings like eagles; they will run and
not grow weary, they will walk and not be faint.*
ISAIAH 40:31 NIV

ave you ever felt so discouraged, so disappointed, so drained that you thought you might just fall over in your tracks? And maybe this time you won't bother getting up! Perhaps tears stream down your cheeks, wetting the hard earth. Perhaps you lift your head to look around, but no one seems to care about your fallen plight. People—your fellow sojourners—find you there, stare at you, and then frown as if they see only a problem and not an opportunity to help. Or maybe in reality they are afraid that they see themselves in your weary state. And the sight frightens them in ways they can't quite explain. So they run from you.

But God does not run from us. He knows our weariness, and in this beautiful verse in Isaiah we find hope. Yes, the Lord promises to renew our strength. We will soar on wings like eagles; we will run and not grow weary. We will walk and not be faint. Praise God for His mercy!

*I cry out to You, Lord. I trust Your mighty hand to
deliver me, and I believe that I will once again
soar on wings like eagles. Amen.* —AH

Your Daily Dose of Awe

How many are your works, Lord! In wisdom you made them all; the earth is full of your creatures. There is the sea, vast and spacious, teeming with creatures beyond number—living things both large and small.
PSALM 104:24–25 NIV

There is that moment—that one gasping moment in the woods—when you catch sight of a fawn nursing its mother. You stay perfectly still for the longest time. Why? Because you want to glimpse the exquisite marvel of God's creation. To receive what is quietly sublime, juxtaposed with the whirling and noisy routine of our modern lives.

Taking the time to pause, to seek out these earthly delights, is such a wonderful way to unwind from this tightly wound world. And God has provided a magnificent supply of these curiosities and wonderments for us to enjoy. Just to name a few—there are the resplendent snowy Alps, the northern lights, ocean plankton that glow like the stars at night, insects camouflaged as the leaves that surround them, the sweet trill of a yellow warbler, and coverlets of wildflowers perfuming the earth. So much to savor and take pleasure in!

Have you had your daily dose of awe today?

How glorious is Your creation, Father God! I thank You for all the awe-inspiring moments You provide! Amen. —AH

I Desire to Be Son-Drenched!

When Moses came down from Mount Sinai with the two tablets of the covenant law in his hands, he was not aware that his face was radiant because he had spoken with the LORD.
EXODUS 34:29 NIV

The more time we spend in God's presence, in seeking Him, communing with Him, and praising Him, the more radiant our spirits will become. People will take notice. They may not see the same physical radiance that Moses possessed after he spoke with the Lord, but they will recognize an undeniable glow from within. Perhaps one parallel might be the many solar lights that have become popular in recent years. After they absorb the sunlight all day, they put off a beautiful glow at night, illuminating the darkness.

People will find our luminous countenance so captivating, they will ask, "You look so happy and at peace. Please tell me, what is your secret?" And then you'll have the glorious opportunity of telling them.

This is what the world desperately seeks. They need to know the source of our glow—Jesus—the one who can give them all light, all life. For now, and for all time.

Oh Lord, please let my light shine before everyone!
In Jesus' name I pray. Amen. —AH

You Can't Do It All

*"But when he, the Spirit of truth, comes,
he will guide you into all the truth."*
JOHN 16:13 NIV

No matter how much we'd like to be omnipresent—we cannot be. Nor can we be all things to all people. If we tried even for a day, we would lose our faculties. Our health. And we would no longer be in God's will. The Lord never asked us to save the world. That is *His* job.

The whispers from the enemy might come as, "More, more of everything, including ministry." Satan knows the secret goal is for a massive meltdown and, ultimately, a complete burnout. Humans were never meant for the intense pressure of continuous labor, no matter how saintly the pursuits.

So, how do we find the balance, peace, and fulfillment for a satisfying Christian life? By allowing ourselves to be guided by the Holy Spirit. Since we can't do it all, we need to have discernment and wisdom in our daily walk.

Even Jesus knew when He had to retreat from the demands of the crowds. He knew how to live perfectly because He spent time in prayer. There lies one of the key truths to balance and the means to a life well lived.

*Holy Spirit, please guide me in all
the ways I should go. Amen.* —AH

Encouragement Does Wonders!

*Therefore encourage one another and build
each other up, just as in fact you are doing.*
1 THESSALONIANS 5:11 NIV

If you look deep into the eyes of people, or you listen very carefully to what they say—or what they don't say—you can sometimes sense their emotional needs. Perhaps your boss brags on herself so much that she comes off as arrogant. Or maybe your coworker becomes the queen of put-downs in an effort to make herself appear superior. Adults act out in ways that seem more than a little childish, and yet the background story behind these deeds may be riddled with pain. Perhaps vital words of encouragement were withheld along their journeys when it mattered the most.

When we know that we can offer kind and uplifting words to a child or an adult, may we never hesitate to give it. Not indulging in flattery, which can bring more harm than good, but offering genuine praise and support and reassurance.

The book of Proverbs reminds us that "Anxious hearts are very heavy, but a word of encouragement does wonders!" (Proverbs 12:25 TLB). *Aah,* yes, that heart-smile you put on someone else's face, well, it's deeply soul satisfying. May we never withhold words that can build up our fellow sojourners!

*Holy Spirit, show me the people I need
to encourage today. Amen.* —AH

Ode to Beautiful Feet

And how shall they preach unless they are sent? As it is written: "How beautiful are the feet of those who preach the gospel of peace, who bring glad tidings of good things!"
ROMANS 10:15 NKJV

Mmm—nothing like a good pedicure. We slide our aching tootsies into that warm footbath of lavender water and sigh all the way down to our toes. Then we sit back, close our eyes, and let a trained professional take over the arduous task of making something beautiful out of those calloused gargoyles we call feet! And amazingly, they do!

There is another way to procure beautiful feet, which is written about in Romans 10:15. When we go from place to place and share the love of Christ and His incredible news of mercy and grace, well, that makes our feet lovely. In essence, our feet are carrying the answers to the biggest questions of mankind—why are we here, why is this world so broken, and is there any way to fix it? May we carry the good news on our beautiful feet all the days of our lives!

Holy Spirit, help me to share the good news of the Gospel with all those who will listen. May I be full of Your boldness and abounding in Your love! Amen. —AH

The Cool of the Evening

*Then the man and his wife heard the sound of the LORD God
as he was walking in the garden in the cool of the day, and
they hid from the LORD God among the trees of the garden.*
GENESIS 3:8 NIV

The path is lined with silvery ponds and cascades of water
and sumptuous gardens so exquisite, you sigh with delight.
Ahead is a meadow covered in wild plants stained with colors
and infused with perfumes you've never known before. And
when a zephyr passes by, oh my. What is that sweet melody?
Can those trumpet blossoms somehow create music in the lea?
What a good question to ask the Lord.

You pause under an arbor. A pure, hallowed kind of radiance that seems to penetrate your whole being warms you from
the inside out. *Aah*, yes. The Lord approaches, and it's time to
stroll with Him for a spell—and enjoy the cool of the evening
together. *Mmm.* Best part of eternity. . .

From reading Genesis 3:8, mankind grieves over our loss of
paradise. But there is great news. The Lord Jesus said He would
go and prepare a place for us. And as followers of Christ, let us
rejoice over that promise of heaven. Hallelujah!

*Thank You, Jesus, that You will someday call me home
to be with You in this marvelous place! Amen.* —AH

Remembering the Basics

*The angel of the LORD came back a second time and
touched him and said, "Get up and eat, for the journey
is too much for you." So he got up and ate and drank.
Strengthened by that food, he traveled forty days and forty
nights until he reached Horeb, the mountain of God.*

1 KINGS 19:7–8 NIV

Being human isn't an easy road to travel. It wasn't back in
Bible times, and even with our modern conveniences, it still
isn't easy today. We can be weak and fragile in many of the
same ways that people have been throughout history.

Elijah had some important tasks to fulfill as a prophet of
God, and yet he needed the basics—support, rest, and good
food to complete his journey properly. How are you doing on
your journey in the many tasks that God has given you to do?
Do you rest enough? Studies have shown that more and more
Americans don't get enough sleep. How is your diet? Do you
eat enough of the right foods to propel you on with your day?
Do you get spiritual backup by praying and reading God's
Word and being still before Him?

Refreshment sometimes comes in the basics.

*Lord, remind me to take good care of myself
so that I might fulfill my calling. Amen. —AH*

Loving Your Way through the Day

A gentle answer turns away wrath,
but a harsh word stirs up anger.
PROVERBS 15:1 NIV

Harsh words are like boomerangs. They tend to come back to you, and they can really hurt. The caustic barbs not only harm the recipient, but they damage the sender too. Yes, there might be an initial thrill of conquest and pride in that clever and perfect comeback, but later those words will settle into your spirit in a way that isn't so perfect. In fact, far from it. It's a lose-lose situation all the way around.

So just when we feel like flinging out some barbed comments, can we instead try to say something kind? Not flattery, not untruths, but words that show understanding and compassion, rather than the "I'm going to set you straight, since I am the knower of all things" comment or "I'm going to give you what you deserve" judgment. This new approach will not only put smiles on people's faces, but in the end, it will put a big one in your heart.

Want to experience an easier walk through this life? Use Proverbs 15:1 as one of your life verses.

Lord, show me how to love my way through
the day with gentle answers. Amen. —AH

In Need of a Wise Tongue

*The tongue of the wise adorns knowledge,
but the mouth of the fool gushes folly.*

PROVERBS 15:2 NIV

Have you ever been stuck by someone at a luncheon who refused to stop talking? Her food went cold, and you never saw her take a breath so you could offer even the briefest comment. And to add to the general misery around the table, the epic marathon of chin-wagging was all about her. Oh, wow, now there's a scenario that could make you want to hide under the table for refuge!

But lest we raise our chins a bit too high in judgment and we poke our fingers too much at the yammering masses, we must admit that we too have suffered from the ailment of "gushing folly" of one kind or the other.

So, what's the cure?

Let Proverbs 15:2 sink into your soul. Tape it to your mirror. To your fridge. On your forehead, if necessary. Know that God sees everyone as precious, and it should show in our dialogue with folks. Or in some cases, it should show in the lack of yak!

*Teach me Your ways, Lord. I want to speak when I should
speak and be quiet when I should be quiet. Give me
a wise tongue. In Jesus' name I pray. Amen. —AH*

More Than Flesh and Blood

*"Do not be afraid of those who kill the body
but cannot kill the soul. Rather, be afraid of the
One who can destroy both soul and body in hell."*
MATTHEW 10:28 NIV

We haphazardly toss used coffee grounds, leftovers, empty cans, broken toys, and random slop into the trash bin. But later when we finally take out the trash, we never expect to find a sweet-smelling bouquet of roses. We expect to find a bin of stinking garbage, right?

We are far more than flesh and blood according to the scriptures. So if we dump all manner of the world's offerings into our spirits, it can have the same effect. A few examples of those offerings might be entertainment with no redeeming value, sites on the internet that don't edify, friendships that cause us to stumble spiritually, as well as a host of other questionable choices that could stain our souls and grieve the Holy Spirit.

Proverbs 23:7 reminds us that we are what we think about in our hearts. That's a pretty powerful declaration, and one we should take seriously.

So treasure what is eternal. God does.

*Guide me in all my choices, Lord, that I might always
please You. In Jesus' name I pray. Amen.* —AH

I'm New!

*Therefore, if anyone is in Christ, the new creation
has come: The old has gone, the new is here!*
2 CORINTHIANS 5:17 NIV

What a spring day! Your favorite meadow is singing with bugs, blooming with buttercups, and there's sunshine from here to heaven. You call your friend and grab your kite. Yes, this day was meant for fun and freedom and beauty.

But wait. You look back. You almost forgot a few things. You'll need that umbrella, since the weather might turn ugly. Then there's that bag of worries you almost forgot. Oh, and the record of wrongs that you've been compiling on your friend. Can't leave that behind.

Suddenly, you are weighed down. That bliss you felt fades, and you no longer feel that lightness of being. Your kite flutters to the floor, and you wonder why you ever thought the moment could be glorious.

Thank God you know just what to do. Talk to God about it. He's waiting for you. Ready to put the beauty back in your day. Ready to fly that kite with you!

*Lord, when I get into worldly thinking, bring me back to You
and Your divine ways. May I always remember that, as a
Christ follower, I am now a new creature! Amen. —AH*

A Love Letter to God

I love you, LORD, my strength.
PSALM 18:1 NIV

We have our little love routines. We tell our spouse good-bye at the door with a kiss and an endearing, "Love you best." We tuck our kids in at night, read little lamb stories, and as we snuggle one more time, we say, "Love you to the moon and back." We say lovey words to family and friends and even pets. Most people know how to love, and we do it freely and publicly and every which way.

But how often do we tell God how much we love Him? The Lord desires our attentions, our fellowshipping, our love. You can even shout it or sing it if you want to. "I love You, Lord!" Doesn't that feel right in your soul?

Or maybe you could write a love letter to God during one of your devotional times with Him. What would you say in your note? What would you thank Him for? How would you express your deepest affections for Him? The Lord would love to hear from you. After all, He's the one who gave us the ability to love in the first place!

*Oh Lord, my God, I love You dearly—
with all my heart and soul. I'm so sorry I fail
to tell You as often as I should. Amen.* —AH

A Wild-Eyed Bunch

*One handful of peaceful repose is better than two
fistfuls of worried work—more spitting into the wind.*
ECCLESIASTES 4:6 MSG

This modern era might offer us a plethora of conveniences and techno fun, but we can get so plugged in, we no longer know how to disconnect. Our eyes, as well as our spirits, become wild. Too many glowing screens and instant news updates and the stresses of constant communication with more people than we can possibly befriend properly in a lifetime. We can't rest right. We can't play right. We can't quiet ourselves long enough to listen to a babbling brook or a sweet birdsong—let alone the still, small voice of God.

So, how can we ever learn to slow ourselves? Ask God for help. He is willing and able. If God can make you from head to toe—every cell from your gait to your giggle—then He can teach you how to quiet yourself to live life the way it was meant to be. As it says in Ecclesiastes, "One handful of peaceful repose is better than two fistfuls of worried work!"

*I need to learn to unplug, Lord. Teach me how
to calm my spirit. Remind me to take the Sabbath
day off and to spend time with You. Amen. —AH*

101 Smiles

"Now therefore, fear the LORD,
serve Him in sincerity and in truth!"
JOSHUA 24:14 NKJV

Humans are capable of the most welcoming smiles. As warm and wonderful as creamy Irish butter melting on a biscuit right out of the oven. *Aah*, yes. But humans are capable of other kinds of smiles too. There is the loaded smile that reminds you that the person hasn't quite forgiven the past mistakes yet. There is the smile that says, "I'm laughing *at* you a bit more than *with* you." There is a smile that is full of shadowy mischief, spite, aloofness, or ill will. There is the overly bright, gritted version that has more to do with obligation than sincerity. These are the kinds of smiles that make our spirits cringe instead of sigh with delight.

What kind of smile do people see on our faces when we approach? We can choose any one we want from our bag of 101 smiles. It's our choice. Every day. Every moment.

I want to please You, Jesus, with all my life—from what I ponder in my heart to the smile on my face. Let my light shine before men and let my smile be full of sincerity. May it bring peace and joy to all those who cross my path! Amen. —AH

Sweet to the Soul

*May these words of my mouth and this meditation of my heart
be pleasing in your sight, LORD, my Rock and my Redeemer.*
PSALM 19:14 NIV

Words are such simple things and yet, so very power filled and enduring. They can speak love or hate, lies or truth, curse or blessing, hope or despair, calm or chaos, life or death. Maybe that is why the Bible gives us plenty of guidance when it comes to what we should say to others.

The book of Proverbs says, "Gracious words are a honeycomb, sweet to the soul and healing to the bones" (16:24 NIV). What a beautiful saying, and so true! May we wake up daily with the mind-set of guarding our words, knowing their power to harm or to heal. May we wield them not as a sharp sword, but with the gentle touch of wisdom and compassion. Yes, may our words be as sweet and satisfying as honeycomb.

And what is sweet to the souls of others and healing to their bones will feel the same in our hearts as well. Because we will know we are fulfilling God's Word, and that brings joy to our souls!

*Holy Spirit, may I never grieve You with my
words, but instead may my words please
You all the days of my life. Amen.* —AH

Rough Waters Ahead

The Lord detests all the proud of heart.
Be sure of this: They will not go unpunished.
PROVERBS 16:5 NIV

We hear that word *pride* more and more in modern times—as if it is a positive way to think and feel about ourselves. But according to the Bible, God considers a haughty person to be detestable. In fact, the Lord promises that this attitude will not go unpunished.

Yikes! How can we make our lives right with God then?

Simply put, we must repent from our arrogant ways of thinking and follow the precepts of the Bible. The Lord gave them to us for a good reason—to benefit us, not to harm us. His guidelines will bring us joy and peace and comfort. So when we are enticed to live in accordance with the world's mindset, run from the enemy and flee from temptation. The Lord will make sure we have a way to escape.

God really does want the very best kind of life for us. He desires to hem us in with His divine love, not to stifle us but to protect us from more sin and suffering. So that we can know Him better as we stroll those green pastures and those beautiful still waters.

Lord, forgive me for the times I've been full of
haughtiness and self-importance. Help me to be
humble in heart and follow You always. Amen. —AH

Condemnation or
Sweet Compassion?

When Job's three friends, Eliphaz the Temanite,
Bildad the Shuhite and Zophar the Naamathite,
heard about all the troubles that had come upon him,
they set out from their homes and met together by
agreement to go and sympathize with him and comfort him.
JOB 2:11 NIV

Friends can either comfort us like a warm blanket on a cold night or they can toss us out onto a snowbank! In the Bible, Job's friends came to visit after he lost everything—his wealth, his family, and his health. They said they came to comfort him, but it turned into bitter arguments and judgments. You might say they lost the *r* in the word *friends*. If I had been Job, I would have been tempted to say, "If this is your idea of comforting me, then please feel free to give your camels a rest by staying home!"

As it turned out, God was not pleased with Job's friends either. He reprimanded them for their cruel comments. Would God be pleased with the way we comfort our friends in their hour of need? Do we give them words of condemnation or sweet compassion?

Lord, please give me genuine love for all mankind and a
special compassion for all those in need. Amen. —AH

Sail Away with Me

*Now the Lord is the Spirit, and where
the Spirit of the Lord is, there is freedom.*
2 CORINTHIANS 3:17 NIV

The lake glistens as if there are millions of diamonds strewn across the surface of the water. Our little sailboat dips and sways, and in these moments we become almost dreamlike, since our troubles have drifted far away on the breeze. We are so released from our burdens that we can now be filled with so much more. *Aah*, yes, room for so much more. Love, peace, forgiveness, gladness of heart, and laughter!

And so it goes with the way we should feel about spending time with the Lord. He encourages us to let Him be all the energy that we need to propel us through our days and our nights. To live in freedom and to be so filled with joy that the whole world wants to come along and sail away with us too.

Yes, that is the way of the Gospel—the way of His mercy and grace and freedom. May we daily sail away with our Lord.

Lord, please be at the helm of my life and show me Your joy as I glide across this glassy sea of life! Amen. —AH

Servanthood

*"For who is greater, the one who is at the table
or the one who serves? Is it not the one who is at
the table? But I am among you as one who serves."*
LUKE 22:27 NIV

TV shows that portray the upstairs/downstairs lives of the aristocracy have become enormously popular in recent times. We can't help but wish (a little or a lot) for the "upstairs" life with the best of everything at our fingertips—the latest fashions, the most opulent surroundings, and the most decadent delicacies. And all of it served on a silver platter! We're also fascinated by the "downstairs" lives of the servants, and yet few of us would line up to be one of those servants.

Amazingly, Christ came to serve—not just the aristocracy but all mankind. And we are to emulate His ways. The riches in servanthood aren't the kind you deposit in the bank. They are treasures of the heart. The sigh of relief you receive when you reach out to help someone. The gentle touch of gratitude when someone feels less lonely because of your attentions. The hope-filled smile you take in when you've brought someone to Christ. Such joy of the soul. May we be so blessed!

*Lord, may I always think of others before myself,
for I know this is Your way. Amen.* —AH

Come as You Are

The Spirit and the bride say, "Come!" And let the one who hears say, "Come!" Let the one who is thirsty come; and let the one who wishes take the free gift of the water of life.
REVELATION 22:17 NIV

Oh to have a housekeeper! Such a blessing, right? But the moment she's scheduled, what do you do? You clean. After all, you wouldn't want her to see the stacks of dirty dishes, the unmade beds, and those piles of junk in your closets. You might say, "She'll think I'm a slob." But then you realize, that is why the housekeeper is coming—to clean up!

Don't we do the same thing when we think of Christ and His grace? We think we're not good enough to reside in His holy presence, or that we're too sinful and dirty for Him to even gaze upon our lives. We might think, *Maybe I should clean up first—well, as best as I can.* But Christ came to save—to wash us clean from sin. The definition of *grace* is mercy and forgiveness that we don't deserve.

May we come to Christ no matter where we are spiritually. Whether it is for the very first time or whether it's for forgiveness for a repeated transgression we're particularly ashamed of. He simply asks us to come.

Lord, thank You for Your unmerited favor. May I never hesitate in coming to You for anything. Amen. —AH

A Life Assessment

*"He who is faithful in a very little thing is also
faithful in much; and he who is dishonest in
a very little thing is also dishonest in much."*
LUKE 16:10 AMP

Most people like to live large. You know, traveling around the world to exotic places. A career that brings what we think is big purpose, oh, and big money. A couple of kids thrown in as well as a plethora of close and influential friends to complete the "living large" image. But if we were actually given tremendous blessings, could we be trusted with them? Do we use our gains and godsends wisely and generously and honestly? Do we thank God genuinely and frequently for all blessings, no matter how big or small?

We can trust God fully, and we are to follow His guidance and example. So, how are *we* doing? If you don't know, ask a friend. But be ready for sincere input, and be willing to make some changes!

Everyone should make an assessment of their lives when it comes to Luke 16:10. Does God find us wanting, or can He trust us in all things?

*Oh Lord, please show me how to be faithful
with all Your blessings whether big or small.
In Jesus' name I pray. Amen.* —AH

Bouts of Loneliness

Turn to me and be gracious to me,
for I am lonely and afflicted.
PSALM 25:16 NIV

Have you ever felt like a party balloon with all the air squeezed out of it? You are flat on the ground, empty and alone, and drained of anything that remotely resembles a festive atmosphere? You have been used up with no one left to revive you, to cheer you up, or cheer you on. Lonesomeness has become a close and familiar thing in your life, but it doesn't feel like a good friend.

Know that in the midst of your loneliness, God understands, and He is by your side. While on earth, Jesus endured stretches of solitude and sorrow. He experienced abandonment and rejection. He understands how lonely this life can be, and He encourages us with promises in His Word such as, "The LORD is close to the brokenhearted; he rescues those whose spirits are crushed" (Psalm 34:18 NLT).

So take heart, the Lord sees your affliction. His arms wrap around you. He loves you beyond human measure. He is so very close. Reach out to Him.

I am grateful for Your understanding during my
bouts of lonesomeness, Lord. Thank You for Your
promises and Your love for me. Amen. —AH

A Daily Helping of Love

"My command is this: Love each other as I have loved you."
JOHN 15:12 NIV

We have a big choice every day when we wake up. We can love or we can hate. Even though we may think many of our feelings and reactions are out of our control, they are not. Will we choose to hate or to love the people at home, church, work, and all others who cross our paths? If we choose to hate, there will be consequences. We will be going against how the Lord wants us to behave in this life, and that will never have a good outcome. Choosing hate will also stress our minds and bodies, sometimes to the point of serious illness.

If we say we can't do this love thing alone, that is also truth. We can't. But the Lord can help us to love others, even if they are not lovable. It doesn't mean we should be forced to endure an abusive relationship, but it does mean we need to forgive others and keep our hearts clean of hate and bitterness.

So let us ask the Lord for help—that we can choose the healing and happiness that come from forgiveness and love.

Lord, please help me to love all the unlovables out there, including unlovable me! Amen. —AH

My Cup Overflows!

You prepare a feast for me in the presence of my enemies. You honor me by anointing my head with oil. My cup overflows with blessings.
PSALM 23:5 NLT

Humans are serious when it comes to gobbling up blessings. We expect a feast of them. Just as a grand buffet can boast many kinds of delights, we desire and sometimes even expect a splendid smorgasbord of good gifts to pick over. But how often do we thank the Giver of all these gifts? Or are we a little like a grasping child at Christmastime who—after tearing through a mound of glorious packages—is caught scanning the tree skirt for more?

Maybe we should pause and look up to the Giver of all good things. The holy Word says, "Every good and perfect gift is from above, coming down from the Father of the heavenly lights, who does not change like shifting shadows" (James 1:17 NIV).

Christ was and is the greatest of all gifts from our Father in heaven. Have we thanked Him today?

Father God, I deeply appreciate the many good gifts
You shower on me. I'm sorry I have not always remembered
to thank You. I am especially grateful for the sacrifice Your
Son made on the cross for the forgiveness of my sins.
I praise You, Lord Jesus! Amen. —AH

Third Helpings, Anyone?

*Their destiny is destruction, their god is their
stomach, and their glory is in their shame.
Their mind is set on earthly things.*
PHILIPPIANS 3:19 NIV

There is one last piece of dark chocolate cake in the fridge—
layered with homemade fudge frosting—and even though
the fridge door is soundly shut, you can hear that decadent
piece of confection calling out to you! *However*, it would be
your third piece and your clothes are already beginning to
feel a bit snug.

What to do?

The answer is easy, but the follow-through is not. Many
Christians do pretty well living their faith, but for some reason
we turn a blind eye to the sin of gluttony. Could it be because so
many of us are guilty of it? Have we allowed a belly to become
like a god to us? Oh dear.

Why would we choose to do anything that might grieve the
Holy Spirit who lives in us or do anything that would damage
our bodies? Moderation and discipline and self-control don't
sound like fun things to us, but does that stomachache—after
gobbling three pieces of cake—really give us a sense of wellness and joy and freedom?

*Lord, help me to exercise self-control at
mealtime and at all times. Amen.* —AH

A Cup of Kindness

He has told you, O man, what is good; and
what does the LORD require of you but to do justice,
to love kindness, and to walk humbly with your God?
MICAH 6:8 NASB

The world has lost some of its goodness and kindness. We see this problem getting more and more serious in the news, on the streets, in the schools—everywhere. When kindness does show up, we might even poke at it to see if it's real. But God wants kindness to become a way of life, a common sight among us all.

Do we offer a cup of cool water and a hot meal to the hungry? Are the widows and orphans cared for? Do we treat the elderly with respect? Do we love justice and truth? Do we treat others as we wish to be treated? We can't possibly do everything for everyone, but we can walk humbly with our God and be kind to the people who cross our path.

If you want to please the Lord and live a more peaceful and joy-filled life, let kindness and justice rule your heart.

Lord, help me to remember the Golden Rule. I really want to
please You in all I do. In Jesus' name I pray. Amen. —AH

The Beauty of Redemption

*This righteousness is given through faith in Jesus Christ
to all who believe. There is no difference between Jew
and Gentile, for all have sinned and fall short of the
glory of God, and all are justified freely by his grace
through the redemption that came by Christ Jesus.*
ROMANS 3:22–24 NIV

It's your favorite movie. Why? Because even though the hero can sometimes be as mean as a junkyard dog, you know where he's headed—toward redemption. Who doesn't love a movie that ends with a complete change of heart for the main character? You leave the theater with a spring in your step, inspired, knowing that life is good again. That all has been made right. Even some secular movies use the general theme of redemption. We long for it, even if we don't know why.

Of course, the ultimate deliverance and true restoration of the heart—the one that will change our lives both now and for all eternity—is the salvation Christ offers us through His sacrifice on the cross. May we embrace His forgiveness and freedom and know the absolute beauty of that redemption all the way to our souls. Yes, God loves redemptive stories, including yours!

*I praise and thank You, Lord, for Your salvation.
It has changed my life forever! Amen.* —AH

Always Available

*"Be strong. Take courage. Don't be intimidated.
Don't give them a second thought because GOD,
your God, is striding ahead of you. He's right there
with you. He won't let you down; he won't leave you."*

DEUTERONOMY 31:6 MSG

Your friend doesn't answer the phone as often as you would like, and she keeps forgetting to return your call. The email you sent comes back undeliverable. The phone finally rings, but it's a sales call. Nobody wants to talk on the phone anymore, and nobody has time to meet for a cup of coffee. If you can't text it or deal with it on the latest social media outlet, you're out of the loop. You're alone.

Where did all the real communication go? And why do so many people seem emotionally unavailable?

No matter how profoundly someone follows Christ. No matter how much he or she loves you. No matter the vows made before God and man, well, humans will fail you.

But how wonderful it is that we serve a God who is not only emotionally available; He is there for us in every other way. He won't let us down. He's right there with us—ever listening, ever caring, ever loving. . . .

*Oh Lord, how happy it makes me to know that Your
promises are real. That You listen to all my prayers
and that You care for me always! Amen.* —AH

One Starry Night

*That night there were shepherds staying in the fields nearby,
guarding their flocks of sheep. Suddenly, an angel of the
Lord appeared among them, and the radiance of the Lord's
glory surrounded them. They were terrified, but the angel
reassured them. "Don't be afraid!" he said. "I bring you
good news that will bring great joy to all people."*

LUKE 2:8–10 NLT

If you've ever visited Israel, you may have seen the hillsides nestled between Bethlehem and Jerusalem. It is a rocky area but also lush with green grasses, and it's the spot where it's commonly believed that the shepherds heard the miraculous news of Christ's birth!

What a night that was for those herders who were tending their flocks of sheep! There must have been a breathless wonder in the air—an expectation of something divine, something marvelous to come. And then it happened. An angel arrived. The magnificent splendor of the Lord shone all about them. Good news was proclaimed. And oh, that angelic news. Nothing has ever had such an impact on this aching, troubled earth as the glorious news from that angel. Yes, since that starry night, nothing has ever been the same.

But Christ's birth was good news for you too. Have you responded? Is Christmas in your heart as well as in your home?

*Lord Jesus, I know You came for the whole world,
but You also came for me. Along with the angels,
I thank You and praise You! Amen. —AH*

A Glorious Tree

"A good tree cannot bear bad fruit,
and a bad tree cannot bear good fruit."
MATTHEW 7:18 NIV

The branches on the cherry tree are shriveled and the trunk looks rotten. The leaves are crispy and ready to fly away in the hot wind. So it seems very unlikely that we would find a crop of cherries, ripe and juicy and ready to eat. Why? Because a bad tree cannot produce good fruit.

So it is with us, if we are exhausted from never taking a day off or a Sunday to refresh, or we never spend one-on-one time with our beloved Savior. If we never rejoice in the wonder of our Lord in song or praise. If we never challenge ourselves, inspire others, or choose to mature in our faith. We will become puny cherries that get stunted on the branches—food that the worms don't even want!

Are you taking care of your mind and body and spirit? Are you becoming a glorious tree, bearing beautiful fruit? You can with the Lord's help. Just ask. He would love to hear from you!

Lord, I want to produce good fruit for You, for the world,
and for me. Help me to be that delicious fruit ripening
on a healthy tree! In Jesus' name I pray. Amen. —AH

A Pleasant Aroma

Our lives are a Christ-like fragrance rising up to God.
2 CORINTHIANS 2:15 NLT

The Israelites got caught grumbling—a lot. This complaining got old, and one could say that the aroma coming off all that whining wasn't pleasing to God. Their mutterings showed that they didn't fully appreciate all the many miracles God had done for them and continued to do for them. Their persistent griping showed disrespect for the Almighty, and it showed a lack of faith.

However, it's easy to find ourselves falling into the same rut, grousing like the Israelites—rising up with a whine first thing in the morning and still grumbling as we climb into bed. It is better to rise up and say, "I thank You, Lord, for all You've done for me. I trust You, Lord, for my needs today. In fact, I am excited to see how You are going to work things for my good."

Won't that kind of attitude, that kind of faith, that kind of thankfulness rise up like a pleasant aroma to God as well as bring peace to our souls?

Please, Lord, help me to rest in You for all my needs. Help me to appreciate all that You've given me, rather than constantly asking for more. In Jesus' holy name I pray. Amen. —AH

Spiritual Safety Gear

*Therefore put on the full armor of God, so that when the day
of evil comes, you may be able to stand your ground, and
after you have done everything, to stand. Stand firm then,
with the belt of truth buckled around your waist, with the
breastplate of righteousness in place, and with your feet fitted
with the readiness that comes from the gospel of peace.*
EPHESIANS 6:13–15 NIV

We have become a nation of safety fanatics—and, well, we
should. There are hazards out there everywhere. We have
helmets and earplugs, eye protection and knee pads. There is
safety gear for pretty much every sport, industry, fix-it task, and
hobby. We want to be ready for anything!

But how about outfitting our soul for protection? There are
spiritual dangers out there—some sly, some bold—including
perils from demonic influences. When the world comes at us
with its evil intentions, are we standing firm with truth and righteousness and the Gospel of peace? There is no need for us to
live in a state of fear, but there is a real need to be ready with
our spiritual safety gear!

*Lord, help me to always be ready to stand up to evil.
May I always love justice and truth and Your
salvation message! Amen. —AH*

The Path of Life

You make known to me the path of life;
you will fill me with joy in your presence,
with eternal pleasures at your right hand.
PSALM 16:11 NIV

*A*ah, the path of life—how beautiful is the sound of that? From the moment we're born it seems like we're trying to outrun death—staying in a whirlwind of anxious thoughts and busyness, wishing desperately to not even think about mortality. And yet the Lord loves to speak of life. Real life in Him, the kind that lasts for an eternity!

And there is such joy, basking in His presence. He even promises eternal pleasures. In the midst of every kind of tumult this earth can conjure up, these hope-filled words are like a welcoming, comforting, divine hug. "Follow me," Christ says. Who wouldn't want to follow Him when the best and finest gifts are awaiting us there in His divine company?

What eternal joy awaits those who surrender their hearts to Him! He loves each of us more than we can imagine. He has sacrificed everything for us—for you. The time is now. Take His hand and step into His light, into His love. . . .

Show me the path of life, Lord. I want to
follow You now and into eternity. Amen. —AH

A Place Called Heaven

" 'He will wipe every tear from their eyes. There will be no more death' or mourning or crying or pain, for the old order of things has passed away." He who was seated on the throne said, "I am making everything new!" Then he said, "Write this down, for these words are trustworthy and true."
REVELATION 21:4–5 NIV

What if our distorted view of life and love and beauty was suddenly made crystal clear and we could see and feel what was really meant to be? What if we could hear the dissonance in the earth's straining lament finally get its resolution? What if the landscape of trees and flowers—and you and me—would never again wither and die? What if the tears shed—if they were to ever fall—would come from joy and delight and not despair and sorrow?

Well, we'd be in a place the Lord is preparing for us. Yes, as followers of Christ we will one day breathe in the air of heaven where God is making everything new! Fresh. Fragrant. Forever. Where promises are fulfilled. Where hope is realized. Draw on this "knowing" whenever you have a need for comfort, for peace.

I am so very grateful to You, Lord, that I have the hope of heaven. May I tell everyone about Your mercy and grace! Amen. —AH

Sizing You Up

For God does not show favoritism.
ROMANS 2:11 NIV

You're at a party, and a woman strolls in—a person you've never met. Within seconds you're able to make a zillion calculations, judgments, and conclusions. This instantaneous "sizing up" may come so naturally to us, we don't even know we're doing it. We may consider how well she's dressed and groomed. Is she rich and educated? If we do decide she's worth some of our time, we may then ask ourselves, "Does she have good connections? Can she help me advance in my career? What can I gain from this encounter?"

We've all made various kinds of instant social assessments, but if they were suddenly exposed on a big screen for all to see, our hidden thoughts would come off mortifying, to say the least. God does not show favoritism. He considers all people to be important, precious, and greatly beloved, no matter their education, background, culture, level of wealth, social status, or anything else we humans can cook up as a way to appraise the value of humanity.

So the next time we are tempted to make those evaluations of the flesh, may we ask God to control the meditations of our hearts. And the beautiful thing is—He will.

*Lord, please help me not to show favoritism and
to see all people through Your eyes. Amen.* —AH

Unlikely Peace

"Lord, save us! We're going to drown!"
MATTHEW 8:25 NIV

The droplets race each other down the smudged glass, sometimes joining together to create streams, and then rivers, washing away the pollen and seeds and little kitten footprints that had been there just this morning. You peer out through the intermittent waterfall at the gray landscape and wonder when traffic will get moving again. Noticing the rhythm of the wipers mixed with the hum of the motor and the periodic squeak of brakes, you smile at the song. Even when we are all sitting here, unmoving, somehow we can't help being moved by the heartbeat of the busy city.

And in the middle of that traffic jam, with the stress of the morning schedule waiting, God calms the waves of anxiety and quiets the honking horns. God guides the sighing semis and the wheezing wagons and the muttering minivans.

We ask Him to speak to the storm, to control the cars, to unjam the jam. But instead He speaks to us. We ask Him to help us out of the mess, and instead He tells us that we can't do without it—that we'll find our peace right in the mess. Right where He is.

Lord, save me in my mess, and let me not be afraid to find You in the middle of it. Amen. —ML

For We Trust

We wait in hope for the LORD; he is our help and our shield.
PSALM 33:20 NIV

Nation against nation, the lines have been drawn, the sides taken, the peace denied. Now each side builds up their defenses, gathering what they can to protect their people. And each side pours resources into their armies—strengthening their units and gearing up their weaponry. They believe with all their might in their might. They trust in the weight of steel and speed of bullets.

But they forget. "No king is saved by the size of his army; no warrior escapes by his great strength" (v. 16). No one can save us. No one can vanquish the enemies of envy and want, of fear and ignorance. No one has the power to overcome death, except God.

And perhaps the real trouble is that we just aren't that courageous. We don't have it in us to let go—to release control. We can't believe in things we can't see and measure and spend money on. Even though we've heard the stories and know God as the source of all truth, somehow we can't quite give up on the idea that we can save ourselves.

And that's exactly why we must place our hope and our trust in Him. Though it may even seem foolish, we must let go of the reins and let Him show us the way, let Him protect us, let Him save us.

Lord, remind me that there is no one else so worthy of my trust—and no one who wants more for me than You. Amen. —ML

Walking Free

I will walk about in freedom,
for I have sought out your precepts.
PSALM 119:45 NIV

Children run at top speed, racing against one another to be first to touch the big tree that provides shade for the playground. The whine of the swings accompanies a pair of friends who reach up, up, up with their toes and giggle all the way down. Other kids are making an obstacle course out of the playground equipment, dashing from one area to the next, performing feats of courage, such as jumping off the top of the (not-so-tall) slide.

They play freely, not concerned about any danger. Even though cars travel on the roads bordering the park, none of the kids are afraid of a car smashing into the playground. Parents sit on the benches all around, so children come and go as they like, never worrying about getting lost.

But what if their parents just left? What if the laws of the land suddenly didn't apply? The children's lives are upheld by a well-designed structure, created by parents and by a society that values them. Without that framework, they would be bound in fear and imprisoned by insecurity.

But within that framework, they are free. Just like you and me. Within the laws the Lord has set up for us, we can live freely, abiding securely within the sight of our loving Father. We can run. We can swing up high. We can jump. We can grow.

Lord, thank You for the freedom
created by Your law. Amen. —ML

Reflections

For now we see only a reflection as in a mirror;
then we shall see face to face. Now I know in part;
then I shall know fully, even as I am fully known.
1 Corinthians 13:12 niv

One of the most beautiful aspects of a clear mountain lake is the upside-down world that can be seen in it. Colors and patterns are softly mottled as gentle ripples travel through the water's surface, set off by the touch of a water bug, or perhaps a bass coming up for a bite.

The watercolor landscape mirrored in the waters is lovely. It is quiet—no sound disturbs that country. It is more at peace than our world—no wars break out there.

But we cannot walk there. We cannot climb the mountains reaching down into the depths of the water. We cannot pick the black-eyed Susans that wave their pretty heads at us. As beautiful as it is, that world can never be as alive and as wonderful as the true creation all around us.

We are living in an upside-down world. And sometimes it's beautiful, but it can never be as beautiful or as real as the world God has created for us to live in for eternity. It is good to see here. It is good to know what we can know.

But it will be so much better there!

Dear Lord, help me remember every day that You have more in mind for me than I could ever imagine. Amen. —ML

Springing Up

Faithfulness springs up from the ground,
and righteousness looks down from the sky.
PSALM 85:11 ESV

Staring out of the airplane window, the rounded rectangle reveals a view that is unlike any we have on the ground. The layers of white blankets part, and there below is a patchwork of field squares—golden browns and light greens are bordered in gray or tan lines, country roads sewn into the land of generations. What we cannot see from our high vantage are the roots—the curling toes of the feet of thousands of plants, reaching out into the fertile soil, searching for refreshment and fuel. All the ingredients for life are there, waiting for them—buried beneath the ground and coming on the rays that blind the passengers of this morning flight.

In our lands of generations, broken by the pathways to industry, our roots reach out, searching for the refreshment that comes only from the Maker of life. His faithfulness breathes us into being. His solidness gives us something to land on, when we have flown away on emotion or ambition or arrogance.

He surrounds us, looking down from on high, but not with pity or disdain. He looks down as the sun shines—with perfect warmth meant to nourish us. With His faithful love fertilizing our path—how could we do anything but grow?

Maker of life, let me grow more faithful
and righteous every day in You. Amen. —ML

Not Too Still

"Rivers of living water will brim and spill
out of the depths of anyone who believes
in me this way, just as the Scripture says."
JOHN 7:38 MSG

Look upon a pond on a calm day and the surface appears to be a mirror reflecting sky and trees, and perhaps a goose flying by. No relentless waves hit the shore, splashing out their rhythmic song. No rushing rapids erode the rocks, smoothing them to a high shine. No, in fact, if the conditions are right (or rather, wrong) and the pond is very still, the balanced system of the pond fails. The pond, and all the life in it, begins to die.

Ironically, this death occurs because of too much living. If algae and weeds grow faster than the bacteria in the water can break them down, the plants begin to choke the life out of the watery world underneath that stagnant surface. So much lively action has to occur under those smooth, still waters for life to keep going. Harmony must be maintained for this song to be sung.

And if we are to spill over with the life of Jesus, we have to keep moving. Not in a rush or with a dramatic crash, but with the constant cycle of growth and maintenance and repentance and renewal. We must believe with every stage, whatever obstacles come or setbacks we may suffer. We must keep reaching up and up, moving toward the light.

Lord God, help me to keep reaching for You. Amen. —ML

He Leads Me

He leads me beside peaceful streams. He renews my strength.
He guides me along right paths, bringing honor to his name.
PSALM 23:2–3 NLT

Have you ever tried to guide a sheep? For all their fluffy exterior, they are hefty animals. They want what they want, and what they want is whatever is under their noses. Getting them to follow a particular path, without straying off after the nearest bit of clover or dandelion or anything really, requires constant prodding and nudging and sometimes pulling.

Without someone to guide them, sheep would be lost. They might survive, wandering here or there, eating whatever they happened upon. But they would miss out on the best feeding opportunities. They would not have shelter in the storms. And if they got sick or injured, they would be easy targets for the nearest predators. Sheep would not thrive alone.

We sheep need a shepherd—someone to guide us to sources of life that are clear and pure. We need to be shown the way to honor, not just any way. We often choose whatever steps seem the easiest, whatever way will get us what we want the fastest. But what seems fast and easy sometimes turns out to be ridiculously convoluted and hard. And in the end, we get nowhere. Or worse—we find ourselves stuck in states of shame or confusion.

My Shepherd and my God, lead me to places of peace. Show
me the best way that leads to honoring You. Amen. —ML

Thoughtful Obedience

We demolish arguments and every pretension that
sets itself up against the knowledge of God, and we
take captive every thought to make it obedient to Christ.
2 CORINTHIANS 10:5 NIV

What if? What if it rains tomorrow during our picnic? What if it gets too hot? What if my new job is too much work? What if my kid gets bullied? What if she bullies someone else? What if my spouse isn't happy with me? What if we can't stop fighting? What if I can't forgive? What if I can't be forgiven? What if I'm forgetting something to worry about?

The what-ifs can drive you crazy! They can weigh down your heart and exhaust your spirit. They can tangle up your thoughts and cause excessive distraction. They can stunt your spiritual growth with unproductive doubt.

Instead of allowing these destructive thoughts to occupy your brain, take them captive. How do you do that? Pray. Ask God for help. Lay out all your what-ifs before Him. Think them all the way through—what if the worst of the worst situations comes to pass? What then? Will God still be in charge? Will God help you? Will God love you?

As you answer your what-ifs with truth and knowledge of God, you will demolish all the anxiety-laden arguments. Bind up every wandering thought and make it obey you. And then make sure you keep obeying God.

What if you did that?

Dear Lord, help me make my every
thought obey You. Amen. —ML

Such Authority

When the crowd saw this, they were filled with awe; and they praised God, who had given such authority to man.

MATTHEW 9:8 NIV

One wonders if the paralyzed man on the mat perhaps had second thoughts about being brought to see Jesus. As Jesus looked down into his eyes and said, "Take heart, son," the man might have felt hope rising up in his chest. *This is it! I will walk again!*

But Jesus wanted to heal his heart, not his body.

When Jesus then said that the man's sins were forgiven, a ripple of disbelief went through the crowd that had gathered to witness a miracle. Forgiven sins? No one can do that! Only God!

It was true. Only someone wholly good could be in the position to forgive. Only the person offended by the act of sinning, the person against whose rules the sin was performed, only the person in authority over all could be the one to say, "Your sins are forgiven."

When Jesus then demonstrated the dominion over physical properties as well, the crowd had to face the truth. This was not an ordinary man. He was not just a powerful healer. He *was* the power.

And so they praised God for bringing this authority close enough for them to see. Humans love the thrill of a happy ending. But better still is the idea of a peaceful forever.

Dear Lord, thank You for showing us what real authority looks like. Amen. —ML

Looking for Mercy

We're watching and waiting, holding our breath,
awaiting your word of mercy.
PSALM 123:2 MSG

A world that lacks mercy is a world full of strife. Insults are spoken, fights break out, and because no one can turn away, because no one has the courage to be the first one to say, "I'm sorry," the anger escalates, the punches come harder and faster, weapons are drawn. People get hurt.

But mercy is born out of a peaceful heart. The person who has more desire to love than a lust for pride is able to bring calm to the tensest situation. They speak peace by offering forgiveness. They breathe relaxation by speaking words of kindness. They ooze relief by overlooking offenses.

Some who have lived lives of fear, who have known what it is to be imprisoned or abused or neglected or bullied, these people watch with anxious eyes. They wait for sharply delivered orders—orders they worry they won't be able to follow. When they make a mistake, they wonder, *Will we be struck again?* They expect to be answered in pain. What a joy when God starts them on a path to healing instead!

We watch and wait today, with one breath, together in spirit with our persecuted brothers and sisters. We wait for mercy. We wait to breathe again.

Dear Father of all, everyone comes to You with
a different story. Help us all find the way to
receive and give mercy. Amen. —ML

Understanding Life

*With your instruction, I understand life;
that's why I hate false propaganda.*
PSALM 119:104 MSG

We sometimes see pictures from other countries that feature oversized posters of country leaders, making them look strong and mighty. Big images and bold colors shout about confidence and power. We see messages that proclaim the superiority of societies—even when reliable reporting tells of suffering and injustice.

And what is our response? "I'm so glad we don't live there."

But look around. False messages are woven in our advertising. Assumptions lie behind images. Prejudices are painted right into the colors of our culture. It's not just hard to know who to trust—it's hard to believe our own eyes. Some lies have been told to us for so long, we don't even remember the truth.

But when we look in God's Word, truth leaps from the pages. When we study His story, we soak in His wisdom. We can use the worldview He gives us to silence lies and reveal false thinking. We can use His light to help us steer away from the acceptance of wrong-headed philosophy. We can learn that true love doesn't always translate to tolerance—sometimes it means saying hard things that hurt for a time and then bring healing. We can understand life, so we can treat others with understanding and compassion.

*Lord of the Word, help me to settle down
into studying what You have to say to me. Help
me to use Your light every day. Amen.* —ML

Exalted Even When

*I know that through your prayers and God's provision
of the Spirit of Jesus Christ what has happened to me
will turn out for my deliverance. I eagerly expect and
hope that I will in no way be ashamed, but will have
sufficient courage so that now as always Christ will be
exalted in my body, whether by life or by death.*
PHILIPPIANS 1:19–20 NIV

Sometimes it seems the world is against us. The dog throws up
on the new carpet, the car battery dies, and the kid who never
gets sick decides today is the day—on the same day you have
an important meeting that you absolutely, positively cannot miss.

When things go wrong, even when they go really, really
wrong, we always have a choice. We can choose to let the
circumstances weigh us down, or we can choose to climb up
on top of them. In hard times, it is good to remember that there
are people praying for us—that we are never alone. If we have
accepted Christ as our Savior, then the Spirit is in us. God will
not forget us. And we cannot forget Him.

Instead we can focus on what we know to be true. Our hope
is in Christ, not in this world. And even in the worst of times,
Jesus can be exalted in the way we act with courage, love consistently, and put others first.

*Lord, help me to have sufficient courage to do what I
need to do, even on really, really bad days. Amen.* —ML

Even in This Place

When Jacob awoke from his sleep, he thought, "Surely the
LORD is in this place, and I was not aware of it."
GENESIS 28:16 NIV

The place may not be all that you hoped for. The plumbing is leaky and the windows rattle. There are seven layers of wallpaper and none of them are good.

The job isn't all it seemed it would be. "Connecting with people every day" turned into filing forms for people every day. The other cubicle occupiers have it in for you. And no one will tell you where the *good* coffee is.

The dream life is not exactly a nightmare, but certainly not a pleasant vision either. There's too much to do and not enough time. Too many decisions and no one to help you decide.

Have you ever felt stuck somewhere? Have you ever felt like you just couldn't see why in the world God brought you to a place? Take heart. God has the same promise for you that He made to Jacob: "I am with you and will watch over you wherever you go" (v. 15).

Keep looking for where God is moving and the work He is doing. Don't give up. There might just be a surprise under that eighth layer of wallpaper.

God, You are everywhere. Help me to recognize
Your hand wherever I go and join You in the
work You have for me to do. Amen. —ML

Find Your Heart

*Let us not lose heart in doing good, for in due
time we will reap if we do not grow weary.*
GALATIANS 6:9 NASB

One more load of laundry. One more pile of dishes. One more dinner to make. One more toilet to clean. One more event to serve at. One more gift to give. One more thing to do.

Sometimes doing things for others just tuckers the life right out of you, doesn't it? It's not that it's not rewarding in some way. It's not that you even dislike doing it. It's just physically trying, energy-sapping, mind-tangling, emotionally draining work.

That's all. And that's okay. Just don't lose your heart in doing it. This admonition comes from the same letter that says to "Bear one another's burdens, and thereby fulfill the law of Christ" (v. 2). Paul is telling you—you're not alone! Don't feel like you have to do it all, be it all, make it all on your own. "For if anyone thinks he is something when he is nothing, he deceives himself" (v. 3). You are not Super-Wonder-Ultra Woman. And that's okay. Because apparently other people are supposed to bear your burdens (it's the law!), and no one really carries stuff for imaginary superheroes.

Don't lose heart. Don't forget why you are doing what you are doing, and who you are doing it for.

*Lord, help me to recognize that I don't have to
do everything. Help me to lean on You. Amen. —ML*

After the Storm

They were terrified and asked each other, "Who is this?
Even the wind and the waves obey him!"
MARK 4:41 NIV

The storm was over. The waves were calm. The boat had not capsized. Every person was accounted for. No one had died. No one had even been hurt.

They should have been grateful. Or at least relieved. But no one cheered. No one applauded. No one even said, "Thanks, Jesus."

Instead, those disciples in the boat—those friends of Jesus, who would one day be responsible for telling the world about Him—were terrified. They looked at Jesus—still standing there with His tunic dripping and His eyes flashing, waiting for anyone to answer Him—and they were completely, utterly, deeply terrified.

"Who is this?"

Just imagine for one moment that one of your best friends turned into a god right before your eyes, wielding all the power and authority and majesty that comes with being a divine being. Wouldn't you be just a little weirded out?

They thought He was their pal. They didn't know He was the Prince of Peace.

Sometimes we need to be reminded that the God we serve, the Lord we follow, is not just our friend. He is our Father God. He is the almighty King. He is the Master of the storm.

Lord, I live in awe of Your power. Thank You for using
that power in my life to calm my storms. Amen. —ML

Crushed

*"Then I took your sin, the calf which you had made,
and burned it with fire and crushed it and ground it
very small, until it was as fine as dust; and I threw its
dust into the brook that descended from the mountain."*

DEUTERONOMY 9:21 NKJV

Israel is about to cross the Jordan. They are going to fight the formidable descendants of Anak. They will fight nations much stronger and greater than they are. And Moses delivers to the people an interesting (and very long!) pep talk.

He does not talk about how wonderful the people of Israel are. He doesn't list their mighty deeds or their incredible strengths and skills.

Nope. He reminds them about all the times they messed things up. He reminds them of their stubbornness, and their unfaithfulness, and their rebelliousness. He tells them that they will enter this land and God will drive out the nations—but it won't be because they are so righteous and obedient.

It's because God is so good.

Moses speaks of the people's former idolatry—about the time they made an idol of gold and worshipped it instead of the almighty God. "Then I took your sin. . .and crushed it and ground it very small." And so their sin was crushed, yet the mighty and awesome God would not crush them.

*God, crush the sin within me so I can
live in peace with You. Amen.* —ML

Like a Great Deep

Your righteousness is like the mountains of God;
Your judgments are like a great deep.
PSALM 36:6 NASB

Imagine diving deep down into the ocean. Past a beautiful coral reef. Past a school of colorful fish. Deep down, where the waters get colder. Deep down, where you feel the weight of tons and tons of ocean pressing on your body. Deep down, where you struggle to see in the darkness.

God's judgments are as vast and as unknowable as that great deep—we cannot see into His thoughts. We just feel the weight of His wisdom and might. We feel the enormity of His existence.

Everything about God is unfathomably vast. His loving-kindness, as the psalmist writes, goes on and on to the heavens. His faithfulness has no end, like the ribbon of blue sky that wraps around and around us. His righteousness stands up tall and sharp, higher than anything, like the mountains.

And this limitlessness, rather than being scary and threatening, is somehow curiously comforting. So when we want to find refuge—where else do we find it but in the shadow of Him who is the light. We know there is space there—for all of us.

Endless God, love me forever, protect me everywhere,
lead me to eternal life with You. Amen. —ML

Sacred Submersion

*"You hurled me into the depths, into the very heart
of the seas, and the currents swirled about me;
all your waves and breakers swept over me."*

JONAH 2:3 NIV

Talk about not getting the answer you expected! First, God tells Jonah to offer the gift of discipline to a people Jonah fears and wants destroyed. When Jonah runs away—escaping to the sea—God calls him back via a test of the very first emergency broadcast system. He sends a storm to stop Jonah in his tracks.

And God's next answer looks very much like a final answer for our friend Jonah.

Let's examine the scene. Jonah, at his own request, is thrown into the sea as a form of sacrifice to God—a way to save the poor men who got caught up in Jonah's life drama when they unwittingly gave a ride out of town to the top guy on God's "most wanted" list. As Jonah is plunging down into the water, he calls out to the Lord in his distress (v. 1) and the Lord listens.

What's the answer? What solution does God propose to Jonah instead of being overwhelmed by the sea?

More sea.

For Jonah, the way out was the way down. Submerged into an ocean that rushed at him, current after current, with the message of God's sovereignty. "I am in control here, Jonah." Jonah couldn't help but rely solely on God—there was nowhere left to run.

*Lord, when my arrogance gets in the way,
submerge my pride in Your power. Amen. —ML*

Echoes of God

*There is something deep within them that echoes
God's yes and no, right and wrong.*
ROMANS 2:15 MSG

Picture yourself down in the ocean depths. You hear, somewhere in the distance, a sound that is not quite a cry, not quite a word—an alien sound to your ears. It's beautiful and weird, and somehow a little sad. The sound rises and falls. It seems to swirl around you, echoing off some distant rock formation and then returning. It comes from the deep and returns to the deep.

Somewhere hidden from you in the dark waters, a mammoth beast sings, calling out to its mate, or its child, or just calling to hear its own voice. The sound you hear is whale song.

Whale song is mysterious and strange to our ears. We don't know exactly what it means—it's unlikely we will ever be able to fully understand the language of whales (though scientists do try)—but we can tell that it's not just random noise. There's a purpose and a pattern to the notes. There's a message there for the one who can hear it.

God's messages speak to us in deep places. We don't always know exactly what they mean. But His truth is woven into the world He created. It echoes in our hearts, telling us there is a way to follow. There is something more than this world—something beautiful and weird, but where there will no longer be sadness. There is God.

*Lord, help me listen for the echoes of
Your truth all around me. Amen.* —ML

Tears of Joy

"Tears of joy will stream down their faces, and I will lead them home with great care. They will walk beside quiet streams and on smooth paths where they will not stumble."

JEREMIAH 31:9 NLT

Have you ever been crying so hard, you couldn't see well enough to walk straight?

In this part of Jeremiah's message, God is talking about a time when He will rebuild and restore His people, the nation of Israel. After a long period of living outside of God's favor (though never far from His care) and in rebellion, and then being scattered far and wide, away from their homeland, the Israelites will be gathered together again. In fact, God says He will gather His people "from the north and from the distant corners of the earth" (v. 8).

After being so long scattered and feeling cast out by God, the sweet relief and pure joy of the Israelites would have been overwhelming. And God, in His tender care, planned to bring them home softly—making sure no one would be lost or hurt on the way back. He would give them rest and calm, with quiet streams as their traveling companions and smooth paths for their feet.

Have you felt cast out by God? Have you been mourning on your own, feeling far away from the pleasant, refreshing company of God's faithfulness? Let God lead you home again. Let Him replace your grief with gladness and turn your sadness into celebration.

Lord, when I am far away from You,
keep calling me back. Please. Amen. —ML

Calm under Terror

*"I know the LORD has given you this land,"
she told them. "We are all afraid of you.
Everyone in the land is living in terror."*
JOSHUA 2:9 NLT

*A*nd the award for the best performance in a major role supporting God's people goes to. . .(insert drumroll) Rahab the prostitute!

This story from Joshua tells how he sent two spies to scout out Jericho—a hub for trade and something of an oasis in the desert. Scripture tells us Rahab's house was part of the town wall—as such, she was located in the perfect position to receive customers. But this also meant her house was vulnerable to attack.

The two spies were putting Rahab at great risk. The king of Jericho would have certainly killed her had he found out she was helping the Israelites. But Rahab hid the spies and calmly lied to the king's men when they directly questioned her.

Not only was Rahab calm in the face of certain death—as she admitted to the spies, she was living in terror of the Israelite God! She told Joshua's men that her people's "hearts have melted in fear" (v. 11).

With fear layered on top of terror, Rahab stayed calm and did what she had to do to support the work of "the supreme God of the heavens above and the earth below" (v.11). And by doing so, she saved her whole family.

*Lord, make me brave like Rahab—
willing to do anything for You. Amen.* —ML

Do Not Fret

Be still before the LORD and wait patiently for him;
do not fret when people succeed in their ways,
when they carry out their wicked schemes.
PSALM 37:7 NIV

That crooked politician wins a seat in local government. The woman who brazenly steals her recipes from a famous celebrity chef (everyone knows it) gets the Best Cake award at the county fair for the fifth year in a row. The drunken driver kills a beloved family pet and drives away, with no consequences.

Wait. Be still. But why? Shouldn't we want to get rid of wickedness? Shouldn't we fight against evil schemes?

Our first job as followers of Jesus is to trust in Him. Over and over throughout this psalm, the writer reminds his listeners where their hope lies. He reminds us to keep our minds focused on what God wants us to do and who He wants us to be—instead of fretting over and getting angry about what wicked people do. He writes, "Consider the blameless, observe the upright; a future awaits those who seek peace. But all sinners will be destroyed; there will be no future for the wicked" (vv. 37–38).

By standing strong for God, and living by His ways, we will show that the way of the wicked is in fact worthless.

Lord, when I'm tempted to envy people who
succeed in evil schemes, remind me that You've
got everything under control. Amen. —ML

Invisibly Purposed

*For everything, absolutely everything, above and below,
visible and invisible, rank after rank after rank of angels—
everything got started in him and finds its purpose in him.*
COLOSSIANS 1:16 MSG

He flits from spot to spot, always moving, never settling. He is, in fact, always eating. His wings are in constant motion.

Dragonflies are fascinating creatures. And one of the most interesting things about them is their wings—which are often almost invisible, looking like pieces of etched glass. Made of a strong network of veins and a thin film of chitin—a variation of starch—the dragonfly's wings at once seem powerful and absolutely fragile. But these beautiful, lacy wings allow these creatures to fly farther and higher and faster than most other insects. They are nature's drones—able to move deftly up and down, backward and forward, side to side, or even just to hover in the air for periods of time.

And though we may watch them and wonder what in the world they are so busy about, certainly they know their purpose. They are just busy trying to live and do what God created them to do—eat, reproduce, grow, and eat some more.

What a creator God we serve, who made every little and big thing in this world and took the time to make them beautiful and perfectly suited to do their work.

*God, I praise You for all the visible and invisible
wonder of Your creation. Amen.* —ML

Be Responsive

Be responsive to your pastoral leaders. Listen to
their counsel. They are alert to the condition of your
lives and work under the strict supervision of God.
Contribute to the joy of their leadership, not its drudgery.
HEBREWS 13:17 MSG

When you take time to be calm, find peace, and rest in the Lord, you not only receive refreshment for yourself; you are able to offer it to others.

As you follow your Good Shepherd in the life of faith and let Him lead you to rest beside still waters, take some time to look around and notice the work of those who are ministry leaders in your area—whether they are paid ministry staff or volunteers. Consider how much they do. Think about their families. Watch out for those not just in your church, but also those who lead organizations that care for the needs of others.

Then do something to be helpful and encouraging to them. Write a note thanking them for their service. Volunteer your time or skills. Find out what their family needs are and supply them where you can.

As they are often so caring and responsive to the needs of others, be an example in the way you are responsive to them. Contribute generously to their joy.

Good Shepherd, lead me to the acts of service and
encouragement that will be most useful. Amen. —ML

Hold Your Memories

*"But watch out! Be careful never to forget what
you yourself have seen. Do not let these memories
escape from your mind as long as you live!"*
DEUTERONOMY 4:9 NLT

Are you finding it hard to remember things as you get older?
Some things seem forever embedded in our brains, while
others flit away so easily—like little moths in and out of the
closet of our minds.

Memory experts say the memories that we hold on to the
best are our most meaningful, but also those that we interact
with. That is, if you witness or participate in an event, and then
look at pictures, or tell stories, or journal about that event, you
will have a better chance of committing that moment to memory.

Often we are running on such hurried schedules, we jump
from thing to thing with little time for reflection. Days blur into
days and we start losing track of even the most commonplace
bits of information.

Take a moment as you sit here by still waters, and think
about what has happened in your day. Write about it. Draw
about it. Tell someone about it. Daydream about it. Make this
practice part of your daily life.

Then do this with your time with God as well. As you
read His Word, consider it carefully. Take time to read each
word and interact with it. Savor the experience of sitting with
and learning about our God.

*Lord, help me to hold on to every
memory of Your presence. Amen.* —ML

Too Small

If you fail under pressure, your strength is too small.
PROVERBS 24:10 NLT

At first, this verse from Proverbs seems like a statement of the ridiculously obvious. Think of a bridge over a river. When a heavy truck drives over that bridge, the supports start to buckle and the sides crack. The road begins to crumble underneath the truck as the bridge fails. Its strength is clearly too small. It cannot withstand the pressure of the truck's weight.

But why is the bridge not strong enough? It all comes down to two things—the way that it was built and the materials it was built with.

Both of these things have to be excellent in order for a bridge to be strong. If the materials are solid, but the construction is wonky, the bridge will still fail. If the construction is well engineered, but the materials are weak, the bridge will still fail.

And so it is with us. We must be mindful not just about how we are becoming strong in our minds and hearts and souls, but we also have to be careful to go to the right source for that strength.

If our source is God and we follow His construction plans, then our strength will always be able to withstand any pressure.

*Master Creator, Lord of my life, make me strong
in every way and every day. Amen. —ML*

No Lack

The LORD your God has blessed you in all the work of your hands. He has watched over your journey through this vast wilderness. These forty years the LORD your God has been with you, and you have not lacked anything.

DEUTERONOMY 2:7 NIV

Can you imagine wandering about, with no permanent home, in the middle of desert territories, for forty years? And with the same bunch of grumbling people?

It's kind of amazing that those Israelites lasted four days together, much less forty years.

But they made it. Even with the complaining and arguing and disobeying and battling and struggling, they made it. And they made it because God supplied everything they needed.

No, He didn't give them coolers full of purified ice water. No, He didn't supply them with velvet-covered air mattresses. No, He didn't lay out a seven-course gourmet meal every evening.

He didn't give them everything they wanted. And He certainly didn't give them everything they coveted from others. He gave them everything they needed, when they needed it.

And that's what our God does for us too. The big difference is we don't have to wander around for forty years in the desert to discover this. We can see it right now, where we are. God supplies everything we need, when we need it. And we can always trust Him to do that.

Lord, I am filled with gratitude for all the ways You bless me every day. Amen. —ML

DAY 118

Under His Wings

He will cover you with his feathers,
and under his wings you will find refuge;
his faithfulness will be your shield and rampart.
PSALM 91:4 NIV

Father God and Mother Hen? Seems a little comical to think of the God of the universe as a clucking bunch of feathers, doesn't it? But the metaphor holds true.

Mothering birds have an instinct to take good care of their eggs. The actual hatching process is fairly miraculous, because different kinds of birds have different kinds of temperatures and processes that must happen in order to allow a healthy chick to develop well and be strong enough to peck its way out of the shell at the proper time. A bird, for example, may turn its eggs at certain precise intervals to ensure the egg is properly heated all the way through.

Then, once the chick has made its way out of the egg, it has to be fed constantly and sheltered diligently. Mother birds are often fierce protectors of their offspring—hens threaten to peck to death any other fowl that pick on their babies. And you'll often see tiny birds in the sky rousting larger birds of prey out of their territory.

God is our gentle nurturer, diligent provider, and fierce protector too. And He will not let His children be taken by the enemy.

Father and Protector, thank You for
providing a safe place for me. Amen. —ML

Controlled

*For the grace of God. . .teaches us to say "No" to
ungodliness and worldly passions, and to live self-controlled,
upright and godly lives in this present age, while we wait
for the blessed hope—the appearing of the glory of
our great God and Savior, Jesus Christ.*
TITUS 2:11–13 NIV

Controlled. Isn't it interesting what certain words bring to mind? Isn't it funny how just the sound of a word can make you feel a certain way?

Some people would find comfort in the idea of control. They might picture themselves being the one in control of a situation, or in control of others and able to call the shots.

Other people might be repelled by this word and the concept of controlling. They immediately see themselves as the ones being controlled by others, and they don't like that idea at all.

Some people see controlling as equal to taming, domesticating, repressing. Other people hear controlling as responsible, calming, or productive.

God wants us to have lives of self-control. He doesn't want to force us, although He easily could. He wants us to take charge of who we are, using Christ as an example through the power of the Holy Spirit!

*Lord, I know You've given me free will.
Please guide me to godly choices. Amen.* —ML

So Much Blessing

"Bring the whole tithe into the storehouse, that there
may be food in my house. Test me in this," says
the LORD Almighty, "and see if I will not throw open
the floodgates of heaven and pour out so much
blessing that there will not be room enough to store it."
MALACHI 3:10 NIV

It's interesting to note that many people who are now hoarders grew up in or were affected by times of severely depressed economic growth. Having spent many years of their childhood watching their parents scrimp and save and make do with nothing, they developed the habit of holding on tightly to what they have, no matter whether it was worth it or not.

But if we look back on our lives, we can see that we have never undergone a time when the God economy was not doing well. That is, God has always been producing, always blessing us, always causing us to grow. There have been no times when we had to worry about there not being enough God to go around. God's promises have always been a good value.

So what then keeps us from giving generously and cheerfully to God? What keeps us from offering the best and first bits of what we have back to the One who has given us every little bit of everything? God is waiting. He longs to bless us. Won't you let Him?

God, stretch my heart and grow my
spirit of generosity. Amen. —ML

Worthy

With this in mind, we constantly pray for you, that our God may make you worthy of his calling, and that by his power he may bring to fruition your every desire for goodness and your every deed prompted by faith.

2 THESSALONIANS 1:11 NIV

She had measured carefully. She had kneaded. She had proved. She had baked. And she had prayed over her work, hoping that her every wish for a good result would come true.

The baker at the county fair watched as her beautiful, golden-brown loaf was tapped and sliced and tasted by the judges. What would the verdict be? Was it worthy of a blue ribbon?

We want good things. And we want goodness to be a large part of our lives. But we can't achieve goodness on our own. No amount of good deeds will make us worthy of God's calling on our lives. Only by His power can we hope to produce a good work in our lives. Only by faith in Him can we hope to create a life worth living—the kind of life that produces good fruit, or good loaves.

Lord, I ask for Your power to be a prominent ingredient of my life. Help me produce goodness in my heart and mind and soul. Amen. —ML

In the Whirlwind

*His way is in the whirlwind and the storm,
and clouds are the dust of his feet.*
NAHUM 1:3 NIV

Strong winds and storms have done a lot of damage to people around the world lately. Hurricanes have wiped out the infrastructure on islands and brought devastating flooding to cities. Winds have kicked up fires that made them all the harder for emergency crews to fight.

In the midst of natural disasters, people often wonder where God is. And it's somehow comforting to know that He is in the storm. He is in the flood. He is in the fire. He is in the clouds. Not that He is causing people to suffer for no reason, or that He is everywhere in some sort of fuzzy way. But He is in the disasters helping—He's the force of love and generosity and care that rises up in the worst situations and causes men and women to take risks, to pull lives out of destruction, to uncover treasures of spirit and strength. He's in the power that can whip winds into furies but can also tame them. He's in the world, standing with us, crying with us, and loving us.

But He's also in the world calling out truth and calling us to justice. And in the end we know He will hold the unrepentant wicked accountable; this also is a sacred comfort.

Lord, let me never fail to see You in the world. Amen. —ML

Rend Your Heart

So rend your heart, and not your garments; return to the LORD
your God, for He is gracious and merciful, slow to anger,
and of great kindness; and He relents from doing harm.
JOEL 2:13 NKJV

In Bible times and in certain cultures, tearing one's clothes is a way of showing intense grief. We all have our own ways of showing grief or shock. Some of us throw things. Some of us light candles and cry. Some of us destroy our diets with chocolate. Lots of chocolate.

But how often do we really let our hearts break over the things that break the heart of God? How often do we grieve over our own sinfulness? How often do we get angry with ourselves for disappointing Him?

"Rend your heart, not your garments." Don't get caught up in the show of sorrow or holy anger without checking what's going on inside of you. If you're not getting angry or upset by the twisting of justice, the corruption of children, the oppression of the poor, and so many of the other issues that are plaguing our world, find out why. Examine your thoughts and see if your pride is keeping you from bowing before the Savior.

Man of Sorrows, I want to know what saddens You.
I want You to speak to my heart and move me to the
best way to serve You in this world. Amen. —ML

Blessing

*"May the LORD bless you and protect you. May the LORD
smile on you and be gracious to you. May the LORD
show you his favor and give you his peace."*
NUMBERS 6:24–26 NLT

We rarely engage in the practice of speaking blessings over one another these days. Sometimes we will bless a couple as they begin their marriage together. Or we might recite a blessing at a funeral or at a ceremony for a new baby. But speaking a blessing over others is a beautiful way to join together before God and invite God's goodness and love and peace to be shown in a specific way.

Speaking a blessing brings peace to the listener, but also peace to the speaker. In order to give the blessing, you spend time thinking on the good things of God. In receiving the blessing, you go away thinking about how those good things might appear in your life. It's a bless-bless situation.

Consider people in your life who are facing big decisions, complex life transitions, or hard situations. What blessing could you speak over them? What good qualities of God might make their lives better, healthier, or more complete?

*Lord, You have blessed us all in so many ways. Every time
I read Your Word, I am shown new gifts from You. Help me
to share these gifts of grace with others. Amen.* —ML

Acting for Peace

"If you remain silent at this time, relief and deliverance for the Jews will arise from another place, but you and your father's family will perish. And who knows but that you have come to your royal position for such a time as this?"
ESTHER 4:14 NIV

Esther was in an impossible situation. She could either speak out of turn or choose to remain silent. But either way, she risked destruction.

Her mentor and adoptive father, Mordecai, helped her to seize the moment by showing her that God was in control, no matter what happened. She could have hope that her action would not be some kind of prideful power grab, founded on a desire to get attention. She could hope that her speaking out might allow others to have a voice. She could hope that her action, done with fear and much trembling, might bring peace.

In what area of your life are you being pulled to act? What people need you to be a voice of courage for them? Speaking out doesn't mean giving big speeches or shouting others down. Sometimes speaking out just means telling the truth. That's all Esther had to do. That's what you can do too.

Lord, make me bold enough to speak truth wherever it needs to be spoken. Amen. —ML

Peaceable Lives

*Therefore I exhort first of all that supplications, prayers,
intercessions, and giving of thanks be made for all men,
for kings and all who are in authority, that we may lead a
quiet and peaceable life in all godliness and reverence.*
1 TIMOTHY 2:1–2 NKJV

Meaningless talk was coming from the pulpit. People were
teaching confidently in areas where they had no knowledge, making statements that they couldn't back up. False doc-
trines were circling throughout the body of believers. Some were
getting overly concerned about details that just didn't matter.
Others were allowing themselves to be swept up in the belief
of myths, without giving careful consideration to understanding
the truth.

Sound like any church you know?

These things reminded Paul of someone he knew—himself.
He said, "Christ Jesus came into the world to save sinners—of
whom I am the worst" (1:15 NIV). But Jesus showed patience
and mercy with Paul as an example to the world of how He
came to save sinners. And so Paul urged Timothy to hold on to
faith and a good conscience so he could live a peaceful and
quiet life. And by doing so, Timothy could also be an example
to those believers in Ephesus who were *not* so peaceful or quiet.

*Lord, when I come to You in prayer, help me to lift up
all believers around me. Let me be thankful for all who
are in authority, and let me live in a way that brings
peace and shows Your mercy. Amen.* —ML

Covenant Friendship

*And Jonathan made a covenant with
David because he loved him as himself.*
1 SAMUEL 18:3 NIV

If their story had happened in modern times, certainly someone would have made a "bromance" movie about them. King Saul's son Jonathan and the king's rival David had a close relationship—like brothers. As Saul's jealousy grew, he hated David all the more and wanted to kill him. But Jonathan risked his father's wrath to protect David.

The conflict came to a head at the New Moon feast, when Saul had plotted to kill David once again, but Jonathan helped David escape, risking even his own life at the end of Saul's spear in the process.

As the two close friends parted company, they promised to show kindness to each other's families and invited God as a witness to their promise, saying "The LORD is witness between you and me, and between your descendants and my descendants forever" (20:42 NIV).

Even under the worst conditions, a close bond can bring peace to friends. When it seems like everyone else is against you, having even one friend who is willing to look out for you can make all the difference in the world.

*Father God, thank You for the friendships I
have in my life. Help me to honor my friends
by keeping my promises to them. Amen.* —ML

Wiped Clean

Every living thing on the face of the earth was wiped out;
people and animals and the creatures that move along
the ground and the birds were wiped from the earth.
Only Noah was left, and those with him in the ark.

GENESIS 7:23 NIV

The waters flooded the earth for 150 days. That's a long time to be stuck in one place with the same people. And it's a long time to wonder about what is going on outside in the world.

Imagine knowing that every human in the world, except for your little family, was being wiped away from the earth. Every person you'd ever met or done business with. Every neighbor. Everyone you passed at the market or on your way to work. All gone.

Noah, having a close relationship with God, must have grieved along with God for what the world He had created had become. Genesis 6:6 (NIV) says the Lord "regretted that he had made human beings on the earth, and his heart was deeply troubled."

How quiet the world must have seemed when they finally were able to come out of the ark—not a single other soul in the world to greet them! And in that quiet, they were able to start new, in the very best place to start, offering themselves humbly before the Lord.

Lord, may every morning be my time to start new with You—
offering my heart as a place for Your light to shine. Amen. —ML

Let Him Fight

"The Lord will fight for you;
you need only to be still."
Exodus 14:14 NIV

Pharaoh and his massive army were after the Israelites. They had been let go from Egypt and had come so far, only to find their former masters still chasing them. The Israelites panicked—stuck between the life of slavery and what seemed like an impassable obstacle. They forgot all that God had just done for them. They forgot all the plagues that God had sent upon their enemies, and they forgot how God had protected them all along.

Have you ever been caught in a hard place, feeling that panicky feeling of being unable to get out, unable to break free from your past? What do you do at times like those? Do you lean into God's presence, or do you lean on your own power?

We would do well to remind ourselves of Moses' answer to the people of Israel and make these words the ones we remember when we are feeling stuck: "Do not be afraid. Stand firm and you will see the deliverance the Lord will bring you today. . . . The Lord will fight for you; you need only to be still" (vv. 13–14).

God of Israel, help me to stand firm in my convictions and on the promises You have made to Your people. When trouble comes, I know I can depend on You. Amen. —ML

Changed

We will not all sleep, but we will all be changed—
in a flash, in the twinkling of an eye, at the last trumpet.
For the trumpet will sound, the dead will be raised
imperishable, and we will be changed.
1 CORINTHIANS 15:51–52 NIV

Have you ever watched a butterfly emerging from its chrysalis? You have to be on butterfly-watch for days and days to see it happen. And like the proverbial watched pot, it seems like it is never going to happen as long as you are looking.

Then, just about when you wanted to give up, some movement happens. A tremble. A quiver. This is the moment to pay attention, because literally, if you blink too long, you will miss it. The whole process from that first fidgeting until the energetic emerging happens in a flash.

All of a sudden, the drab greenish-gray chrysalis is shed, and everything about the striped caterpillar has changed—legs, body, antennae, color. Everything! But it's still the same creature. The butterfly that now frees its vibrant, fragile wings is the same being as the caterpillar that imprisoned itself in the firm cocoon.

And someday we too will be changed, leaving behind prisons of our own making for majestic, grace-given freedom.

Lord, there is so much beauty in the world that happens in these still, quiet moments. Let me be looking out all the time for the beauty of eternity that You show us every day. Amen. —ML

Undisturbed

*The fruit of that righteousness will be peace;
its effect will be quietness and confidence forever.
My people will live in peaceful dwelling places,
in secure homes, in undisturbed places of rest.*
ISAIAH 32:17–18 NIV

How is the neighborhood where you live? Is it sleepy and quiet, perhaps nestled away from the busy world in a calm cul-de-sac? Or is it speedy and spastic, with people running to and fro on their full schedules and cars zipping about in large numbers?

No matter where you live, you can create a culture of calm in your relations with your neighbors. Start by getting to know your neighbors. Find out what their needs are. Find out their pet peeves. Seek out moments to show kindness. Be humble in your communications. Put others' interests above your own as you make changes to your house or your yard. Make sure any noise coming from your house doesn't disturb others.

Everyone wants to dwell in peace and security. Do your part to bring a little of God's blessings to His people to your street or your community. And while you're at it, bring His peace into your heart and vow to live, as much as it is in your control, a life of calm—undisturbed by the drama of others' lives, and yet being moved with compassion when people are troubled by suffering or hardship.

*Lord, make me a good neighbor and a
good witness of Your love. Amen.* —ML

Don't Miss a Word

When they heard him speaking Hebrew, they grew even
quieter. No one wanted to miss a word of this.
ACTS 22:2 MSG

The scene was set. Paul had come to Jerusalem and been dragged from the temple by angry, riotous Jews. These men were trying to kill him! Then the Roman troops heard the uproar and came running to calm the mob and find out what was going on. Unable to discern who exactly was at fault, the soldiers took Paul into custody—most likely for his own protection, in the first instance.

But as they were taking him away, Paul asked for a chance to speak to the people. The crowd became silent. And Paul, who knew several languages, addressed them in Aramaic, a dialect of Hebrew—the language of the people. And in his first words, he caught the crowd's ears even more: "I am a good Jew" (v. 3).

Paul took this opportunity to speak and tell all who were listening about his testimony and his belief in Jesus—even though he knew that would turn the crowd against him. What follows in the accounts of Acts is Paul's track through various courts and prisons, and even a shipwreck scene, as Paul slowly made his way to Rome. Everywhere he went, Paul used every opportunity to speak about Jesus—telling his story to some of the most powerful people in the land. And many learned about Jesus through Paul's willingness to speak.

Lord God, help me not miss a
chance to tell Your story. Amen. —ML

Healing Mercy

"O Lord," I prayed, "have mercy on me.
Heal me, for I have sinned against you."
PSALM 41:4 NLT

There is nothing more humbling than admitting you've done wrong. But admitting you've done wrong against God is perhaps the most humbling experience any human can ever have. It's that moment when you realize that, even though God created a world for you, breathed life into you, shaped you, led you, guided you, protected you, provided for you, and died for you, you still chose a moment of sin over obedience to Him.

But it seems like there is not any other moment in which we can feel the weight of God's mercy than in this moment of confession. Because as we bow before the King of kings to admit our sins, in that stillness, in our sadness, we can't help but feel His never-ending, amazing, healing love.

What a miracle it is that God continues to love us and claim us, even when we turn away from Him! How gracious is our God—who bends toward us, picks us up, and heals our wounds, even those wounds that we have carved out with our own hands.

Father God, I praise You for Your loving mercy! I accept
Your forgiveness. I want to try again. Lord, heal my
heart so that I can live for You. Amen. —ML

Life-Giving Water

"For the Lamb on the throne will be their Shepherd.
He will lead them to springs of life-giving water.
And God will wipe every tear from their eyes."
REVELATION 7:17 NLT

Have you ever visited a spring? It's such a wonder—to see the water bubbling and bubbling up, never ceasing, and to know that there's no machine making it happen, no pump, no man-made interference. Just pure, clean, natural, untouched water.

God promises to lead us to springs of life-giving water. The image presented to John in Revelation is one of continual, eternal refreshment as opposed to the image of our current world—where people go hungry and thirsty and face long days in the heat of the sun. We live in a world where supplies run out, where there's never enough to go around, where struggle is the name of the game, and where our resources are often polluted.

Our hope in heaven is hope in a place where there will always be enough, and even more. It's a hope in a time when sorrow and struggle will disappear, because scarcity and strife will no longer exist. It's a hope that bubbles up, never ceasing, coming from our eternal Life Giver.

Eternal God, I look forward to the day when I can drink forever from Your life-giving springs. Amen. —ML

Born for Trouble?

*"People are born for trouble as readily
as sparks fly up from a fire."*
JOB 5:7 NLT

Poor Job. Besides his devastating personal losses, he had to put up with being surrounded by his less-than-helpful friends. Job's friend Eliphaz presented the idea that no innocent people die. In other words, someone somewhere along the way must have done something wrong for this calamity to have fallen on Job's household.

In the previous chapter, Eliphaz challenged Job: "Stop and think! Do the innocent die? When have the upright been destroyed? My experience shows that those who plant trouble and cultivate evil will harvest the same" (4:7–8 NLT).

Eliphaz argued that people create their own trouble and that Job should go to God to receive correction. But in doing so, Eliphaz made the same mistake we all often make—he pushed God out of His position as Sovereign Lord. He negated the idea that God is in control—in hardship or in triumph, God is in control. When we suffer and when we thrive, God is in control. When we don't have any idea how to make sense of the situation, God is very much in control.

Yes, people are indeed born for trouble—born into a broken world with hearts that desire to disobey. But that doesn't change the fact that God is in control.

Lord, I know my heart is not pure. But I know You can rule in my heart, and in my world. Let me serve You. Amen. —ML

Deep Roots

"They are like trees planted along a riverbank,
with roots that reach deep into the water."
JEREMIAH 17:8 NLT

The drain was plugged. And as we watched the hole in the basement floor with some anxiety, we realized the next thing that could happen could very well be a stinky, sludgy, sewage mess all over the basement floor. And what might be the cause?

Roots.

As trees grow, they stretch out their roots, seeking water and nourishment. If what they need cannot be found in the ground—during a drought or in the dry, cold months of winter—the roots will keep stretching and searching, until they find those house pipes.

Wouldn't it be wonderful if we were a little bit more like the trees—always stretching and searching for the life-giving water of the Lord? In spiritual dry times, times when we just don't feel the passion that we once had, we could be driven to keep seeking out nourishment from God's Word, listening hard for His counsel during prayer, and looking at His faithfulness in the lives of His saints. As recorded in Jeremiah, we could then be like those "who trust in the LORD and have made the LORD their hope and confidence" (v. 7).

Lord, I want my roots to be firmly planted, embedded,
and completely satisfied in You. Amen. —ML

Pour Out Your Heart

*Trust in him at all times, you people; pour out
your hearts to him, for God is our refuge.*
PSALM 62:8 NIV

Do you have a bosom friend? Someone whom you can trust with anything? Someone who is always there for you, through good and bad times? How often do you pour your heart out to your friend? How often do you listen to your friend's heart?

Even the very best friends sometimes disappoint us. They can't always be there exactly when we need them. And sometimes we are the ones who fail—sometimes we just can't bring ourselves to express what is going on inside.

But God can always be trusted with our deepest secrets, our innermost longings, our most intense hurts. He knows us inside and out, and He alone knows exactly what we need to heal, to recover, and to renew. When we come to Him, He protects our hearts. He is a mighty protector and a stalwart refuge! And even when we can't find the words to say what is going on in our hearts and minds, our Lord and Savior is the one person who knows exactly what we are going through, before we utter a single word.

Cultivate trustworthy friendships that can stand the test of time. But always remember that you have a Friend who is constantly and consistently ready to hear your heart.

*Lord God, my Friend, thank You for being a safe
place for me to share my heart. Amen.* —ML

Not Shaken

"Though the mountains be shaken and the hills be
removed, yet my unfailing love for you will not be
shaken nor my covenant of peace be removed,"
says the LORD, who has compassion on you.
ISAIAH 54:10 NIV

When was the last time you felt that the rug was being pulled out from under your feet? When did you last feel a crushing blow that took your breath away? Was it a friend who left you in the lurch? Was it a spouse's harsh words? Was it the sudden and tragic death of someone whose absence has now left a giant, gaping hole in your life?

What do you do when your mountains are shaken? What do you do when the landscape around you shifts into some kind of foreign territory? Sometimes it's hard to know where to put your first step.

But though relationships and careers and finances and even our own bodies are subject to change, one thing will never change. God's love for us will never be shaken. God's compassion for us never fails. God's promise to give us peace will never be broken. When everything around us seems to be falling apart, we can go to His Word and be reminded that He does not change.

Lord, thank You for Your constant presence. Amen. —ML

Search Me

*Search me, God, and know my heart; test me and
know my anxious thoughts. See if there is any offensive
way in me, and lead me in the way everlasting.*
PSALM 139:23–24 NIV

What keeps you up at night? Or even more so, what wakes you up in a cold sweat? What makes your stomach churn?

Sometimes we don't even know what's bothering us. We just know something is.

Whenever anxiety plagues your soul, ask God to look into your thoughts. And not just once. Keep asking. Taking time to consider what subjects are rising to the top of your mind on a regular basis can help you sort out which things are most important to you. And it could also help you see which problems are taking up too much of your mind space, and which ones aren't really that important.

Are there any topics that are taking up your thoughts so much that they are distracting you from your relationship with God? Are there issues that are blocking your relationships with others? Ask God to point out anything that is hurting your connections to Him or other people.

Consider all these questions in light of eternity. Will these worries really matter much then?

*Lord, help me to discern the issues that are significant
from the things that are only fleeting. Amen.* —ML

A Pact

"We will not neglect the house of our God."
NEHEMIAH 10:39 NIV

Nehemiah and the Israelites had come together to gather tithes, the portions of what they had, to go toward the service of the house of God. Nehemiah and his crews had been working for some time together rebuilding the wall around the holy city. And though they were people from all different kinds of jobs and with a broad range of skills and assets, they were united in their purpose—restoring the holy city of the Israelites, Jerusalem.

As they finished the work on the wall, they paused to take stock—not just of their material resources, but of their history with God—where they had come from, all that God had done for them, and what they wanted to do next. And they promised together, as one body, to serve the house of God.

It's a good example for us. As bodies of believers, how often do we take time together to think about what God has done for us? How often do we hear each other's stories of how God has blessed us or changed us or led us? And do we gather together to decide together what mission we are united in—or do we let the pastoral staff take that all on their own shoulders? Are we just coming and occupying seats? Or are we actively participating in the work of the church?

Lord God, help me to think more carefully about what I can do for You as part of my local congregation. Amen. —ML

New Heart

*"I will give you a new heart and put a new
spirit in you; I will remove from you your
heart of stone and give you a heart of flesh."*
EZEKIEL 36:26 NIV

Stubborn. That's what she is. The toddler sits in her chair and refuses to eat the mashed potatoes. She says they aren't mashed enough. She says they aren't white enough. She says they are "ucky." And she won't have it.

But she is not the boss.

And so the battle of wills begins. It happens so early, doesn't it? Sometimes even before we learn to speak, we learn to want our own way.

The thing we don't learn until much later is that our own way is often not the best way for us. The One who knows us inside and out and can see all the paths before and beyond us is the One we need help from. But to ask for that help requires submission. It requires us to give a little. Or a lot. It requires us to let go of our stubborn hearts and open them up to Him—the shaper of hearts. And if we do that, He will gladly make our hearts new.

And He probably won't even make us eat the mashed potatoes. Maybe.

*Lord, thank You for creating a new
heart within me. Amen.* —ML

Don't Be Puffy

*"See, the enemy is puffed up; his desires are not upright—
but the righteous person will live by his faithfulness."*

HABAKKUK 2:4 NIV

We all know this guy. He owns every room. He controls conversations. He interrupts. He monopolizes time. He pushes his way into situations where he wasn't invited. He always wants his way, and if he can't have it, he just leaves or gets irritated.

His desire is for one thing and one thing only. All attention, from all eyes, on him, all the time.

Okay, so it's pretty easy to point fingers at characters like this and say, "That guy is so full of himself—he's as puffy as a marshmallow!" But what about us? Can we ever be accused of being a little puffy? Do we sometimes think our issues matter more than someone else's? Do we ever take advantage of someone's time? Do we get so caught up in our plans that we forget to consider others first?

Before pointing fingers at our puffy friends and enemies, we should evaluate our own souls. Are we living in a way that is faithful to God's commands, or are we only faithful to our own plans?

*Lord of lords, be Lord of my life. Be Lord of my words
and my actions. Help me to be a faithful follower
and not a puffed-up fool. Amen. —ML*

Partners

*I pray that your partnership with us in the faith may
be effective in deepening your understanding of
every good thing we share for the sake of Christ.*
PHILEMON 6 NIV

Partnerships are helpful in many different areas of life. Workout partners can help spur each other on to work harder, push muscles further, and eat better. Business partners can bounce ideas off each other, divide up complex projects, or raise funds together.

Who are your faith partners? Do you have people in your life who walk alongside you as you work out your life in Christ?

Faith partners can help one another remember to stay in the Word, can hold each other accountable about tricky temptations, and can pray for each other. As you share your lives with each other, you learn about how God is working in each person's life, and you see how that happens in a myriad of ways. Your understanding of the good gifts God gives us grows. And then, when hardship comes your way, you can fall back on those lessons of faith you've learned through sharing in the life of another person.

Partnerships create many valuable outcomes that can change one person's single endeavor into something that impacts a whole community. Make sure you have a faith partner in your life!

*Lord, help me to support other people as they seek
to follow You. Help me be humble and helpful as I
walk together with other disciples. Amen. —ML*

Enough Is Enough

Now this is what the LORD Almighty says: "Give careful thought to your ways. You have planted much, but harvested little. You eat, but never have enough. You drink, but never have your fill. You put on clothes, but are not warm. You earn wages, only to put them in a purse with holes in it."

HAGGAI 1:5–6 NIV

Planting much, harvesting little. Eating and drinking without ever being satisfied. Putting on all sorts of layers but never getting warm! And making money one day only to turn around and see it all gone the next.

Sounds like a nightmare. And. . .sounds kind of familiar.

The Lord delivered a message through the prophet Haggai to the governor of Judah and to the high priest. God wanted them to see that their efforts to make progress kept failing because they were not giving proper attention to the work of the Lord. They had not obeyed Him and were not concerned enough with rebuilding His dwelling place.

Could that be why our efforts sometimes fall flat? Do we push God's work for us aside and leave it as the last item on our to-do lists? God wants to be first in our lives! And when we put Him first, somehow all the other things miraculously fall in line.

Lord, I want You to be first on my list. Help me to focus my heart and mind on You every day. Amen. —ML

Sharing All

For if we are faithful to the end, trusting
God just as firmly as when we first believed,
we will share in all that belongs to Christ.
HEBREWS 3:14 NLT

The heavens. The earth. The seas and all that is in them. The birds of the air. The words of our mouths. The thoughts of our hearts. The whole universe. All the riches in the world. All the blessings of God. All the power in heaven and on earth. All the hope. All the strength. All the peace. All the joy. All the love. You. Me. Everyone.

Just think of all the amazing things that belong to Christ! And that is what we will share in, if we remain faithful to following Him and trust God just as much as when we first believed.

In this moment by still waters, think of how you were when you first believed. What did you feel? What did you think? How sure were you of God's presence? Try to recall who you were and what your attitude toward God was then, right when you first gave your heart to Him. Do you think you trust Him as much now? If not, what can you do to get closer to that place of trust?

Lord Jesus, I want to share in all the wonderful gifts
You have waiting for me. Help me to get back to the
kind of trust and passion and confidence I had in
You as on the day I first believed. Amen. —ML

DAY 146

Too Tired to Be Cool

"Come to me, all you who are weary and burdened, and I will give you rest. Take my yoke upon you and learn from me, for I am gentle and humble in heart, and you will find rest for your souls. For my yoke is easy and my burden is light."
MATTHEW 11:28–30 NIV

Have you ever thought, *I am exhausted from trying to be cool, from trying to have the right clothes, the right Christianese, the right smarts and witty comebacks, the right everything? I don't have all the answers. I don't really stand out in the crowd. The world seems to need me to be chic and with-it and unique and tech-savvy and slang cool. But in all honesty, I'm discouraged, and I'm tired of the merry-go-round. I'm tired of the nonsense. I want off this ride called earth. What now?*

Everyone knows discouragement from time to time. If you need a good long rest from the pressures and expectations and demands of this world, God knows just who you can turn to. . . .

Oh Lord, I'm really worn out from jumping through so many earth hoops. I can no longer be everything to everybody. I'm going to trust You to get me through this wearisome time. Help me to learn to rest in You always. Amen. —AH

Just Stand in Your Position

*Each man stood at his position around the camp
and watched as all the Midianites rushed around
in a panic, shouting as they ran to escape.*
JUDGES 7:21 NLT

This chapter in many Bibles is titled "Gideon Defeats the Midianites," but the Lord's hand was all over this victory. First, God chooses a man to lead His army who claims to be anything but a warrior. "How can I rescue Israel?" Gideon asks (6:15 NLT). He claims to be the least person in the weakest clan of Manasseh. The least of the least.

He's also full of doubt, asking God to go through several tests to prove what He says is true.

Then for good measure, God thins out Gideon's army—reducing it from 32,000 men to only 300.

But as we see in the account of the confrontation with Midian, even these 300 weren't really necessary. Gideon and his 300 men circled around the Midianite camp. All at once, they broke their clay jars with torches in them and sounded their horns.

But it was the Lord who caused the Midianites to rush around in a panic, fighting against themselves, like sleepwalkers awakened in a groggy dream. All Gideon's men had to do was stand still. God, as He often does, created the climate for victory.

*Lord, help me stand firm in the position You give me and trust
You to claim the victory over my enemies. Amen.* —ML

Be Careful Who You Copy

*Dear friend, do not imitate
what is evil but what is good.*
3 JOHN 11 NIV

Have you ever tried to dress like someone else? Or maybe you've got your hair cut to look like a celebrity's hairstyle. Or perhaps you've taken to using a certain catchphrase that has been popularized by someone on social media.

It's tremendously easy to get caught up in sounding or looking like someone else—especially if we get a positive reaction from doing so. But we have to be careful about whom we are trying to copy. Do a self-evaluation. Why do you want to adopt these styles or habits? What good does it do for you? What bad does it do?

We have to be mindful, as followers of Christ, to not take on behaviors or images that will not be in keeping with a godly life. Sometimes the attitudes and actions we adopt on the outside begin to change the way our thoughts and feelings work on the inside. Thus, John advises his readers to not imitate anything that hints at evil, but instead to model what is good.

*Lord, help me seek to uniquely represent You.
I don't want my image to get in the way of
people seeing Jesus in me. Amen.* —ML

Nothing

But godliness with contentment is great gain. For we brought nothing into the world, and we can take nothing out of it.
1 TIMOTHY 6:6–7 NIV

Babies are bundles of pudgy wrinkles, snuffley noses, and wriggly toes. They come with no expectations and no reservations, and their main motivation is hunger. They ask for nothing but food, and nothing but cuddles, and nothing but love. And they take us by surprise with their all-consuming cuteness and the deep connection we feel to them forever. They don't need anything but their eyes to catch our attention. They don't need anything but their smiles to wield power over us.

We bring nothing into this world but ourselves—our capacity to love and consume and grow. And a life of contentment is marked by those same simple satisfactions—love, nourishment, and learning.

If we can learn to go after those things, instead of worldly possessions, passions, or power, we will come closer to living a godly, and a more contented, life. Instead of falling into the trap of craving riches and scrambling for control, we can achieve the fullness of generosity and the righteousness of humility. And by so doing, we'll avoid ruin and destruction.

God of the universe, thank You for bringing me into this world to learn about Your love. Amen. —ML

Oceans

You rule the oceans. You subdue their storm-tossed waves.
PSALM 89:9 NLT

Oceans are powerful—hurricane winds or massive earthquakes can cause the oceans to wave and turn and spiral and churn, creating huge flooding waves that crash on the shores.

Oceans are mysterious—there are still many places in the ocean that have not been observed and recorded. Still so many creatures we've never even seen.

Oceans are predictably unpredictable—so many factors can affect the speed and direction of ocean waves. It's hard to know whether a small storm is going to turn into something disastrous, or whether a hurricane might fizzle out into a few showers.

Only our God is big enough to see all the oceans. Only He can see down into the farthest depths. And only He knows every turn and twist of every wave. Only He can speak calm into the ocean's chaos.

And because He can do all that, He can calm our chaos too. He can order our disordered days. He can subdue our stormy souls. No wonder the "highest angelic powers stand in awe of God" (v. 7)!

God of angel armies, God of ocean storms, take my life and blow a wind of peace over my rebellious waves. Amen. —ML

Space to Reflect

I will study your commandments and reflect on your ways.
PSALM 119:15 NLT

Where do you go when you really need to concentrate? Students during finals week often seek out coveted library tables. But so many students descend on these areas that a quiet buzz starts to rise up, making it difficult to keep one's eyes on the page, and not on who might be sitting close by.

Performers sometimes practice in little closet-like rooms where they can stick on some headphones and hone in on the sound of their own instruments. But eventually they will need to rejoin the larger band in order to make good music.

The proverbial image of someone who wants to find peace in meditation is generally a lone person sitting on top of a mountain. But if we even had a mountain close by, who among us could have enough breath by the time we got to the top of it to focus on anything other than trying not to fall off the edge?

Thankfully, taking time to reflect on God's ways doesn't have to mean climbing a mountain, hiding in a closet, or braving a crowded library. We can reflect a little every day, in our own homes, by just opening up our Bibles and reading His Word.

My great God, I love spending time with You.
Thank You for the gift of Your Word and the
glimpses I have of You in it. Amen. —ML

Silent Night, Joyous Morn

*Early on Sunday morning, while it was still dark,
Mary Magdalene came to the tomb and found that
the stone had been rolled away from the entrance.*
JOHN 20:1 NLT

Joseph of Arimathea had perhaps the saddest, loneliest job there ever was. On his own, due to the risk involved, he approached Pilate to ask for Jesus' body. We're told in the Gospel of Mark that Joseph was a member of the high council and that he was waiting for the kingdom of God. Perhaps Joseph, like so many, had hoped that Jesus would bring that kingdom. And now, his hopes would be buried along with the body of the rabbi.

Joseph took Jesus' body, wrapped it in the cloth he had purchased with his own money, and then laid Jesus gently down on the stony, cold bed in the dusky light before the Sabbath, perhaps whispering a farewell prayer before he sealed the tomb with the stone.

Contrast that with the morning of the third day, when the breathless, hectic discovery of the empty tomb rocked the world of Jesus' disciples. Imagine Peter's surprise being caught in his throat as he beheld the quietly folded wrappings that had enveloped Jesus' dead body just hours ago. And as the realization dawned on him while the day dawned outside, joy and bewilderment bubbled up inside the fisherman.

*Lord, You speak to me through the stillness of Your tomb
and through the glory of Your resurrection morning.
Thank You for dying and living for me. Amen. —ML*

Be Holy

"I am the LORD, who brought you up out of Egypt to be your God; therefore be holy, because I am holy."
LEVITICUS 11:45 NIV

Often we think of holiness as some unattainable state of godly perfection. We think it's something to wish for, perhaps something we may have in heaven, but not something we can ever hope to achieve here on earth.

But that is not what our Lord says. God would not tell His people to do a thing that He would not equip them to do. Much of Leviticus is God's way of helping the Israelites to be holy. And this holiness does not equal perfection—it equates rather to a position of being set apart before God.

God tells the Israelites how to be holy—He spells it out for them in specific ways that seem hard for us to imagine in modern times. We can't understand the concept of living by a hundred different rules on what to eat and wear and drink and do. But God gives the Israelites clear instructions on how to set themselves apart from other people in the world because He wants the Israelites to succeed. He wants them to set themselves apart. He wants them to be His. He wants to be their God. And He wants that for us too.

Lord, teach me how to be holy,
as You are holy. Amen. —ML

Beautiful Garden

*"You will be like a well-watered garden,
like an ever-flowing spring."*
ISAIAH 58:11 NLT

Imagine for a moment, in this time of stillness, that you are walking in the most beautiful garden you've ever seen. Everywhere you look, there is a different kind of blossom, or leaf, or color, or creature to discover. There are fruit trees laden with juicy, delicious apples and pears and oranges. There are sweet blooms that attract butterflies and bees with their heady fragrances. Every plant seems to have a place. There are no bare spots, no patches of brown grass, no wilted stems, because through the garden runs a small stream, which comes down from a hill at the base of a mountain—sourced in the cool, ever-running waters of the mountain spring.

This beautiful garden is what we can be like if we let the Lord guide our lives. If we follow Him to feed the hungry and help those in need. If we let His light shine through us out into a dark world. If we rebuild what has been damaged and restore broken homes. Then God will fuel us, give to us, and restore us—refreshing us with His living water.

*Lord of the Sabbath, let me set aside time to learn how to
follow You. Teach me Your will. Show me how to give
from the heart. Restore my spirit, Lord. Amen. —ML*

Into the Depths

Once again you will have compassion on us.
You will trample our sins under your feet and
throw them into the depths of the ocean!
MICAH 7:19 NLT

Consider what it would be like if God kept a record of our sins. Instead of wiping them away, what if He kept a tally up on a big cosmic board? Then every time we sinned again, He'd point out when and where we'd done that sin before.

What if He compared our record of sins with that of others? What if He valued those of us with less sin in our lives as better than those of us with more? And what if we could only get to live with Him if our sin count was right?

If our God was a God who kept all records of wrongs, would you feel loved by Him? Or would you instead just feel like a number? Would you feel as though He was watching over you with compassion? Or would you just feel watched?

Thankfully, we serve the God of grace and forgiveness. He shows us unfailing and unconditional love by utterly crushing our sins and throwing them away. No records. No tallies. No scores. Just love.

Thank You, Lord, for keeping Your promises to
forget our sins and forgive us. Amen. —ML

Out of Deep Waters

*"He reached down from heaven and rescued me;
he drew me out of deep waters."*
2 SAMUEL 22:17 NLT

This chapter of 2 Samuel records a powerful song of praise from David. In it he lists all the ways that God saved him from his enemies. He also describes in detail the way he felt as his enemies surrounded him. But most of all, he praises God for the attributes that make Him able to save.

"For who is God except the LORD? Who but our God is a solid rock?" David asks (v.32).

Who indeed? This God who saved David from the hands of Saul and all his other enemies is the same God who comes to our rescue when we are in distress. The God who gave David the strength and courage to stone giants and battle armies and face off against kings is the same God who enables us to face our greatest fears. The God who protected David on the battlefield is the same God who guards our hearts as we battle temptation.

And when we feel lost and alone and like we are drowning in deep waters of doubt, God reaches down from heaven and rescues us. He lifts us up and claims us as His own.

*God of David, I am so glad You
are my God too. Amen.* —ML

Give Thanks

We give thanks to God always for all of you, making mention of you in our prayers; constantly bearing in mind your work of faith and labor of love and steadfastness of hope in our Lord Jesus Christ in the presence of our God and Father.
1 THESSALONIANS 1:2–3 NASB

Who do you see doing the work of faith? Those quiet servants who show up every week to set up chairs and clean up rooms and hand out programs and welcome visitors—who else do you see?

Who do you see working at a labor of love? The elderly widow who makes quilts for newborns, or the piano teacher who works with kids with special needs for free, or the scientist who diligently spends long hours in the lab trying to find the cure for the disease that has hurt his own child—who else do you see?

Who do you see with steadfastness of hope? The retired preacher who spends his days still reading and learning from the Word of God, the parent of the runaway who keeps searching and sending out messages of love, the people in tornado-ravaged towns who rebuild and renew their promises to one another—who else do you see?

Give thanks for those followers of Christ among you who show us every day how to walk in faith and love and hope in our Lord Jesus Christ.

God, I'm thinking of the examples in my life right now of faith and love and hope. Thank You for putting these people in my life. Amen. —ML

The Age of Infusions

*But when the Holy Spirit controls our lives he will
produce this kind of fruit in us: love, joy, peace,
patience, kindness, goodness, faithfulness.*
GALATIANS 5:22 TLB

Have you noticed that infusions seem to be "the thing" now? Peach-infused white tea. Rosemary-infused almonds. Lavender- or rose-infused chocolates. Oh my! Basil-infused olive oil. Cinnamon-infused coffee. The list goes on and on. We live in a world of every kind of culinary delight—enough to make a body swoon. And there is still so much left to be dreamed up and savored. All to bring new and merry adventures to our taste buds!

Spiritually speaking, wouldn't it be wonderful if we could get as excited about the Holy Spirit infusing our spirits with joy as we do about infusions to the palate?

Today's culinary delights seem to expand by the day, but no pleasurable infusion will ever come close to the wonder and power and rapture of allowing the Holy Spirit to permeate every part of us—to produce love, joy, peace, patience, kindness, goodness, and faithfulness. Now that's an infusion!

*Holy Spirit, please infuse me with every
good thing, that I might be holy and joy filled
and useful in Your kingdom. Amen. —AH*

What God Can Do with Nothing

"Your servant has nothing there at all," she said,
"except a small jar of olive oil."
2 KINGS 4:2 NIV

The widow was in a desperate situation. She had to come up with the money to pay her creditors, or sell her two sons into slavery. What a choice! With no husband alive to bring in money, she didn't know how to get out of this problem. So she called to Elisha for help.

Elisha asked what she had in her house, and the woman replied that she had nothing there at all, except. . .

And God could work with her exception. God can work with yours too. What is the little bit of something you have that God could work with? Perhaps you have just a little money. Or maybe you have just a little bit of talent. Maybe you have only a faith the size of a mustard seed or only a shred of hope.

God can work through what you lack. He can work with the smallest offering to make big things happen. Elisha took the woman's small amount of oil and filled up all the jars they could find. Through the power of God, enough oil was produced to sell for enough money to save the woman's sons.

God, I never cease to be amazed at the big things
You can do with the little I have. Amen. —ML

Speak

Then Samuel said, "Speak, for your servant is listening."
1 SAMUEL 3:10 NIV

Samuel was dedicated to serve the Lord from the time of his birth. From a very young age, he ministered under the care of Eli in the temple. This was a special assignment for a special boy.

We are told at the beginning of chapter 3 that, in those days, "the word of the LORD was rare; there were not many visions" (v. 1). This fact sets the scene for the young Samuel's confusion as he lies down at night and three times hears someone calling his name. He thinks it's Eli calling to him, but Eli realizes it is in fact God.

Eli tells Samuel that, if God calls to him again, the boy should answer humbly, "Speak, for your servant is listening." So, that is what Samuel does. And then God delivers an important message to the boy.

How often do you ask God to speak to you? How often do you take time to listen? Samuel became an important messenger for God because he listened well and did what God asked him to do. What might you become if you let God speak to you more?

Speak, Lord, Your servant is here,
by still waters, ready to listen. Amen. —ML

Dear Martha

*But the Lord said to her, "My dear Martha,
you are worried and upset over all these details!"*
LUKE 10:41 NLT

Have you ever known someone who finds it impossible to keep still? They are multitasking every moment—always on the move. Martha was one of these movers. The queen of hospitality, she welcomed her friend Jesus and His disciples into her home. Chances are, she was a little bit concerned about what others might think of her and how she maintained her household. So, of course, she couldn't take time to sit down.

But her sister, Mary, had a different personality. While Martha rushed around looking after everyone's needs, Mary sat at Jesus' feet, just listening. After all, it wasn't every day someone like Jesus stopped by to chat. It wasn't every day the Son of God came to dinner. So Mary sat and cared for Jesus by giving Him her full attention.

Martha, with a mouth that moved as much as the rest of her, complained to Jesus about her sister's actions—or lack of action. But she didn't get the support she was expecting. Rather, He said that there was "only one thing worth being concerned about" (v. 42)—and that thing was not the dinner being cooked or the dishes to wash or the table to be set. That thing was time with Jesus.

*Lord Jesus, let me sit at Your feet by these still waters and
listen to what You have to say to me. Amen.* —ML

Deep Within

Mary kept all these things to herself,
holding them dear, deep within herself.
LUKE 2:19 MSG

What a night it must have been for that young girl! The long journey, ending in the crowded city. The labor pains coming—an experience she had never had before. Her baby son appearing for the first time—reaching for her, nuzzling her, crying and wriggling and breathing in her arms. The warmth of the animal bodies surrounding her as she wrapped her newborn in cloths and laid Him in His manger bed. Joseph gently watching with care, concerned for his wife-to-be, and amazed at the idea of bringing up this miracle child—this Son of God!

Mary might have even wondered if that whole scene with the angel coming and talking to her had just been some dream. Doesn't pregnancy sometimes do strange things to one's mind? But then, oh yes—the pregnancy! If the angel hadn't come, then how had *that* happened? And whose child was this?

Then, before she could even get those thoughts straight, the shepherds were arriving, talking in hushed voices about the angels they had seen in the sky, praising God. The looks on their faces were all the proof Mary needed. It was real. All of it.

And as the shepherds rushed off, excited to spread the news of this newborn King, Mary looked into her baby's eyes and hid her thoughts—her fears and wonderings—deep inside her heart.

Lord, Your coming to earth is the most
amazing gift. Thank You! Amen. —ML

Harmony

So then, let us aim for harmony in the
church and try to build each other up.
ROMANS 14:19 NLT

Baptist, Methodist, Presbyterian, Catholic, Church of Christ, Christian Church, and so on and so on. We have so many divisions and denominations and deviations, the idea of harmony in the church seems almost impossible.

But can we make that our aim?

Can we find commonalities in our potlucks and rummage sales? Can we find relatable points in our service projects and outreach events? Can we find ways to join forces and knock our heads together and make the most of our common bonds—our belief in Jesus Christ, in His death on the cross, and in His glorious resurrection?

The problem is, if we don't try to do this, if we don't attempt to work together and care for each other and build each other up, we are in grave danger of destroying each other—if not deliberately, then through the indirect impact that our divisions have on the witness of the body of Christ among nonbelievers. If we don't help each other grow, we will end up helping each other fail.

Lord, help me to work in my community to find ways
to connect with those in other churches. Help me to
see where we are similar and what goals we share in
showing Your love to people everywhere. Amen. —ML

One Voice

*May the God who gives endurance and encouragement give
you the same attitude of mind toward each other that Christ
Jesus had, so that with one mind and one voice you may
glorify the God and Father of our Lord Jesus Christ.*
ROMANS 15:5–6 NIV

Have you ever been in a room where everyone in the area is talking at once? No one can hear each other, so the volume levels just keep rising and rising, until you have to scream at someone just to get them to PLEASE PASS THE PEPPER!

Maybe this is what your family celebrations look like. Or maybe it describes the dinner table at your house every single night. (If that's the case, we feel for you!)

While this type of atmosphere can sometimes work out all right for a family gathering, where one assumes at least a small amount of goodwill pervades the room, it doesn't work at all for other settings—for example: business meetings, team practices, or choir rehearsals. In those settings, people need to be able to work together, and they need to be able to hear each other, and they really, really need to be able to hear a leader's instructions.

And that is true for the body of Christ as well—we need to be able to hear one another, to hear our Leader's guidance, and to work together to offer one voice of praise and worship to our wonderful God, who joins us all together with His Holy Spirit.

*Lord, help me be part of one voice
that worships You. Amen.* —ML

Fitted Together

He makes the whole body fit together perfectly. As each part
does its own special work, it helps the other parts grow, so
that the whole body is healthy and growing and full of love.
EPHESIANS 4:16 NLT

O ur brain sends us a message. It travels down through our spine and out into our arm, and down through the muscles, and out to our fingers. Our fingers move. Our brain dictates the actions. Our fingers move again. And somehow, without even thinking too much about it, we have a whole page of letters and spaces that form words and sentences and paragraphs and stories—and we can understand it all. Better yet, we can hand it off to someone else, and they'll understand it too.

The body is simply a miraculous bundle of cells and spirit. And each part of it has a purpose. Even the appendix—just don't ask anyone what it does.

Somehow God formed all the elements of our anatomy to perfectly suit the jobs they needed to do. And that is how He has formed us to work and live and grow together as a body of believers as well. We each have some special work—things we can do better than others or that we are uniquely gifted to achieve. We each have ways to support the other parts. And God designed us to do this together—not alone. He designed us to need each other, so we could learn how to love each other.

Lord, thank You for designing us to live
together and to love You. Amen. —ML

Unity

*How good and pleasant it is when
God's people live together in unity!*
PSALM 133:1 NIV

If you've ever been a part of a disorganized, large group event, you'll know how unpleasant it can be. Even if someone has planned lots of activities, fun giveaways, music, and party food—all of that will fall flat if there's not some sense of order. That's one reason so many people hire wedding coordinators to organize their wedding ceremonies and receptions. It just makes the whole experience more enjoyable for everyone. (And it doesn't hurt that it gives the mother-in-law a person other than the bride to target with any criticisms or challenging questions.)

Among believers, there is just no place for petty arguments and jealousies and grievances to get in the way of loving our Lord and loving each other. We must live in unity. It's an imperative, not an option. For if we don't live peacefully with one another, then we aren't working together as one body, and all our efforts to show how much we worship and honor our one God will crumble, and our witness will be severely damaged.

As we work and live and serve and play and learn together, we should ask this question: Are we living as one body or just a collected bunch of busybodies?

*One true God, we want to worship You as one
whole body. Help us to do that! Amen. —ML*

Teachable Moments

*Teach them to your children, talking about them
when you sit at home and when you walk along
the road, when you lie down and when you get up.*
DEUTERONOMY 11:19 NIV

Reading a story on your lap. Playing a game together and learning the rules. Sharing a cookie. Counting the stars. Taking care of pets. Picking up toys.

There are so many opportunities we have every day to teach our children about how to live rightly as followers of Jesus. We can teach them through stories. We can show them through the way we act toward them. We can talk about hard questions. We can serve people together and talk about how that feels. We can do our jobs around our houses and learn about obedience and putting others first.

You don't need to have a dedicated Bible teaching time (though there's nothing wrong with that!) to help your children and grandchildren understand who Jesus is, what He wants us to do, and how we need to love others. Honestly, the concept of "quiet time" is often lost on little ones. But what you can do, and should do, is talk about and live out your walk with Jesus when you wake up, when you eat together, when you play together, and when you tuck those kiddos in for bed at night.

*Lord, help me to seize those teachable
moments whenever they occur. Amen. —ML*

Silence Them

*For it is God's will that by doing good you should
silence the ignorant talk of foolish people.*
1 PETER 2:15 NIV

Peter wrote to the believers and asked them to do a thing that we often find hard to do today—to submit to every human authority. We like to be able to freely criticize our leaders, and we often find it hard to respect people in positions of authority if we don't agree with their beliefs, don't like their behaviors, or don't care about their business goals. But people who are in the position of developing and enforcing the laws of our land should be respected, because they are instruments, however flawed, for justice and peace—two things God cares very much about.

We are free under God's law to use our minds to figure out problems and come to our own solutions. But just because we have free use of our hearts, minds, and mouths, doesn't mean we always need to use them, and especially not in ways that undermine civility and authority.

When we live in a way that shows "proper respect to everyone" (v. 17), we avoid giving any appearance of bias or bad attitudes. And by doing that, we'll be sure to present an honorable, and even admirable, reputation among those who might seek to dismantle the cause of Christ.

*Lord, help me to silence critics and instead draw
them into a desire to talk about You. Amen.* —ML

Heard

"What you have said in the dark will be heard in the daylight, and what you have whispered in the ear in the inner rooms will be proclaimed from the roofs."
LUKE 12:3 NIV

There are some poor folks who live every day with the idea that every single conversation they have is bugged. They think someone is listening in, all the time. Never mind that the most controversial statements they've made in a week revolved around whether to use mayo or mustard on their tuna fish sandwiches. They just can't get over their problematic paranoia.

Jesus wasn't talking about bugs when He advised His disciples to be aware of what they said in secret and how it might be made known to all. He was trying to urge His disciples to live lives of integrity—to make sure that whatever they talked about in the dark, or behind closed doors, late at night, or under their covers would be honorable and upright. He didn't want His followers to be like the Pharisees, who sometimes acted one way in public and another way when no one was looking. He didn't want them to be double-minded, to think one thing but say something else. He wanted them to be aware that anything they said or did could reflect on their testimony and cause people to not want to accept the message of God's love.

Lord, help me be always aware that You hear my words, whether spoken or silent, and that I need to live with integrity for You. Amen. —ML

Watch Your Flock

Care for the flock that God has entrusted to you. Watch
over it willingly, not grudgingly—not for what you will
get out of it, but because you are eager to serve God.
1 PETER 5:2 NLT

Let's face it, folks. Working with people ain't always a party. People are weird. They do awkward things and say things that don't make sense. They fight. They criticize. They complain. They cut each other down. Sometimes they just don't have a clue, and sometimes they want to tell you about every single clue they have. They hold grudges and hold too tightly to possessions and hold back from loving each other well. They stray. They disobey. They delay. They are suspicious and pretentious and contentious. They will step on your toes and get under your skin and on your last nerve.

But these people are the most important treasure God has given us. And whether or not we are a paid church staff leader, whenever we are part of a family of believers we have a responsibility to look out for each other. To share wisdom. To support one another emotionally, spiritually, and even physically. And no one does any of this for what we get out of it (including those paid staff members). We do it because it is what God wants us to do. It is how we show Him we love Him. And it's how we show others His love.

Lord, have mercy on me and give me strength to
deal with people—including me! Amen. —ML

Soft but Tough

*Patience can persuade a prince,
and soft speech can break bones.*
PROVERBS 25:15 NLT

It's hard to think of a single time when shouting at someone has ever really been a success. Think about it. Even if shouting stops a child from running out in the street, it usually also ends in tears, and you go away thinking that surely there could have been a better way to deal with that situation. Or if you shout to catch a person before they get on the wrong bus, you might stop their error, but you probably embarrass them in the process.

It's better, when possible, to use soft speech to get attention. Many seasoned elementary school teachers know this trick—instead of raising your voice to be heard over classroom chaos, get very quiet. As the children, often one by one, start to realize you are saying something, they get quiet too, not wanting to miss out.

The same principles apply when you are trying to persuade someone—whether that someone is a prince or a pauper. Shouting or being overly aggressive will generally get you nowhere. Patiently presenting your case and using kind, confident words can make all the difference.

*God, as I sit quietly with You, I realize that Your
calm makes me calm. Help me to remember
this as I speak to others. Amen.* —ML

DAY 172

I Can't Do This Anymore!

They were at their wits' end. Then they cried out to the Lord in their trouble, and he brought them out of their distress.
Psalm 107:27–28 niv

Have you ever said that to God? "Lord, I can't do this anymore. Life. Work. Relationships. None of it. I am hanging on by a thread here. I have bags under my eyes from lack of rest. When I do nod off, my sleep is riddled with nightmares. I don't know how to carry on. Please, God, You're the only one who can help me!"

Humanity has cried this plea throughout the centuries. We may occasionally fool ourselves into thinking we are invincible, but humans can become helpless in the twinkling of an eye. All it takes is for someone beloved to walk away forever. A car crashing into a tree. A sudden crisis of faith.

It only takes a moment for us to see how truly vulnerable we are. But it only takes a moment for us to see how big and how good and how great our God is. No matter what century we live in, He is there with His heart of mercy. Call out to Him when you are in danger and distress. His mercy endures forever. . . .

Lord, help me now. I need You to rescue me from all my many troubles. Amen. —AH

Waiting

Let all that I am wait quietly before God,
for my hope is in him.
PSALM 62:5 NLT

The dishes will wait. The laundry pile will grow. The dust will settle. The papers will stay in their stack. The pages will remain unturned. The television can stay silent. The internet chatter can be quiet.

We don't have to work our way down a to-do list of good deeds. We don't have to visit a certain quota. We don't have to serve x bowls of soup at the soup kitchen. We don't have to memorize a hundred verses. We don't have to pray eight times a day. We don't have to touch our knees to our noses. We don't have to exercise before breakfast. We don't have to eat foods we cannot pronounce.

As free children of God, there's a lot we don't *have* to do. We are not bound by the kinds of codes and books of law that define and constrain the actions of members of some other religions. Because our hope is in Christ, and not in our abilities or endeavors, we know that He will not let us fall. But there's also a lot that will help us grow in our knowledge of the Lord, and help make us into better disciples for Him.

Lord, let me just sit here for a minute with You. Amen. —ML

Quiet Strength

This is what the Sovereign LORD, the Holy One of Israel, says:
"In repentance and rest is your salvation, in quietness and
trust is your strength, but you would have none of it."
ISAIAH 30:15 NIV

Don't we sometimes just make life too hard? We race around from place to place, trying to find just the right thing to go with the thing that sits on the thing that we never wanted in the first place. We fill up our schedules with meetings and appointments, not leaving any time for ourselves. We try a million different diets and fitness plans instead of just settling on and sticking to one. We send a hundred different emails when just one phone call could have achieved our goal. We stress, and fuss, and make messes of relationships over trivial matters, when really all that is needed is more time together.

And we do this with God too. We analyze and evaluate ourselves, our faith, and our discipleship goals. We spend loads of money on self-help books and seminars and conferences. But all that we really need is more time with Him.

We need the quiet strength that comes from getting to the point of it all. We need the confidence and wisdom to say no to too many distractions. And we need to find our rest and our salvation in the One who matters most.

Lord, I want to trust You more to
be all that I need. Amen. —ML

Kings of Righteousness

Each one will be like a shelter from the wind and a refuge from the storm, like streams of water in the desert and the shadow of a great rock in a thirsty land.
ISAIAH 32:2 NIV

Isaiah gives the message to the Israelites that a righteous king is coming (v. 1). That news would have been welcome to the Israelites, who often had been led by corrupt and idolatrous, or even villainous, kings.

What a blessing it is to be led by strong, honest, faithful leaders! Competent, intelligent leaders inspire trust—you know you can depend on the plans they put in place to be well thought out and engineered. Compassionate, considerate leaders motivate people—when you feel that you are valued and cared for, you want to strive for excellence. Transparent, humble leaders invite accountability across organizations—if you see your leader serving others and being willing to be evaluated, you invite the same kind of accountability and offer yourself up without hesitation to serve others. Faithful, responsive leaders improve working relationships—you know they will do what they say, which allows you to plan for the future.

Good leaders help people to grow and thrive. Good leaders also offer rest and refuge in times of need. When you work under a competent leader, you don't just do a job; you serve a purpose.

King of kings, thank You for the way You lead me every day. Help me to be a good leader too. Amen. —ML

Deep Calling

Deep calls to deep in the roar of your waterfalls;
all your waves and breakers have swept over me.
PSALM 42:7 NIV

Sadness can drag us down to places we never thought we'd be. In the depths of depression, we see hard things about ourselves, and often we realize in those moments that we cannot live our lives on our own. We just can't. We don't have any sources of internal strength that are strong enough to get us moving. Everything good and strong and solid that we know comes from God.

And down in our deep, dark places, we also realize we are not alone. God is there, calling to us. Even as He overwhelms us with a glimpse of His sorrow, He beckons us to come to Him. The weight of His power becomes like a warm blanket around us—never stifling or oppressive, just protective and supporting.

When we are deeply sorrowful, our hearts breaking, His heart breaks with us. And somehow in the knowledge of our oneness in grief, He shows us that all will be well, and we still can have peace. Because He is our peace.

Lord, when I am so sad I can't even speak,
let me remember to come to You. Amen. —ML

My Help

I lift up my eyes to the mountains—where
does my help come from? My help comes
from the LORD, the Maker of heaven and earth.
PSALM 121:1–2 NIV

Why do we so often look up to talk to and refer to God? Have you ever thought about it? We say God is everywhere, and God is inside us. But when we talk to Him, we turn our faces upward.

It seems we look up to see what is always there—a constant reminder of our eternal God who does not change. We look up and are greeted with the sky that stretches farther than we can see. Or we look up to the mountains, carved out of solid rock and pointing up even higher than our imaginations can climb.

And maybe we look up because we want to feel small. We want to know and experience the bigness, the hugeness, and the enormity of our almighty God. We want to know that the God who created the universe is the same God who speaks to us, listens to us, and helps us figure out what to do next.

Lord, in these still, quiet times with You, I remember
You are my help. I will depend on You to lead me.
I will count on You to catch me if I fall. Amen. —ML

Bread and Water and Peace

*A meal of bread and water in contented peace
is better than a banquet spiced with quarrels.*
PROVERBS 17:1 MSG

"He touched me." "No, I didn't." "Yes, you did." "No. I. Didn't!" "YES! YOU! DID!" Sometimes these quarrels start before you even make it to the table, much less through the muttered blessing.

These little arguments are bound to occur whenever people are living close together, and understand how to push each other's buttons, and happen to be really hungry. Someone makes one little comment, and before you know it, the nice family mealtime you had in mind—you know the kind where you sit around and share funny stories from your day and everyone loves each other and listens so sweetly?—is completely shattered. You look around at all the good food you cooked and wonder why you gave it so much effort. Maybe you should have just had bread and water.

It is good to remember at these times that family quarrels are fairly normal. But it's also good to consider how to have better communication in the future. What could you do to help your family members interact with each other in kinder ways? Maybe you are just trying to do too much—maybe you need to simplify. Well, bread and water it is then!

*Lord, I long for contented peace in our family times together.
Show me the way to get closer to that goal. Amen. —ML*

Mysterious Things

*"He gives wisdom to the wise and knowledge to the scholars.
He reveals deep and mysterious things and knows what lies
hidden in darkness, though he is surrounded by light."*
DANIEL 2:21–22 NLT

What drives the mole to dig? Where do insects go in the rain? Why do worms come to the surface of the earth? How do flowers know when to bloom? How many planets exist beyond what we have been able to see? What lives at the bottom of the ocean? How many bacteria are in us right now? What happens at the moment we die?

This world of ours is full of mysteries, from deep philosophical questions to lighthearted scientific inquiries. We could spend decades asking and trying to answer all the questions humans have, and indeed, that is what some scholars do.

It is a relief to know that the God who made us with these curious minds that ask never-ending questions is also the God who knows all the answers. We can depend on Him not to leave us in the dark forever. Someday, every question will be answered in His light.

*Lord, You know the questions on my heart today,
even before I say them. Guide me to the answers I need,
and not just the answers I'd like to hear. Amen.* —ML

DAY 180

Gushing

You make springs pour water into the ravines, so streams
gush down from the mountains. They provide water for
all the animals, and the wild donkeys quench their thirst.
PSALM 104:10–11 NLT

When we need comfort, He supplies whole churches of friendly faces. When we are hungry, He leads us to huge buffets of food. When we are lonely, He gives us a crowd of new friends. When we are hurting, He gives us His calm.

Our God is so generous with His gifts and tender care of us! He does more than we ask or imagine!

The God who cares enough to supply wild donkeys with gushing streams of pure, cool water to drink from is the same God who cares about us more than we can ever comprehend.

Sometimes, like stubborn wild donkeys, we feel the need to be independent—to try to soothe our souls, rest our minds, and quiet our hearts all on our own. But God delights to provide for His children. He won't let us down. And His answers to our problems are always better and bigger and smarter and last longer than anything we could come up with all on our own.

Generous Father, You give me so many good things.
Help me to remember to come to You first
with anything I need. Amen. —ML

Prudent

Therefore the prudent keep quiet in
such times, for the times are evil.
Amos 5:13 NIV

In this message from the prophet Amos, God is pointing out the corruption of leaders who deprive those who have no voice. They lose their rightful justice in the courts simply because they don't have money to offer bribes. We see a system where everything runs on greed and power. Whoever has the most money wins.

Why then do the prudent keep quiet? Why don't they instead speak up for the oppressed? Perhaps because the system has become so wicked that any attention drawn to the weaknesses will only result in retaliation from the powerful ones who feel threatened. Or perhaps they stay silent in order to survive the mess and not be accused themselves of wrongdoing.

Life is not easy. When dealing with people who don't play by the rules, it can be extremely tricky to get ahead without losing one's soul. It's at times like these that it is good to stick very, very close to the Lord, and let Him give you the right words to say at just the right moment.

Lord, the times we are living in now are certainly
filled with evil influences. Please guide me
in the way of truth. Amen. —ML

Transcendent Peace

And the peace of God, which transcends all understanding,
will guard your hearts and your minds in Christ Jesus.
PHILIPPIANS 4:7 NIV

There is no explaining it. The idea that a person could undergo huge personal loss, financial ruin, chronic states of stress, and sudden tragedy all at once and somehow not lose her mind seems impossible. But people manage to get through tremendously bad circumstances and come out smiling still.

This is the peace that transcends all understanding. It goes beyond what we can achieve or wrap our minds around on our own. It's not available in a bottle or in a pill. It doesn't even come in the hugs of a loved one. It only comes to us through the gracious, merciful, kind, ever-loving heart of our Father God.

It is His answer to every trouble we have. It is His way of always leading us back to Him. He is the only source in which we can find it. This transcendent peace. And oh, how we need it! Not just when we are at our bleakest moments, but when we need to keep moving through a sea of stress, when the waves of anxiety just keep coming through our everyday routines. We can rely on His transcendent peace to carry us.

Lord, grant me Your beautiful peace today.
Thank You! Amen. —ML

Heart Replacement Required

A peaceful heart leads to a healthy body;
jealousy is like cancer in the bones.
PROVERBS 14:30 NLT

Jealousy. It causes more stress in our everyday lives than almost anything else. What's that, you say? You're not jealous? Hmm. Let's test that idea out.

Have you ever blocked people's posts on your social media site because you just got tired of seeing how great their lives were? Have you ever criticized another person simply because you didn't like the fact that they were getting so much attention? Has anyone ever irritated you just by existing—because their existence reminds you that you are not as beautiful/thin/smart/wealthy/popular/successful/insert-your-own-adjective as they are?

Jealousy. It's the fuel and the by-product of the great comparison game, all rolled into one green, prickly package. And it is most likely making us sick. Certainly, it's not getting us one centimeter closer to being more beautiful, successful, kind, or any other attribute we've been wishing we had.

It's time to back up and back out of the comparison game. Shut it down. Remember how much God values you, just as you are. Ask Him to restore your peaceful heart.

Lord, help me to get rid of jealousy and
replace it with peace. Amen. —ML

Leaders for the Lord

*Dear brothers and sisters, honor those
who are your leaders in the Lord's work.*
1 THESSALONIANS 5:12 NLT

They work more hours than most Wall Street stockbrokers. They skip meals. They give out of their own pockets. They go way beyond the call of duty. They bend over backward so far, they now need regular chiropractic appointments just to walk upright in the Lord.

These are leaders in the Lord's work. They are the wonderful, unsung, unthanked, underappreciated, overutilized, and overachieving servants for Christ.

So how can we honor them? Well, for starters, we can say thank you more often. We can show them respect by valuing their time and not taking them for granted. We can love them by giving them little surprise treats and gifts that make them realize we were thinking of them. We can invite them out for coffee or dinner. We can get out of their way when they are focused on a task. We cannot argue with them over trivial differences of opinion. And most of all, we can serve alongside them.

In many churches, there are a handful of people who seem to just be everywhere doing everything. If you are not one of those people, make sure you find out how to help the ones who are. And if you are the one who needs the help, make sure to ask!

God, thank You for Your gracious servants! Amen. —ML

But If Not

"Our God whom we serve is able to deliver us from the burning fiery furnace, and He will deliver us from your hand, O king. But if not, let it be known to you, O king, that we do not serve your gods, nor will we worship the gold image which you have set up."
DANIEL 3:17–18 NKJV

*B*ut if not. Those three little words speak volumes of trust and devotion in the speech given by Shadrach, Meshach, and Abednego as they faced King Nebuchadnezzar and the flames of the fiery furnace he had prepared for their punishment. And they ended up speaking volumes about the God these three men served.

But if not. "God, please heal my father. Don't let him die. I know You will save him. But if not, I'll still believe in You."

But if not. "God, the waters are rising. I know You don't want us to lose our house and You, Lord of all, can stop these floodwaters. But if not, I will still praise You for saving our lives."

But if not. "Lord, I really want this promotion, but I think they want me to lie to get it. And I can't do that. Please change their minds. But if not, I will know You have the best plan for me still to come."

God, may I always remember that I can trust You, no matter what happens. Amen. —ML

Distress and Delight

Trouble and distress have come upon me,
but your commands give me delight.
PSALM 119:143 NIV

It may seem a strange thought at first. How could commands possibly give delight? Chocolate chunk ice cream, we understand. Cute puppies are definitely delightful. A beautiful bouquet of flowers—yes, we would feel delight at seeing those arrive on our doorstep, especially in a time of distress. But commands? Who would offer us commands in a time of trouble and distress?

God would, that's who. And He knows exactly what we need. Commands give us a solid framework when our world feels like it's crumbling apart. Commands help guide us when we're struggling to see through a fog of despair. Commands provide us with a solid place to stand when it feels like the ground keeps shifting. Commands give us a plan, a point, and a purpose.

God's commands give us delight because they bring us closer to Him. "Be still and know that I am God." "Draw near to Me." "Love the Lord your God." "Ask." "Seek." "Knock." These commands lead us into His presence, and it's there that we find eternal comfort and relief from the troubles of this life.

Father God, Your commands bless me by bringing
me closer to You. Help me to honor them and
follow through with Your plan. Amen. —ML

Action

So prepare your minds for action and exercise self-control.
1 PETER 1:13 NLT

Peter wrote to God's chosen people as they were scattered among several provinces. He wanted to unify them by reminding them of the hope we all share in salvation—in our knowledge of and access to eternal life with Jesus Christ. He encouraged them to remain consistent in their faith and not to "slip back into your old ways of living to satisfy your own desires" (v. 14).

So how do you prepare your mind for action? Prayer is a good place to start. Make it a habit to spend a little time each day talking with God, listening to Him speak through His Word, and thinking through your spiritual struggles with Him. Then read His Word some more. Read about people who faced challenges and defeated them. Read His commands. Read about His love for you. Read about His miraculous power and realize that is the same power you can access through Him.

Practice physical self-discipline as well. It may sound silly, but testing your physical control and making a habit of exercise will help you to be mentally fit too. The same willpower needed to stop eating cookies and start getting stronger is also needed to fight against other kinds of temptations.

God, I want to be holy, as You are holy. Help me
to be disciplined as I follow You. Amen. —ML

New Clothes

*So, chosen by God for this new life of love,
dress in the wardrobe God picked out for you:
compassion, kindness, humility, quiet strength, discipline.*
COLOSSIANS 3:12 MSG

A beautiful, soft sweater with intricate crochet detailing catches your eye. Or maybe it's a smart pair of pants in this season's latest hue. A cleverly designed jacket with waterproof coating calls your name. Or is it a little black dress that is waiting for you?

Donning some new wardrobe pieces tends to make us all feel a bit sharper, smarter, and more ready to face the world. But, who are we kidding? Five minutes into lunch and that sweater will have a tomato-soup stain, the pants will be wrinkled, and we will have lost the hood to the jacket. Oh, and that little black dress? Well, let's just say it was a little *too* little.

If we really want to be ready to face the world, and to deal with something harder than a tomato-soup stain, it would be much better to clothe ourselves in the wardrobe God has picked out for us—to put on compassionate hearts, kind actions, humble attitudes, quiet strength, and firm, consistent, persistent discipline.

*Lord, help me to wear the wardrobe You've
picked out for me every day. I feel beautiful
when I'm reflecting Your Spirit! Amen. —ML*

Devoted

Devote yourselves to prayer, being watchful and thankful.
COLOSSIANS 4:2 NIV

Paul tells us in his letter to the Ephesians that "we are not fighting against flesh-and-blood enemies, but against evil rulers and authorities of the unseen world, against mighty powers in this dark world, and against evil spirits in the heavenly places" (Ephesians 6:12 NLT). This is one of the reasons we need to be devoted in prayer and watch what is going on in us and around us.

There are forces in the world that will seek to run us right off the narrow way of our walk of faith in Jesus. These forces like to distract us with worldly obsessions or trivial distractions. We should not brush aside the powers of the dark world. Sometimes big struggles begin with small stumbles.

So when you pray, help yourself to focus. One way to do that is to pray through scripture. Read a few verses, think about what they mean, and then ask God to help you live out the principles that are being talked about, or help you see the virtues being presented, or help you examine more closely to see what God is saying to you through His Word.

Be as devoted to praying as you are to binge-watching your latest favorite show or binge-reading your favorite author.

God, help me be watchful as I pray.
Thank You for protecting my heart. Amen. —ML

Share the Load

Carry one another's burdens and in this way
you will fulfill the requirements of the law
of Christ [that is, the law of Christian love].
GALATIANS 6:2 AMP

The woman was clearly trying to win the yes-I-can-carry-everything-in-one-trip game. She had bags around her neck, bags up to her elbows, a pack of soda balanced on one hip, and one bag with the eggs in it hanging precariously off her pinkie finger. And there was just no way she was going to make it up those two flights of steps to get to her apartment.

Thankfully, a pleasant, helpful sort of fellow came along and rescued the eggs along with several other bags of groceries as he carried them up the steps for her. It was a small act, and didn't cost him anything (perhaps a few extra minutes of his time), but it made the woman's day. And it lifted his spirits as well, making him feel useful.

And this is why we are told to carry one another's burdens. Not only do we feel better when someone helps us carry our load, but we also feel better when we are helping someone else. Through little labors, we learn to love more.

God, help me be on the lookout for people
who could use a hand, either with physical,
mental, or spiritual loads. Amen. —ML

He Is Near

Seek the LORD while he may be found;
call on him while he is near.
ISAIAH 55:6 NIV

This passage may make one wonder, *Can the Lord ever not be found?* Surely God is everywhere all the time—when would He hide from us?

That's the key point. God doesn't ever hide from us, but sometimes our vision is so clouded, we can't see Him. It's like peering through a dense fog for a familiar landmark—we know it's there somewhere, but we can't make out its shape, and so we steer far around it, hoping not to crash into the thing. Sometimes we wait to seek God until after we have been long involved in disobedience. And because we know He's there, and yet are afraid to come close to Him, we steer in the other direction.

But Isaiah reminds us of the better-than-human forgiveness levels of our Lord. When we leave our wickedness behind and turn in God's direction, He will have mercy. He will not ridicule us or treat us badly because we have sinned and asked for forgiveness. We might not understand why God so easily offers forgiveness, but that's okay. We can still accept it. As God says, "As the heavens are higher than the earth, so are my ways higher than your ways and my thoughts than your thoughts" (v. 9).

Lord, I know Your thoughts are nothing like mine.
Thank You for that! Amen. —ML

Quick and Quiet Action

"May you be blessed for your good judgment and
for keeping me from bloodshed this day and
from avenging myself with my own hands."
1 SAMUEL 25:33 NIV

First Samuel 25 portrays one of the many mini hero stories of the Bible. In this account, a dispute arose between David and the wealthy, yet somewhat stingy, Nabal. Because Nabal refused to share any supplies with David and his men, David prepared for battle.

Things could have gone rather horribly wrong, but Abigail acted quickly to put an end to the conflict. She gathered a large amount of food as fast as she could, loaded it up on donkeys, and rode off (without alerting Nabal) to take the supplies to David. Then, when Abigail met David, she humbled herself before the king-to-be and asked for his pardon. And along with all the goods she had brought, she gracefully offered David a commonsense argument for keeping the peace that David could not refute.

Abigail's quick assessment of the situation and alert action ended up saving many people that day—both in her household and any men David might have lost in battle as well. And through her easy handling of this problem, she would later be saved from being tied for life to the foolish, wicked Nabal.

Lord, help me to be willing and ready to step into conflict
when I see a way toward peace. Amen. —ML

Taming the Turmoil

You answer us with awesome and righteous deeds,
God our Savior. . .who stilled the roaring of the seas,
the roaring of their waves, and the turmoil of the nations.
PSALM 65:5, 7 NIV

Psalm 65 is a song of praise to God for all His "awesome and righteous deeds." The psalmist praises God for His strength and power—the One who formed mountains and stilled seas. With that same level of power, God calms the "turmoil of the nations."

The turmoil of nations is often more destructive than any natural disasters. When nations battle against each other, divisions are born that can take generations to overcome. It usually begins with some argument over ownership—of rights to a resource, land, equipment, or something else. Each nation wants its people to have the upper hand. Yet no one sees how the people will be hurt in the long run if hostilities between neighboring nations erupt. Suspicion grows between people of different origins— prejudices develop. The attitudes of parents are handed down to their children, and then to their grandchildren. These prejudices become yet another symbol of that nation's pride.

Only God can bring peace to such situations. Only God has the power to open the eyes of powerful national leaders and make them see sense. And only God has the patient endurance to wait out the generations until a new wave of thinkers is born.

God, You save us from so much turmoil.
Please save us from ourselves. Amen. —ML

A Soothing Spirit

*Whenever the spirit from God came on Saul, David would
take up his lyre and play. Then relief would come to Saul;
he would feel better, and the evil spirit would leave him.*
1 Samuel 16:23 NIV

What's your go-to music for relaxation? Do you like classical
strings or piano? Are you a Mozart fan? Perhaps you
like some soft jazz. What about heavy metal? (Note: If you
find heavy metal music calming, you might want to get your
hearing checked.)

Maybe you don't find music relaxing at all. Some people
need absolute quiet when they want to calm their thoughts.
Others like to watch television—something that doesn't make
them think too hard. Others like to go for a walk and get some
fresh air to wake up their brains.

God knows what we need to soothe our hearts, souls, and
minds. When we go to Him, He provides us with a place for us
to rest our weary thoughts. If we ask Him, He will help us set
aside any negative language that threatens to bring us down.
He will speak truth to us too—pointing out where we've made
bad choices and engaged in selfish habits.

Whenever a dark spirit is settled on your heart and mind,
threatening to steal your joy, ask God to come and fill your
mind with Him.

*Lord, my thoughts are heavy sometimes with negativity and
hopelessness. Help me to focus all on You. Amen. —ML*

Forgive and Be Forgiven

*"But when you are praying, first forgive anyone
you are holding a grudge against, so that your
Father in heaven will forgive your sins, too."*
MARK 11:25 NLT

You're standing in the middle of the church service. And you realize that you can't pay attention to anything that's being said. All you can think about is that woman at the end of the row of seats and how she said something harsh to your child last Sunday. Sure, it was a one-time thing, and you weren't there when it happened. But boy, oh boy, is it making you mad now. You can't pray. You can't sing. What to do?

You could catch her later, then tell her exactly what you think of her bad manners. Or you could consider for a moment all the times you have let harsh words fly (perhaps even at your own children!) and realize all of us make such mistakes. Then you could forgive her in your heart. Release the anger and tension, remember God's grace toward you, and forgive.

Forgiving, even if you never hear "I'm sorry," allows you to take back your mind and cleanse your heart. Instead of letting bitterness hijack your thoughts, you can be set free through a conversation—even one you have with yourself in your head. With this new freedom, you will be able to pray and sing praises once again. And you'll be secure in the knowledge that God forgives you too.

*Lord, thank You for forgiving me.
Help me to forgive others. Amen.* —ML

Suffering on Purpose

"So then, it was not you who sent me here, but God."
GENESIS 45:8 NIV

The story of Joseph and his brothers is one of the best stories of brokenness, redemption, and forgiveness ever told. After hostility grows between Joseph and his brothers, and his brothers sell him into slavery, Joseph is granted favor in the eyes of God and eventually becomes Pharaoh's second-in-command, having control over the administration of the entire country of Egypt. When famine strikes, Joseph's family is affected too, and his brothers come to ask for grain, not realizing their brother Joseph was the one in charge.

Now this is the moment when, in some stories, the main character would choose to get revenge on his old enemies. But Joseph didn't do that. He did come up with a plan to assess what had happened to his father and youngest brother. Once he was settled about their care, he revealed himself. And before his brothers could say "Midianite merchants," Joseph pardoned them and told them that everything, even his own suffering, had been done according to God's plan for saving lives.

When things go well for us, we often attribute it to God's plan or talk about God's blessing. But when things are hard and the ending doesn't look happy, it's good to remember that God's still in control, and He may be writing a chapter to our stories that we could never imagine.

Lord, help me remember that You can use my suffering for Your purposes too. Amen. —ML

Sensible People

Sensible people control their temper;
they earn respect by overlooking wrongs.
PROVERBS 19:11 NLT

When you spend time resting and refreshing in God's peace by still waters, the world begins to look a little different. Things that might have caused you anxiety the day before don't seem so out of control now. Problems that had you flummoxed before now seem to have multiple good outcomes. And things that another day might have caused your temper to flare now barely seem worth noticing. In the light of eternal peace, our momentary struggles seem like small potatoes.

You might say that we've taken a healthy dose of common sense. Sensible people don't let themselves get overrun by life's little issues because that just wouldn't make sense. Why let a small problem take up a large amount of time? Why let a finite issue limit your infinite soul? Why let a situation that can easily be fixed turn into a complicated puzzle? And why let something that could be over and done with drag out to last forever?

Be a sensible person. Control your temper and don't let the little stuff get in the way of you becoming a bighearted person with God.

Lord, help me to overlook small offenses
and see Your big plan. Amen. —ML

Never Revenge

Dear friends, never take revenge.
Leave that to the righteous anger of God.
ROMANS 12:19 NLT

If the Bible stopped with just the command to "never take revenge," we might just be fine with that. After all, revenge is hard work. Who wants that?

But that's not where scripture stops speaking on this matter. It goes a step further. It says, "If your enemies are hungry, feed them. If they are thirsty, give them something to drink. In doing this, you will heap burning coals of shame on their heads" (v. 20).

Wow. Really, God? I have to fulfill my enemies' desires? Give them food and drink? And why? What will this do for me?

The answer comes in the last verse of the chapter: "Don't let evil conquer you, but conquer evil by doing good" (v. 21).

If we let vengeful and unforgiving feelings enter our hearts and take over our minds, we will be conquered. We will have let our worse side win. But we were created to be more than conquerors. And what do conquerors do? They forgive.

Lord, thank You for the chance to change my heart. Help me not to even want revenge against my enemies. But help me to love them, just like I would anyone else. Amen. —ML

What Could Have Been

*"Oh, that you had listened to my commands! Then you
would have had peace flowing like a gentle river and
righteousness rolling over you like waves in the sea."*
ISAIAH 48:18 NLT

The waves lap on the shore in a raucous rhythm—splashing,
sucking up sands, then heading back out to the sea. It's a
sound that's loud and soft all at once—there are no harsh edges
here. The sound patterns roll around in your mind, creating a song
only you know. And you are full of peace, and full of goodwill,
and full of grace. You can feel God's truth and wisdom washing
over you, like a bath of blessing.

You walk away to higher ground, where the river runs to
meet the sea. Here the water sings a different song—a bubbling,
swift tune, with notes hooked on pebbles and then pushed down,
down, down. As you watch your reflection shudder with the
moving waters, you realize the peace of a river is never still.
It never takes just one form and sits there. The peace of a river
is in the flow—the ability to move and change as needed to fit
any circumstance. It's in the wisdom that gathers information
and assesses what is the most important. It's in the relationships
that keep on moving, bubbling, and getting all the more deep
as they blend with the sea.

This is the world that could have been, if we had listened
to God's commands.

Lord, let Your gentle peace flow in my life. Amen. —ML

Inexpressible

You love him even though you have never seen him.
Though you do not see him now, you trust him;
and you rejoice with a glorious, inexpressible joy.
1 PETER 1:8 NLT

Imagine you are a little lamb, lost on a hillside. The shepherd spots you and sends his dog after you to lead you back to the flock. You can't see the shepherd, but you know he is the one giving the commands. You know he is the one with the plan for where you can go.

As you settle in among the flock, reunited with your friends, you are pleased. You are filled with a glorious, golden joy because you have complete trust in your shepherd. Complete faith that he wants only what is good for you. And complete hope that he will lead you to good things.

This is what it means to be led by our Good Shepherd, our Lord and Savior Jesus Christ. Even though we cannot see Him, we feel His presence. We know His commands were left to guide us. And we can trust Him to guide us to safe places by still waters. The joy that comes with this certain, unlimited, peaceful dependence on Him is so beautiful and big and ongoing, it's simply inexpressible.

My Good Shepherd, thank You for
leading me so well. Amen. —ML

Why Jesus Sleeps

But Jesus was sleeping.
MATTHEW 8:24 NIV

The story is told a few different ways, but it always goes something like this: Jesus was in the boat with His disciples, when very suddenly a furious storm formed, catching the relatively small boat in it and dashing it about. It was the kind of boat ride that could throw even the most experienced fisherman off his feet.

But Jesus was sleeping.

Doesn't that sound a little familiar? Picture this: You have one of the worst days of your life. A project you've been spending numerous extra hours on fails completely. People around you are tired and angry, and a storm of emotions erupts, throwing you off guard. You turn this way and that, trying to make things better, frantically looking for solutions. Then you remember to pray.

But Jesus is sleeping.

Is He uncaring? No, of course not. He is the one who loved us so much, He died for us! Is He lazy? Again, no. He is the man who heals and attends to crowds upon crowds and only takes short bits of time for Himself. Is He just out of touch? What do you think?

Jesus sleeps because He knows the story's end. He knows they will be okay. He's got the power to make it happen.

Lord, I'm thankful that no matter how riled up I get,
You are always my source of calm. Amen. —ML

With You Always

*"And be sure of this: I am with you always,
even to the end of the age."*

MATTHEW 28:20 NLT

He is always with us. From the moment we gasp for that first breath, till the moment we exhale our last.

He is always with us. In those days of fast growth and multiplying connections, when our chubby toddler legs cannot keep up with where our minds want to run. And then later as we chalk up a whole series of firsts: first haircut, first day of school, first lost tooth, and on and on.

He is always with us. From the first heartbreak to that moment we find our forever love, and all the dates and breakups and relationship messes in between.

He is always with us. From the first time we realize we are sinful and need a Savior, and all the many times afterward when we repent and ask for forgiveness, to the day we look forward to shutting our eyes and opening them again in His glory.

Our Lord, our Shepherd, is with us every step of the way, guiding us, protecting us, loving us.

*My Lord and God, I don't know what I would do if
I didn't have You. Don't ever leave me! Amen.* —ML

Overcome

*"These things I have spoken to you, that in Me you
may have peace. In the world you will have tribulation;
but be of good cheer, I have overcome the world."*
JOHN 16:33 NKJV

What things had Jesus spoken to His disciples, that they might
have peace? He told them what would happen soon, that
the hour was coming when they would be scattered and would
leave Jesus all alone. Hmm. That doesn't sound so peaceful.
But then Jesus said He would not really be alone because the
Father was with Him. Okay, that's better.

Then He went on to say that we'd have great trouble in
this world. Again, not so peaceful. But we should be of good
cheer because Jesus has already overcome the world. Oh yes,
that's good.

It seems it was rather a mixed-bag kind of farewell speech.
But in looking at it again, we find a bigger truth. Jesus knew what
would happen. He knew that these men standing there were
going to run away. They were going to get scared. One would
even betray Him. And they would later have far worse troubles
than just being afraid. But Jesus never left them. He never gave
up on them. Even here in this chapter, when they still seem to
not have a clue, Jesus stays with them.

Jesus can give us peace because He is the Prince of Peace.
He knows He's not going anywhere. He'll be right here, with
us. And He has overcome the world.

*Lord Jesus, I look forward to the day
when I will see Your face. Amen.* —ML

Lifted Up

The LORD lifts up those who are weighed down.
PSALM 146:8 NLT

A lollipop. A beautiful yellow rose. Merry daffodils on a hillside, waving in the breeze. A fuzzy kitten chasing its tail. A brilliant blue sky. Ocean waves, coming and going. Birds flying high among the clouds. A baby's belly laugh.

These are all things that can lift us up when we are feeling down. They might provide momentary relief, but they are still a blessed break from sorrowful faces and glum frowns.

But when the Lord lifts us up, He doesn't leave us to sink down again. Instead, He reigns forever in our lives.

God lifts up those who are oppressed—He brings justice where justice has been pushed out. He brings healing to those who are hurting. He looks after those who are strangers in a foreign land. He brings relief and help to the fatherless and to the widow.

He turns the way of the wicked upside down.

He doesn't help us for a moment and then fade away. He reigns forever—to generations after generations.

Lord, thank You for lifting me up when I am pressed down. Thank You for freeing me from paths of injustice and showing me the way to truth. Amen. —ML

Soul Searching

Tremble and do not sin; when you are on
your beds, search your hearts and be silent.
PSALM 4:4 NIV

In the silvery stillness of the moonlit midnight, you lie on your bed with eyes open wide. You hear the crickets singing outside. You hear the creaking floorboards inside. You touch the sheets on your bed to reassure yourself that, in this magical moment, this bed is real, and you are real in it.

You take a deep breath, and you listen as the air goes through your teeth, over your tongue, and then fills your lungs. You are alive, and you consider all the body processes that keep you breathing.

As you stare into the deepening darkness, you imagine you are pulling out a filing cabinet drawer in your mind. You search through the files, looking for the sins that might be keeping you from a whole relationship with God.

You breathe out, letting the air escape, letting go of hard feelings and grudges and unforgiven trespasses. With no audible words, you ask for God's light to shine on you. You ask Him to fill your well-searched heart with joy and peace. And love. Always love.

God, remind me to take regular times to lie down and be
silent and contemplate the state of my heart. Amen. —ML

God-Supplied

*Do it with all the strength and energy that
God supplies. Then everything you do will
bring glory to God through Jesus Christ.*
1 PETER 4:11 NLT

Peter tells his listeners, "God has given each of you a gift
from his great variety of spiritual gifts. Use them well to
serve one another" (v. 10). But how do we use them well? By
relying on God. If we have a gift of good speaking abilities,
we should use that gift to speak the truths God has given us to
tell the world, rather than using it to make pompous speeches
about subjects we know nothing of. If we have a special ability
to help others, we should rely on our God-supplied strength and
energy to make connections with others and find out what will be
most useful to them, instead of relying on ourselves, and getting
tired or fed up, and then giving up altogether.

If we use God-supplied speech, God-supplied truth, God-
supplied energy, and God-supplied strength, then everything
we do will bring glory to God through Jesus Christ. Everything
we do will point back to Him.

*Lord, thank You for Your special gifts that You
give us through Your Holy Spirit. Thank You
for supplying everything I need. Amen.* —ML

Times of Refreshing

*"Repent, then, and turn to God, so that your sins may
be wiped out, that times of refreshing may come
from the Lord, and that he may send the Messiah,
who has been appointed for you—even Jesus."*
ACTS 3:19–20 NIV

Have you ever been stuck in your seat on a hot, humid summer day? The heat in the air is heavy and wet—it sticks
to everything that moves through it. You feel as though even
lifting your arm and reaching out your fingers to hold your glass
of water takes too much effort. You begin to wonder if the air
will ever feel cool again. Where are the breezes? Where is
some shade? The sun beats down mercilessly on the steaming
landscape.

Then you feel it. One. Little. Drop.

Before you know it, the heavens open, the clouds gather,
and down come sheets of blessed relief—cool water breaking
through the still, thick air and breaking up the heat molecules.
A breeze begins to blow, but you have to help it lift your sweaty
strands of hair off your forehead. Line after line of beautiful
raindrops come beating down, and you don't even mind the
sting. Because nothing has ever felt so refreshing.

And this is the kind of relief our Lord promises us to come.
Times when our heavy sins will be lifted from us and when we
can repent, turn to God, and have our hearts washed clean.

*Lord God, thank You for blessed times of refreshing
and relief, when my heart is made new. Amen. —ML*

Fruit

*He brings gifts into our lives, much the same way that fruit
appears in an orchard—things like affection for others, exuber-
ance about life, serenity. We develop a willingness to stick with
things, a sense of compassion in the heart, and a conviction
that a basic holiness permeates things and people. We find
ourselves involved in loyal commitments, not needing to force
our way in life, able to marshal and direct our energies wisely.*
GALATIANS 5:22–23 MSG

In his letter to the Galatians, Paul says that the acts of the
flesh are clear to be seen. But in today's world it is harder
and harder for people to see the difference between what is of
the flesh and what is of the Spirit—what desires are fueled by
darkness and which ones are wholesome and healthy. We seem
to have culturally landed upon the concept that any desires a
person has, from birth on up, are healthy and natural, in the
sense that they are a normal part of human development. But
many things that are part of being a human are not good for
us. Some of us have a natural desire for sweet things, but that
doesn't mean we should eat every piece of candy in the store.

Paul outlines the kind of virtues and life practices that
should come with a life led by the Spirit. Let us all strive for
these values, instead of continuing to live in the dark.

*Lord, thank You for making it possible
for me to live in the Spirit. Amen.* —ML

I Do Not Understand

*I do not understand what I do. For what I
want to do I do not do, but what I hate I do.*
ROMANS 7:15 NIV

Who hasn't felt the same way as Paul describes here in Romans 7? We know what is right. There's no ambiguity there. We know what is wrong. And we know that doing right will be better, ultimately, than doing wrong—even if the wrong feels good in the short term.

And yet, somehow, we still end up doing the wrong things. Paul says that is because it's sin in us doing it. He doesn't mean this as an excuse—not "The devil made me do it." It is just a logical conclusion—if our minds are straight on what we want to do and what we ought to do, and we are in our right minds, then when we still do not do the right things, that is not because we willed it that way. We did not reason ourselves into wrong. We simply ended up there, because we are humans, and humans are subject to temptation.

Paul asks this question: "Who will rescue me from this body that is subject to death?" (v. 24). We know the answer to that—our faithful Savior, the Lord Jesus Christ. He is our deliverer from the bonds of sin.

Lord, thank You for rescuing me from me. Amen. —ML

No Favorites

*My brothers and sisters, believers in our glorious
Lord Jesus Christ must not show favoritism.*
JAMES 2:1 NIV

In recent years, the issues of racism and poverty have created
more sharply divided lines in our nations than ever before.
And these lines show up in our churches as well. They shouldn't
be there—almost everyone agrees that no true follower of Jesus
should ever shun someone based on their skin color, how much
money they have or don't have, or where they came from. And
yet, we can't pretend that the lines don't still exist.

We need to ask ourselves hard questions to root out favoritism
among us. Questions like, Do you find it more pleasant to strike
up conversation with those who are well-dressed and have the
appearance of having money? Do you ignore those who look
troubled or dirty? Do you mostly have friends who resemble
you? Why do you think that is?

Through asking honest questions and giving honest answers,
we can begin to root out favoritism and love one another as
Jesus would want us to do.

*Lord, help me to uncover traces of favoritism in my life,
and help me truly treat everyone as equals. Amen.* —ML

No Longer

There is no longer Jew or Gentile, slave or free, male and female. For you are all one in Christ Jesus. And now that you belong to Christ, you are the true children of Abraham. You are his heirs, and God's promise to Abraham belongs to you.
GALATIANS 3:28–29 NLT

No longer bound for destruction. No longer alone. No longer oppressed with a sadness that could not be shaken. No longer without a home. No longer hopeless, with no redemption for wrongdoings or mistakes made. No longer worthless. No longer known by what we have or what we can produce or how well we can perform. No longer orphans. No longer forgotten. No longer rejected. No longer.

Once we believe in Jesus and accept Him as our Savior, we can cast off all the labels and definitions that used to bind us to sin. Instead we can go by just one name. His.

We can know that we are all valuable. That we are all loved. That we are all wanted. That we are all heirs. That we are all children of Abraham and children of our Father God.

Lord, thank You for enabling me to leave behind what I once was and take up a new identity in You. I love being Your child. Amen. —ML

Who Am I?

But Moses said to God, "Who am I that I should go to Pharaoh and bring the Israelites out of Egypt?"
EXODUS 3:11 NIV

Poor Moses. Don't you feel for him? This guy is minding his own business, doing his job, watching his sheep. When all of a sudden God interrupts his life and knocks his sandals off. It's no wonder he's a little speechless, a little doubtful, and more than a little afraid.

Besides the fact that he has something of a history with the royal family of Egypt, Moses also has a criminal record in that land—he killed a slave master with his own hands. So it's easy to see why Moses might ask God what in the world He is thinking by sending him back to Egypt. "Who am I?"

But God quite cleverly never answers Moses' question—and in fact, it doesn't matter. Because all that really matters is not who Moses is, but who is sending him. God tells Moses that the God of Abraham, Isaac, and Jacob will go with him. He will not let him go through this alone.

Lord, sometimes I'm afraid to go to the places You are leading me. Help me remember that You are always with me so I don't need to be afraid. Amen. —ML

Sustain Me

*Restore to me the joy of your salvation and
grant me a willing spirit, to sustain me.*
PSALM 51:12 NIV

When we are facing up to the sin in our lives and confessing it before God, it can be a dismal, shameful time. It's hard to own up to our mistakes and to claim our bad choices. It's hard to deal with the fact that we've let stupid things get in the way of our relationship with God and with others. It can be downright humiliating.

In order to get through this struggle, we need to pray and ask God to help us reclaim our joy. We need to remember the truth and hope of salvation. We need the holy sustenance that comes from the Spirit dwelling within us—filling us up with the goodness of God and a willing heart that wants to do better. This is not something we can manufacture on our own. As is clearly shown by the fact that we have to repent, we are not capable of consistently holding on to the will of God for long by ourselves. We need some support.

What is sustaining you right now?

*Lord, bring back the joy I had when I first loved You.
Give me a willing spirit and an open heart,
that I might worship You. Amen.* —ML

Bread of Life

Then Jesus declared, "I am the bread of life.
Whoever comes to me will never go hungry,
and whoever believes in me will never be thirsty."
JOHN 6:35 NIV

Easy as pie, some people say. But making bread is not all that easy. At least, not making beautiful, perfectly baked, golden-brown loaves of delicious bread. It can be difficult to get the reaction between the ingredients to work just right, and to knead the dough just the right amount, and to be sure you are letting it rise just long enough.

Often when first trying to make bread, many failed loaves will result. So if bread is the main item on the menu that day, your guests might just go hungry.

Bread is a staple of life in many cultures, and it's made in a thousand different ways. But no bread is as nourishing and enduring and beautiful as the bread of life Jesus offers. When we go to Him in our quiet moments, we always come away filled and fed with the Word of God. And like the manna given by God to the Israelites in the wilderness, or like the loaves that fed five thousand with some left over, His bread will never run out. He will always fill us up to overflowing.

Lord, thank You for filling us up with
Your bread of life. Amen. —ML

Former People Pleaser

*Am I now trying to win the approval of human beings,
or of God? Or am I trying to please people? If I were still
trying to please people, I would not be a servant of Christ.*
GALATIANS 1:10 NIV

Are you a former people pleaser? Did you ever downplay your relationship with Jesus in order to fit in with others? Have you deliberately not included "church" in your story of what you did on the weekend? Have you ever worried about being seen as a Goody Two-shoes?

When we realize that we are accepted by Christ and that His love for us is all we need, it's much easier to set aside our worries and cares about pleasing others. In fact, there will be many times when following Jesus and pleasing Him will mean doing things that are most certainly displeasing to some people. We may get called "a drag" or "a stick in the mud." We may not get invited to every party. But in light of eternity, the only invitation that matters is the one that gets us in the door of heaven.

*Jesus, sometimes I still get embarrassed or
uncomfortable when I'm talking about You in
front of others. Help me to share my faith easily and
without worrying about what people think. Amen.* —ML

Really?

*"But will God really live on earth among people?
Why, even the highest heavens cannot contain you.
How much less this Temple I have built!"*
2 CHRONICLES 6:18 NLT

These words of Solomon in 2 Chronicles are a joyful reminder of the magnificence and tenderness of our God. Here we see King Solomon concerned with presenting a worthy temple to the Lord—a place for God to dwell and communicate with His people. Solomon wonders how the great and mighty and limitless God could ever live on earth. Little does he know that, many generations away, the God of the universe would shrink Himself down into the little body of an infant, and be born to a common girl, and then be laid in a feeding trough. How amazing! Though even the highest heavens cannot contain our God, He was wrapped up and held tightly in the arms of His mother.

It's hard for us to believe even now, knowing the Gospel, that Jesus lived and walked where we can live and walk. It's hard for us to fathom that He ate and drank and slept and got dressed. But He did do all those things. He came to earth so He could know us. And so He could save us.

*Jesus, my Lord and Savior, I am
forever amazed by You. Amen. —ML*

Not-Gods

*Formerly, when you did not know God, you were
slaves to those who by nature are not gods.*
GALATIANS 4:8 NIV

Can you remember a time when you didn't know God? For some of us who have grown up in the church all our lives, that may be hard to do. But can you remember a time when you were not really on board with following Jesus all the way, every day, in everything you said and did? Can you remember a time when you didn't even really understand what it meant to follow God?

For those of us who didn't grow up in the church, these memories may be very fresh indeed. Even a little too fresh! When we think about the time before we knew God and understood what He wanted from us and for us, we realize that our lives were busy with serving many little not-gods. We served the not-god of money—doing whatever we could to get ahead. Or we served the not-god of pleasure, choosing whatever activities would make us feel good (albeit for a short time). Some of us might have served the not-god of food, or alcohol, or drugs—caught up in an all-consuming addiction. And all of us no doubt served at the altar of the not-god of self.

Thankfully, life with Jesus is much simpler. Just one, real, true God.

*Lord, help me to keep all those not-gods
out of my life forever! Amen.* —ML

Word That Prospers

*"It is the same with my word. I send it out, and it always
produces fruit. It will accomplish all I want it to,
and it will prosper everywhere I send it."*
ISAIAH 55:11 NLT

God's Word can cut through all the falsehoods and deceptions of this world and reveal the truth to us in a way that nothing else can. God's Word can reach into our souls and stick to us in the places where we most need to concentrate on change. His Word is alive and fierce. His Word is inspiring and gentle. God's Word is beautiful, with writing that transcends the best literature of our day.

God's Word always works. When God uses it, when He speaks it, when He sends it, it never comes back without having achieved its purpose. Prophets have confronted kings with it. Men have gone into battle with it. Women have taught generations with it. Leaders have been humbled by it. Hearts have been broken by it. Spirits have succumbed to it. God's Word is powerful and persistent. God's Word always prospers.

Lord, the words of men and women will all fade away. But Your living Word stands forever. Thank You for giving it to us to teach us and lead us and show us Your will. Amen. —ML

The Eyes of the Lord

"For the eyes of the LORD range throughout the earth to strengthen those whose hearts are fully committed to him."
2 CHRONICLES 16:9 NIV

It's a little hard to read this verse without picturing some kind of sci-fi beast—with eyes as big as houses—wandering throughout the earth, sniffing out those who are devoted to the Lord. Perhaps, as long as it was a friendly beast, that would be all right.

But in this case, for Asa king of Judah, the beast might not be so friendly. The words of this verse were spoken by Hanani, the seer. He came to see King Asa to deliver a message. The king had bribed a competitor, the king of Aram, by giving him valuable silver and gold items from the Lord's temple. Instead of relying on the Lord to help him conquer his enemies, Asa took matters into his own hands and stole from the Lord.

Hanani confronted the king, reminding him how the Lord had helped Asa defeat the mighty armies of the Cushites and Libyans. He reminded him how God is always seeking to lend His strength to those who are committed to Him. But Asa had forgotten this, and he did not want to hear Hanani.

What have you taken into your own hands that you need to give to God? In what areas of your life have you been forgetting to rely on God's strength?

Lord, I release my struggles to You. Amen. —ML

The Joy of the Lord

"This day is holy to our Lord. Do not grieve,
for the joy of the LORD is your strength."

NEHEMIAH 8:10 NIV

On those days when you wake up on the wrong side of the bed, when the coffee maker stops working, and when your hair just won't do—the joy of the Lord is your strength.

On those days when your job seems pointless, your spirit is listless, and your bank account is worthless—the joy of the Lord is your strength.

On those days when troubles are mounting, and sorrows are haunting, and your willpower is missing—the joy of the Lord is your strength.

The joy of the Lord. How can joy impart strength? When you know the joy of the Lord, when you are sure of your hope in Him, in His kingdom here on earth, and in your home to come in heaven, you become less concerned with the cares of this world. Your happiness is not dependent on everything working well—you depend on Christ. And having that joy and that quiet assurance inside you allows you to push through hard circumstances to see where God is working in your life.

Lord, I want to know the joy of You.
Strengthen me with Your love. Amen. —ML

More Than Words

You believe that there is one God. Good!
Even the demons believe that—and shudder.
JAMES 2:19 NIV

In chapter 2, we see James pointing out the differences and relationships between faith and deeds. He points out that merely mouthing the words of faith—saying you believe in Jesus but then not actually doing anything that backs up your promises—is not enough. He gives the example of being confronted with the clothing and food needs of people who have no money. If you just told them about Jesus' love, but did not offer them anything from your plentiful supplies, what good would that do for those people? What would they think about this Jesus if His followers seem unwilling to give to others?

Faith requires action to keep that faith alive. We need to continue reading God's Word, learning from godly teachers, and serving others in order to grow in our faith. Without any action, we put ourselves on the same level as the demons—who know the image and name of God but cannot feel or know His love or show that love to others.

Lord, may my faith be more than just statements I make.
I want to do things that show others how much You love them.
And I want to worship You through my actions. Amen. —ML

Winter Is Past

"See! The winter is past; the rains are over and gone. Flowers appear on the earth; the season of singing has come."
SONG OF SONGS 2:11–12 NIV

What a beautiful time it is when we get to say farewell to the long, cold, dark winter days, and we begin to greet the first messengers of spring. The ice and snow melt away from the grass and bushes and trees—leaving the ground ready to do its work. Tiny, pale-green buds start to shoot up through the dirt, promising blossoms to come. Robins return to their stomping grounds and hop about all over the lawn, hunting and pecking for nourishment.

The days grow longer and the smells of spring become sweeter. Crocuses rise up in their golden, lavender, and ivory dresses, dancing in the gentle breezes. Daffodils and tulips begin to unfold themselves. Irises start to stretch up to the sky. And every tree is peppered with tiny buds.

Seasons of life change like the seasons of the year. And with each one, it's good to stop and spend some quiet time reflecting on the blessings that have come to us, and the promises yet to be fulfilled.

Lord, I'm so humbled by the beauty in Your world.
You've created so many wonderful plants and animals
for us to enjoy, all year round. Thank You! —ML

Foundations

With praise and thanksgiving they sang to the LORD:
"He is good; his love toward Israel endures forever." And
all the people gave a great shout of praise to the LORD,
because the foundation of the house of the LORD was laid.
EZRA 3:11 NIV

What are you standing on? Are your beliefs grounded in a long-standing tradition of generational faith in God's promises? Is your faith born out of family trials, times when you saw God working in your lives, helping you to thrive? Is what you believe an eclectic mix of quotations and thoughts from a variety of thinkers, poets, artists, and writers?

What is your faith foundation made of? Is it cemented with the Word of God? Is it laced with worship? Is it strengthened by the testimony of many great and faithful witnesses?

What do you build on when you want to grow in the Lord? Do you rely solely on His Word, or do you turn to other helpful voices? Do you have wise counselors? Do you have trustworthy friends?

The Lord is good. He was good to the Israelites, and He will continue to be good to us too. Take some time today to think about where your faith comes from and where you want to go with it. Think about your foundations. And give a shout of praise!

Lord, I praise You for Your unfailing love. Amen. —ML

Sin Crouching

"If you do what is right, will you not be accepted?
But if you do not do what is right, sin is crouching at
your door; it desires to have you, but you must rule over it."
GENESIS 4:7 NIV

All of us have certain temptations that affect us more than others. These may be weaknesses that have developed over a long time, stemming from some event buried deep in our history. Or they might just be powerful attractions that have surprised us, coming seemingly out of nowhere.

Satan is clever. He knows what things we like. He knows our habits. He knows areas of human frailty. He knows exactly how to trick us into believing that something that is bad for us is actually good. He also twists good things to make them appear as God things.

That's why we have to be alert. We can't just tune the world out and go on our way. We have to tune in to God's Word every day. We have to keep our focus on loving God and loving others, and not on pleasing ourselves. And we have to surround ourselves with people who are willing to speak up and speak truth to us when they see us going in an unhealthy direction.

Lord, I want to do what is right. Help me
to rule over sin in my life. Amen. —ML

Seek His Face

Look to the LORD and his strength; seek his face always.
1 CHRONICLES 16:11 NIV

Imagine seeing God face-to-face. It seems like the glory of Him would be so bright, we'd never be able to look at Him. And what would we see in His eyes if we could? Would He gaze on us as a new father looks at his child—with adoration and admiration mixing together as one? Would there be a little sadness in His smile? Would we see in Him ourselves—the pieces of us that show His love?

There are many times when it is extremely difficult to seek God's face. Sometimes it's because life has become so stressful and busy that we just never take a moment to rest in Him. Sometimes it's because the cares of life—caring for others or scrambling to care for ourselves—are physically so troublesome that when we do have time to rest, all we can do is sleep. But at other times it's hard to see Him when we don't want to see Him. Sometimes we are angry—someone is gone or something was lost—and in our grief, we can't settle down enough to even be civil. Or sometimes we are ashamed—something we've done seems too terrible to overcome, even for our heavenly Father.

No matter what has happened in our lives, we can be sure that God is always with us, and He wants us to seek Him. Always.

*Lord, help me to come looking for You,
even when it's terribly, terribly hard. Amen. —ML*

Shine

Do everything without grumbling or arguing, so that you may become blameless and pure, "children of God without fault in a warped and crooked generation." Then you will shine among them like stars in the sky as you hold firmly to the word of life.

PHILIPPIANS 2:14–16 NIV

Have you ever cleaned something until it sparkled? When a surface is free from grime and fingerprints and dust and lime scale, it's easy for the light to bounce off the surface and come back to you with bright rays that dazzle your eyes. Think about a mirror in a bathroom. When it's smudged and water-splashed and streaked, it's hard to even see your own reflection, much less any kind of shine.

As you gently and carefully wipe away the streaks and smudges, the brightness of the glass starts to appear. And the more clean glass there is showing, the more the light can do its work!

Our lives are like that glass. When our spirits are clouded with grumbling and complaining and fighting, all coming from us wanting our own way, our witness gets murky too. People see us and wonder why we're so joyless if we are supposed to have the Joy-maker in our lives. But if we can set all those cares and complaints aside, if we can focus on putting Him first, then our attitudes shine forth clearly, with joyful and gracious selflessness. The more a pure heart is showing in our lives, the more His light can shine.

God, thank You for shining on me. Amen. —ML

Too Much to Drink

And so the people are dismayed and confused,
drinking in all their words.
Psalm 73:10 nlt

The psalmist who wrote Psalm 73 could have easily been living in modern times. He tells how he almost lost his way due to envy and pride. He saw people who prospered, even though they were wicked, and he wanted to be like them. Listen to his description and see if this scenario sounds familiar at all to you: "They seem to live such painless lives; their bodies are so healthy and strong. They don't have troubles like other people; they're not plagued with problems like everyone else. . . . They scoff and speak only evil; in their pride they seek to crush others. They boast against the very heavens, and their words strut throughout the earth" (vv. 4–5, 8–9).

It's like social media just suddenly showed up in the Psalms. But it shouldn't really surprise us—the problem of pride has been around since Adam and Eve. But these days pride is almost seen as a virtue—as something to desire and flaunt and show off itself. And people who are prideful have so many outlets through which they can boast and spread their wicked words. And we just keep following them and drinking them in.

If you find yourself getting too caught up in wanting to be like the wicked who prosper, why not take a break from drinking in those empty words?

Lord, help me fill my mind with Your
Word instead of wickedness. Amen. —ML

Obstacles

"But sir, you don't have a rope or a bucket,"
she said, "and this well is very deep.
Where would you get this living water?"
JOHN 4:11 NLT

Have you been there? You come to a spot in your life when you could use some advice or a helping hand, and then God is there in the form of a stranger, a friend, a pastor, a family member, reaching out, ready to help. But you come up with all kinds of reasons why whatever the plan is won't work. It's not the right time. It's too hard. It's too easy. It's too complicated. It's too embarrassing. It's too soon.

Have you been there? The Samaritan woman was there. Here she was, her life embroiled in all kinds of stressful relational and societal pressures, hiding out from her peers, and then she comes to the well. And there is Jesus. He offers her a chance at new life. But what does she say? "You don't have a rope." "There's no bucket." "This well is deep." "And who do you think you are to offer help to me anyway?"

She throws up all the obstacles before she even figures out who He really is. And she almost misses the chance to know Him.

Lord, I don't want to miss out on You or Your plan for me.
Help me to stop coming up with false reasons not to
engage with You or with others. Amen. —ML

Busybodies

We hear that some among you are idle and disruptive.
They are not busy; they are busybodies. Such people
we command and urge in the Lord Jesus Christ to
settle down and earn the food they eat.

2 THESSALONIANS 3:11–12 NIV

Just in case it isn't clear, let's consider what is being busy and what isn't. Making meals for a new mom is being busy. Criticizing the way that mommy is taking care of her baby is not. Stopping by someone's house to see how they are doing is being busy. Stopping by to peer in their windows to see what new furniture they have is not. Volunteering to clean up at a church function is busy. Volunteering as a way of looking good to the pastor but then spending the whole time chatting or sitting in the chairs meant for the guests is not.

Busy gets things done. Idleness wastes time. Busy makes an impact. Idleness makes a mess. Busy does the Lord's work. Idleness. . .well, you can see where we're going here.

Friends, there is an awful lot of work to get done in the kingdom of God. Can we all agree that no one's got time for busybodies?

Lord, I don't ever want to be idle or disruptive when I
should be serving You. Help me make sure I have the
right attitude about doing Your work. Amen. —ML

The Days Are Coming

"The days are coming," declares the LORD, "when the reaper will be overtaken by the plowman and the planter by the one treading grapes. New wine will drip from the mountains and flow from all the hills, and I will bring my people Israel back from exile."

AMOS 9:13–14 NIV

The Bible is filled with vibrant, wonderful language. Every time you read it, you can find some new treasure. Here in Amos we see a colorful description that paints a picture in the reader's mind of what will happen when the Israelites are finally able to take back their homeland and get out from under the rule of their enemies.

Imagine the reaper of the harvest being plowed right over by the man pushing the plow. The reaper is going ahead, cutting down the plants, never imagining that the plowman would be out digging new furrows at harvest time. Then whammo! Down he goes!

Or consider the planter inspecting the plants, when he hears a call from the winepress. He goes over to see what the problem is and surprise! He gets pulled right into the vat of grapes and stomped on by the purple feet of the one treading out the juices.

Whoever said God doesn't have a sense of humor surely hasn't read all through the Bible!

Lord, I love how Your Word has new surprises in it for me every day. Amen. —ML

No More Sitting

Then he went with them into the temple courts,
walking and jumping, and praising God.
Acts 3:8 niv

How many days must the man have sat in front of that beautiful temple gate? He had been born lame—unable to walk on his own. He had no way of making an income. No way of supporting himself in that culture and at that time. All he could do was the lowliest thing in that society—beg. Every day some people carried him there, to that busy spot where many people would pass him, and many people would ignore him.

Until that one day. He was locked into his routine, holding his hand out, asking for money from everyone who entered the temple gate. So when Peter and John came by, he asked them for money too. Peter stopped. Peter looked straight into the man's eyes (he couldn't even remember the last time anyone had made eye contact with him!). And Peter made sure the man was paying attention. "Look at us!" he said. And then, with a few words and the power of the name of Jesus Christ, Peter healed the man.

All those days, all those years of sitting and begging and now this! The man jumped to his feet. And he went with Peter and John into the temple courts, walking and leaping for joy. And praising God with every step. No more sitting for him. He had too much to do!

God, I am amazed by the power of Your name. Amen. —ML

Like Spring Rain

May the king's rule be refreshing like spring rain on
freshly cut grass, like the showers that water the earth.
PSALM 72:6 NLT

You can almost smell it right now, can't you? It smells like green, and earth, and growing things. It smells like pond water and rain. And it might even smell a little bit like wet dog.

The lovely look of a fresh-cut lawn combined with the cool, delightful experience of a gentle spring shower provides a beautiful image of what Solomon wants his rule to do in the land. He wants it to be a time of rest and refreshment for his citizens.

One way of bringing that refreshment follows a bit later in the psalm, when he writes that "he will rescue the poor when they cry to him; he will help the oppressed, who have no one to defend them. He feels pity for the weak and the needy, and he will rescue them" (vv. 12–13).

A leader who is willing and committed to looking after the least powerful people will set at ease every person under his authority. His care for the least of these shows great humility, great compassion, and great power.

Lord, may all our leaders be like this king—
caring for the least in the best way. Amen. —ML

Silent Awe

They will cover their mouths in silent awe,
deaf to everything around them.
MICAH 7:16 NLT

This passage from the prophet Micah starts off in a pretty bleak tone. He talks about how miserable he is due to God's punishment. At one point he exclaims, "Don't trust anyone—not your best friend or even your wife!" (v. 5). Everyone is turned against everyone else in this horrible time when judgment is coming.

But then a glimmer of hope appears: "For though I fall, I will rise again. Though I sit in darkness, the LORD will be my light" (v. 8). The writer's hopefulness and confidence grow with each mention of how the Lord will restore him. Finally, we see the Lord doing mighty miracles for His people, the nation of Israel. And because of this, all the nations will stand back, looking on with amazement, covering their mouths in awe. Through the wonders that He does for His people, God always draws a crowd!

Lord, as I sit here with You, enjoying this peaceful time, I too am struck with silent awe at Your wonders. I am amazed by Your compassionate action. And I am stunned by the love You pour out on all Your people, everywhere we are. Amen. —ML

Just a Whisper

*"And these are but the outer fringe of his works;
how faint the whisper we hear of him! Who then
can understand the thunder of his power?"*
JOB 26:14 NIV

In his responses to his friends, Job lists many illustrations of God's great and awesome power. Here he talks about God spreading the skies, wrapping up the water in the clouds, marking out horizons, and churning up the sea. And all these things are just the merest glimpse—a flash, a whisper, a hint—of what our almighty God is capable of doing.

God is so big and so amazing, we can't even begin to imagine the extent of His power. But we can have some hope of understanding His love. The closer we get to Him—the more we read His Word, the more we talk with Him, the more time we spend sitting in His presence—the more we see all the ways that He cares for us, thinks about us, has made plans for us, and just loves us as His children. Though we hear just a whisper of His might, we can see a full, beautiful display of His love through His Son.

*Lord, thank You for all these little glimpses and
whispers that show us more about You. Amen.* —ML

Wise Counsel

Let the message about Christ, in all its richness, fill your lives.
Teach and counsel each other with all the wisdom he gives.
COLOSSIANS 3:16 NLT

Put His Word up on the first thing you see in the morning. Send yourself reminders with verses in them on your phone. Use a Bible app for daily reading. Write His Word in a journal. Make beautiful signs using His Word. Hang up prints featuring His Word in your house. Attend classes and small groups where you can dig into His Word. Be at church every week to listen to teaching on His Word. Listen to podcasts of speakers who base their talks on His Word. Write poetry including His Word.

In this day and age, there are certainly at least a thousand ways for you to fill your life with His Word. Pick a few, or several, and try them out. See what happens. No doubt your life will be made better by the injection of God's Word, and you will get to know His Word so well, you might even find yourself teaching others about it!

Lord, You know how much I love Your Word. Help me
find new and trustworthy ways to explore it and
use it in every detail of my life. Amen. —ML

Selfish Ends

*An unfriendly person pursues selfish ends and
against all sound judgment starts quarrels.*
PROVERBS 18:1 NIV

One by-product of spending time with God by still waters is that you stop being so consumed with the sound of your own voice, with your own desires, and with your own needs, and you start getting used to listening for His wisdom.

There are many people in the world (perhaps you've been one of them sometime!) who push, push, push their way through their lives and the lives of others, always looking out for themselves. They approach every situation from the perspective of "What's in it for me?" They are always striving to get the upper hand, to be in control, to get the best deal.

Instead of trying to understand anyone else's point of view, these sorts of people only hear the sound of their own demands. Instead of listening, they are always scheming about what their next move will be. And so, they start a lot of quarrels since they don't care to take the time to have better understanding and successful communication. They just want to dictate instead.

And though at times such people do get their way, the problem for them is that there is likely so much more that they could be experiencing, if they only would take the time to find out.

Lord, I don't want to be selfish in the way I interact with the world. Help me to be more aware of others. Amen. —ML

Not So Still

*They are wild waves of the sea, foaming up
their shame; wandering stars, for whom blackest
darkness has been reserved forever.*

JUDE 13 NIV

The ungodly people Jude describes, those who deny Jesus as Lord and pervert the grace of God, were positioning themselves among the believers. Jude wanted to warn them not to let these rebellious people destroy their fellowship.

These people are the very opposite of the kind of people we all want to be—the kind of people that God leads by still waters. For these people are never still; they are always stirring up trouble and creating controversy. At the same time, one feels sorry for them, for they are empty—"clouds without rain" (v. 12)—and dead, or even "twice dead" (v. 12), as Jude put it. They have no substance in them—nothing they are really working for. They just seek to upset everyone else and destroy relationships. They have no anchor or foundation—they are concerned only with finding fault in what others have built.

The best that we can do for such people is not let them get to us, but instead, pray for them. Ask God to change their hearts. Don't listen to their empty words, but take every opportunity to share with them the story of Jesus Christ. And keep yourself focused on that message too.

*Lord, help me know how to love people
who seek to hurt others. Amen.* —ML

As You Have Done

"The day of the LORD is near for all nations.
As you have done, it will be done to you;
your deeds will return upon your own head."
OBADIAH 15 NIV

What kind of reaction does that statement cause in you? "As you have done, it will be done to you."

Think about your interactions this week—with your kids, your spouse, your coworkers, the telemarketer, the mail carrier, the guy taking too long in line at the dry cleaner's, your pastor,and so forth and so on. Think about every single person you've talked to, just this week. And think about every person you've neglected or forgotten about this week too.

Now, what do you think? "As you have done, it will be done to you."

Are you comfortable with that promise? And if you're not, what can you do about it? How can you change your interactions with others so they are more fruitful? How can you be more kind? How can you be more considerate?

Think about a few small steps you can take in the coming week to improve your connections with others. Then take action!

Lord, the idea of my own actions coming back to me
is a little worrying. But that shouldn't be the case!
Help me to treat other people better, Lord. Amen. —ML

Unresolved

*Is your love declared in the grave, your faithfulness in
Destruction? Are your wonders known in the place of
darkness, or your righteous deeds in the land of oblivion?*
PSALM 88:11–12 NIV

God is not afraid of our dark places. At times when you are
sinking into depression, remember this one thing: God is
always, always with you. Even in the pits of despair. Perhaps
especially in the pits of despair.

Psalm 88 is a little unusual in that the writer leaves it un-
resolved. Often the Psalms explore themes of sorrow and grief
and punishment, but then eventually the writer comes to the
conclusion that we can trust in God's unfailing love or that His
love endures forever. But this psalm ends in absolute despair—the
person feels destroyed, engulfed, swept over. The psalm ends
with this haunting claim: "Darkness is my closest friend" (v. 18).

But the beautiful comfort of this piece lies in the answers
to the questions posed. Is God's love declared in the grave?
Yes, even in the grave, God's love is there. Is His faithfulness
in Destruction? Yes, even if everything is utterly destroyed, God
remains faithful. Are His wonders known in the place of darkness
and oblivion? Yes, even in the places farthest from His light,
God's power reaches out.

*Lord, in my darkest places, I can depend on You.
Thank You. Amen. —ML*

Called to Be Free

You, my brothers and sisters, were called to be free.
But do not use your freedom to indulge the flesh;
rather, serve one another humbly in love.

GALATIANS 5:13 NIV

People sometimes get very hung up on what it means to be free in God. They either want to define it and set limits on it, or they want to throw caution to the wind and let everyone do anything they want to do. But the way to understand freedom in Christ is the same way we understand other parts of God's plan for us. We just have to ask ourselves, What's most important to God?

And the answer is (1) love the Lord your God with all your heart, soul, mind, and strength, and (2) love your neighbor as yourself.

If you love the Lord, you are going to want to please the Lord. So you will naturally want to do the things that God finds admirable and praiseworthy. And if you love your neighbor, you're going to want to do good things for your neighbor. Your mind is not going to be set on what you can get away with or what you are allowed to do. Your mind is going to be set on considering what would serve your neighbor in the best way.

Lord, help me learn to serve others,
and You, humbly. Amen. —ML

Truly Life

Tell them to go after God, who piles on all the riches we could ever manage—to do good, to be rich in helping others, to be extravagantly generous. If they do that, they'll build a treasury that will last, gaining life that is truly life.
1 TIMOTHY 6:18–19 MSG

There are few things that really last in this world. So many things that are manufactured these days seem to fall apart so easily. And even if an item is of quite good quality, would it really stand up to a flood, or a hurricane, or a forest fire?

No, the things that really last are not things at all. They are experiences, connections, relationships. They are good memories, hugs, and close friendships. They are moments of joy, celebrations of love, and offerings of grace.

If we spend all our time running after money, at the end of our days, we will be disappointed. We will also most likely be alone. But if we instead spend all our time and effort and talents investing in people, then we will get to experience God's glorious generosity of spirit and grace. Instead of a life built on things, we will have a life that is truly all about life.

Lord, I want the life that is truly life.
Help me get moving! Amen. —ML

Hammered Swords

They will hammer their swords into plowshares and their
spears into pruning hooks; nation will not lift up sword
against nation, and never again will they train for war.
MICAH 4:3 NASB

We are living right now in an unsettled time. Even a some-times scary time. There are many nations whose societies are in danger of falling apart. And there are some leaders who seem in danger of falling apart themselves. On the other hand, there are people existing in dire situations. And though no one wants to go to war, it's hard to know what we should do to help these human beings.

This passage in Micah presents a beautiful picture of the promise of peace. We see in this chapter that there will come a time when the nations actually come together and ask each other to meet together on the mountain of the Lord. They want to go there, not to war against each other, or to even negotiate, but they want to go to learn from God: "He may teach us about His ways and that we may walk in His paths" (v. 2).

Then the nations will turn their weapons into instruments of peace—tools for growth and change. Plowshares that turn up the soil and make it ready for planting, and pruning hooks that help cut back plants so they can grow better and stronger—these are the instruments that can help nations grow together in peace.

Lord, make me an instrument of Your peace. Amen. —ML

Stand in the Presence

Now to Him who is able to keep you from stumbling,
and to make you stand in the presence of His glory
blameless with great joy, to the only God our Savior,
through Jesus Christ our Lord, be glory, majesty, dominion
and authority, before all time and now and forever. Amen.
JUDE 24–25 NASB

We all stumble. It's a human characteristic. Sometimes our feet just get going too fast for the rest of us, and we trip. Now, of course, some of us stumble more than others. Some of us, perhaps, stumble every day. On the same ridiculous end table legs, no less. But that's another story.

God is able to keep us from stumbling. Isn't that a wonderful thing to know? But He is not so concerned with our klutzy feet. He is able to keep us from stumbling in our faith—from losing our footing established in the knowledge of Him.

But He doesn't stop there. He doesn't just keep us from falling down; He makes us able to stand in the presence of His glory—to stand blameless. That's a position we only have access to because of Him. There is nothing about us that allows us to be there before our God and Savior—we are purely invited guests at the table of His grace.

Lord, I stand here to give all glory
and honor to You. Amen. —ML

DAY 244

Far and Near

"Peace, peace to him who is far and to him who is near."
ISAIAH 57:19 NASB

Peace. God offers His peace. Peace to the child left behind in a hut while his parents forage for food. Peace to the leader of a nation left in ruins after war. Peace to the woman enduring the pains of a long, long labor. Peace to the wife watching in the night as her husband draws his last breath. Peace to the man holding his wriggling newborn in his trembling hands for the first time. Peace to the worker in the fields, wondering if he can last till the end of the day. Peace to the refugees, living in tented cities. Peace to the revolutionaries, looking for a chance to change their lives. Peace to the boys holding guns that are much too big for them. Peace to the girls who have been stolen and abused. Peace to the researchers who long to find breakthroughs. Peace to the pastors who are caring for troubled flocks. Peace to the rich man who sits alone in his office, wondering what it all means. Peace to the poor man warming his hands by an outdoor fire. Peace to the child who waits for Christmas blessings. Peace to the child in the manger, who is the ultimate Christmas blessing.

Peace near, peace far. Peace everywhere. For everyone, His desire is peace.

*Lord, I want to spread Your peace
all over my world. Amen.* —ML

Speak Up

> *"If anyone sins because they do not speak up when they hear a public charge to testify regarding something they have seen or learned about, they will be held responsible."*
> LEVITICUS 5:1 NIV

We are all familiar with the commandment not to give false witness. Not to lie. Honesty certainly is a highly valued quality—and God commands us to tell the truth. But here He goes one step further. Here we are told that if a situation arises in which someone is charged with breaking a law, or if a case is being examined and a call for information is sent out, we are responsible for telling anything we know. In other words, if we know that we have information that someone else ought to know, and we don't offer that information, then we are sinning. And we will be held responsible for that sin.

Lately, speaking up has become a very important and often powerful action. When we speak up about the truth we know, we help other people to understand the truth. We help other people feel encouraged to speak about what they know. And we persuade people who hide their wrong deeds either to stop hiding or to start doing things right.

If we know truth and don't speak up about it, that's on us. But we have to acknowledge that holding back truth can hurt others too.

Lord, when I have truth to share, help me be confident to share it. Amen. —ML

Preserved

*You, O LORD, will keep them; You will
preserve him from this generation forever.*
PSALM 12:7 NASB

God's promises never fail. That's a concept we find hard to comprehend. We live in a culture filled with broken promises. Marriages are easily broken. Business deals fall apart at the last moment. Promises made on campaign trails quickly drown in a sea of bureaucracy. All kinds of people from all kinds of places find it hard to do what they say they will do.

But God's words are pure. God's words are true forever. God's words don't change.

We can always trust that when God says He will do a thing, He will do it. In this psalm, the writer begs the Lord to help the "godly man." The person expresses the fear that the godly are disappearing. Contrary to the Lord's words, no one in this land speaks the truth. Yet people still feel free to say whatever they want to say: "Our lips are our own; who is lord over us?" (v. 4).

But God promises to keep the godly safe. He will preserve those who trust in Him.

*Lord God, thank You for always being a source of truth. Help
me to speak the truth too. Be Lord of my words. Amen.* —ML

Joyful Insight

*The commandments of the LORD are right,
bringing joy to the heart. The commands of
the LORD are clear, giving insight for living.*
PSALM 19:8 NLT

People don't often rejoice in commands. But then again, they aren't often talking about commands that are perfectly designed to guide us into the best way to live and love and grow together.

God's commands are right. We don't have to worry about following them because they have always been right and they will always be right. His commands don't need to change as times change because they are about sacred things of life that do not change—things like the bonds of love, truth, justice, care for others, humility, integrity, and so on.

His commands are also clear. We don't have to puzzle over them. He gave them in straightforward language that even small children can understand.

His commands bring joy because right living brings joy. When we are living in a way that honors God and respects others, our hearts are content, at peace with God and at peace with our fellow humans.

His commands offer insight because they come from the source of all wisdom. There is no area of life that God cannot shed light on. He is the best guide for any situation.

For these reasons, we can rejoice in God's commands.

*Lord, I love the guidance You provide for me.
Help me to hide Your commands away in my heart
so I can always have them with me. Amen.* —ML

Darkness Isn't Dark

Then I said to myself, "Oh, he even sees me
in the dark! At night I'm immersed in the light!"
It's a fact: darkness isn't dark to you; night and day,
darkness and light, they're all the same to you.
PSALM 139:11–12 MSG

Imagine a world with no darkness. You'd never have to be afraid to walk down a dark alley. You'd never worry about driving at night. You'd have a much easier time finding things that get lost outside.

Of course, you also might have a hard time sleeping—but that problem is for another day.

Darkness isn't dark to God because He is pure light. He is everything that darkness is not. Where darkness hides, God reveals. Darkness keeps secrets; God tells truth. Darkness masks evil deeds; God unmasks all evildoers. Darkness invites sinful actions; God invites holiness.

No matter where we go, in darkness or in light, God is with us. He knows where we are going before we even set the itinerary. He knows when we'll be back. He knows our whole story, from beginning to end. Thus, it is a very good idea to stick close to Him!

Lord, I know sometimes I try to hide from You. But I'm so
glad You always know where to find me. Amen. —ML

From the Dust

"He raises the poor from the dust and lifts the needy from the ash heap; he seats them with princes and has them inherit a throne of honor."

1 SAMUEL 2:8 NIV

Hannah suffered for years. Not only could she not give her husband a child, but her rival, her husband's other wife, kept taunting her. Year after year, she had to endure the cruel words of this woman, Peninnah.

Hannah must have very much felt like a second-class citizen. Even though her husband treated her with kindness, she was brokenhearted.

Finally, the Lord blessed her and she gave birth to Samuel. She was so devoted to God though, and so thankful to Him, she decided to dedicate Samuel to the Lord's service, and she gave him to the priest Eli to live in the temple. Samuel would become a very important prophet of God—the man who would anoint kings of Israel.

Hannah's prayer reflects her heart, as she acknowledges God as the one who can raise the poor from the dust and seat them with princes. Hannah, the barren wife, became the mother of the Lord's own messenger. What redemption!

King of kings, I love that You are able to make king makers out of servants, and princes out of paupers. You bring glory to every life You touch. Amen. —ML

Walk in Love

*As you have heard from the beginning,
his command is that you walk in love.*

2 JOHN 6 NIV

Walking in love sounds beautiful, but it takes hard work. No one should think that loving people is an easy job. People are people. They make mistakes and make life difficult. They cause problems. They hurt each other. They are unpredictable.

Walking in love means walking with all these complexities. It might mean going the extra mile to fight for someone who has no voice. Or it might mean helping someone clean her home when she's sick. It could mean convincing someone to give up an addiction. Or it could mean helping someone handle extreme physical distress as they battle a disease.

Walking in love will often mean walking in tears.

Just as Jesus carried the cross for us, endured beatings for us, and offered Himself as a living sacrifice for us, we are called to be as humble as He was. We may not have to suffer that kind of physical trauma (I hope not!), but we will have to put ourselves in places we never expected to go and do things that we would not normally do. It will be hard. It will probably be awkward. And it may even be painful. But God would do no less.

*Lord, teach me how to walk in love,
and help me have the courage to do it. Amen.* —ML

The Word

*When you received the word of God, which you heard
from us, you accepted it not as a human word,
but as it actually is, the word of God, which is
indeed at work in you who believe.*

1 THESSALONIANS 2:13 NIV

Followers of God believe that His Word is not just a collection of letters and words, not just ink on papyrus. We
also believe that God's Word is not a series of unrelated, unreal
stories. Though people do differ on some points of God's Word,
almost everyone who believes in Jesus also believes there is
something special about God's Word. We believe His Word
is powerful. We believe it carries the truth. And we believe it
is good for us to use to get closer to God.

When we take time to be still and study His Word, we're
not just reading good material. We're reading about Him. We're
learning God's story of His life with His people. We're seeing
where we fit into that big story.

We should thank God for His Word. He didn't have to leave
it for us. We could have had to just figure out things on our own,
or depend on signs and visions and dreams. But instead we have
the Word of God, and we can go back to it again and again,
to learn more and more about the God we serve.

*Lord, please help me to study Your Word well and
thoroughly so that I am ready to answer anyone
who might have questions about it. Amen.* —ML

No Need

I do not treat the grace of God as meaningless.
For if keeping the law could make us right with God,
then there was no need for Christ to die.
GALATIANS 2:21 NLT

The Galatians were having a hard time. They were trying to live by the Gospel of Christ, but at the same time, there were some people among them who were trying to convince them that they had to live by the old laws as well. Paul wanted to encourage the Galatian believers not to become enslaved by the law again. Much of his letter to the Galatians deals with this issue.

Paul points out to the Galatians that no one gets right with God through obeying the law, because no one is able to obey the law 100 percent of the time. If anyone could perfectly obey the law, then perhaps they could be made right with God. But that is not possible. And God has shown us that it is not possible—that's why He sent His Son to die for us. If God had wanted us to try to keep the law perfectly as a way of achieving righteousness, He wouldn't have had to send His Son. There would have been no need for Christ to come to the earth, to suffer as He did, and to die on the cross.

So we must not make the grace of God seem meaningless by forgetting the importance of faith and turning back to a life chained to the law.

Lord, I know the only way to You is through Jesus. Amen. —ML

Woven in Wisdom

*I want you woven into a tapestry of love, in touch with
everything there is to know of God. Then you will have
minds confident and at rest, focused on Christ, God's great
mystery. All the richest treasures of wisdom and knowledge
are embedded in that mystery and nowhere else.*

COLOSSIANS 2:2–3 MSG

Antique tapestries are made with thousands of skillfully woven stitches, all carefully planned out. Look closely at a tapestry and you'll see a story that unfolds throughout the length of the fabric. Every thread is placed where it needs to be to complete the whole picture. If you look at just one corner of the piece, you may not understand the message, but when you back up and take another look, you can see what story is being told.

When we are woven into God's tapestry, we become a part of the rich and colorful story of His love for His people. The beautiful thing is we don't have to do anything to earn a place in this story. We just accept God's love and sacrifice for us, and He weaves us in. Knowing that, and knowing about God, allows us to be confident in Him and to rest in Him. We know He will be there for us. And we know we will never lose our place in His great story.

*God, thank You for weaving my life into the great
story of love that You are creating. Amen.* —ML

No Condemnation

*So now there is no condemnation for those who belong
to Christ Jesus. And because you belong to him,
the power of the life-giving Spirit has freed you
from the power of sin that leads to death.*

ROMANS 8:1–2 NLT

*N*o condemnation. Even those two words by themselves sound like freedom. Because we know there is no condemnation once we accept Christ, we can truly rest. Our hearts and minds can be at ease.

No condemnation doesn't mean no mission, however. And resting doesn't equal laziness. When we belong to Christ, we belong to a whole family of believers, and we have the responsibility to look after one another and encourage one another. We have the job of teaching each other and telling each other our stories about when we learned we were freed from the power of sin and what that means to us.

His life-giving Spirit allows us to continually be renewed—to have our hearts and minds reset as needed to focus on Him. He knows we get distracted and weary and a little muddled sometimes. He forgives us and sets us right so we can be wholly centered on Him.

No condemnation is a pretty wonderful place to live.

*Lord, thank You that I don't have to fear being
condemned to punishment for my sin. Thank You
for Your indescribable gift of grace. Amen.* —ML

Who among You?

Who among you fears the LORD and obeys the word of his servant? Let the one who walks in the dark, who has no light, trust in the name of the LORD and rely on their God.
ISAIAH 50:10 NIV

Walking in the dark without a light can be treacherous. It might be fine if you're on a large, flat lawn that you are very familiar with. But if you are set down in the middle of a path in the woods, you might never find your way out! You would need someone to guide you—someone who knows the way.

The person who fears the Lord, who has a healthy respect for what God has done and can do—this is a person who trusts God. He knows that God knows every path of life. God knows every possible pitfall. God knows every trap. God knows every turn. So if God says to him, "Go out and walk in the dark. I will lead you," then this man will obey—just as he obeys everything else God says. He trusts God not to let him fall. And God would not leave him by himself in the woods. God stays with us on every challenge He gives us, every step of the way.

My God and my Guide, I put all my trust in You.
Lead me in the way I should go. Amen. —ML

Mindful

When I consider your heavens, the work of your fingers,
the moon and the stars, which you have set in place,
what is mankind that you are mindful of them,
human beings that you care for them?
PSALM 8:3–4 NIV

The hands that held the heavens also formed you. The fingers that set the moon and stars in place are the fingers that were scraped up against the cross. The One who created everything in the world thought we were good additions to make.

It's truly amazing that He ever wants to spend even a moment thinking about us. It's mind-blowing that He pursues us, protects us, and provides for us.

It should be an honor to take time to be with our God. It should be a privilege that we get to be in His presence.

When we realize that He wants to love us, there is nothing in the world that can make us feel so secure, so settled, and so safe.

Who is like this God of ours? He creates miracles in heaven and on earth. And He calls us His miracles too.

Father and creator God, I praise You for all the beauty You have placed in the world for us to enjoy. Thank You for caring so much about the smallest of details, even me. Amen. —ML

He Heard My Cry

I waited patiently for the LORD;
he turned to me and heard my cry.
PSALM 40:1 NIV

When we are in a rough spot, especially if we are stuck there for a long time, we might feel like God isn't really listening. We might wonder why He doesn't rescue us right away. Perhaps there are some lessons we need to learn along the way. Or maybe someone else is stuck too, and we need to help them first. But God is never ignoring us. He is always listening. He hears us, and He knows exactly what we need.

In Psalm 40 we see how the psalmist received his answer from the Lord. God lifted him out of his rough situation—"out of the mud and mire" (v. 2). Then God gave him a solid place on which to stand.

When we wait patiently on God, we learn to trust Him even more. And He will bless that trust.

Lord God, sometimes I cry out to You and I'm afraid You
don't hear me. Forgive me for the times when I am full of
doubts. I know I can trust You. Thank You for understanding
me so completely and giving me exactly what I need,
when I need it. Amen. —ML

Undivided

Teach me your way, LORD, that I may rely on your faithfulness; give me an undivided heart, that I may fear your name.

PSALM 86:11 NIV

Our hearts are tricky things. We have so many feelings that get rolled up into this one bundle that we call the heart.

We have strong feelings that often can pull us in different directions. We love our family and want to spend time with them. But we also love our friends. We love our church family, but we also care for our coworkers. We love to play hockey and we love our golden retriever. We have a passion for missions, but we also want to go on a lovely beach vacation with the girls.

Sometimes these feelings can all travel along together in harmony. But sometimes we get pulled in lots of different directions. Like when your mother-in-law wants you to go out to a movie but you'd really rather go shopping with your friends.

But one area we should not be divided about is our love of God. There should be no other things in our lives that we worship above God. We should not chase after wisdom from sources that are contrary to His Word. We should not try to follow spiritual paths that don't honor Him.

Where God is concerned, we need to focus our feelings and follow just one way—the one way to Him.

God, teach me the way to get to You. Give me an undivided heart, fully focused on You. Amen. —ML

Stand and Listen

"Now stand here quietly before the Lord as I remind you of all the great things the Lord has done for you and your ancestors."
1 Samuel 12:7 nlt

Samuel was getting old and it was time for him to go. He offered a farewell address to the Israelites, gathering them together to remind them of what God had done for them, in so many situations and over such a long time. He wanted to remind them of God's faithfulness and urge them to be faithful in return to God.

We need to be reminded in this way as well. That's why it is good to gather together regularly, to attend church services in some form, to hear from God's Word and be reminded by the testimony of others what good things God has done for us. To be reminded of His truthfulness. To be reminded of His promises. To be reminded of what His form of justice and righteousness looks like. And to be reminded of His grace.

We need to take time to stand quietly before the Lord and hear what He has to say to us.

Lord, I can think of all the things You've done for me and my family, but it's good to remember all that You've done for the world. Don't let me forget to gather with other believers and listen to You. Amen. —ML

In the Valley of Despair

"I have no peace, no quietness.
I have no rest; only trouble comes."
JOB 3:26 NLT

There are no words for these moments. The sudden death of a loved one. The long, drawn-out suffering of someone who is dear. The unexpected loss of a job. The betrayal of a close friend. A severe illness that devastates your life.

When Job experienced the sudden loss of his family and almost everything he cared about, even his own health, he was thrown into a horrible pit of sorrow and pain and despair. Even his wife urged him to "curse God and die" (2:9 NLT).

Job refused, but chapter 3 is, in fact, a kind of elaborate death-wish poem—for a pre-birth death. Job longs to wipe this whole story not just out of his memory, but off the face of the earth.

Job is not alone in this feeling. Grief commonly results in the desire for some kind of numbing—either the eternal quiet of death or a freezing of feelings, often obtained, sadly, through alcohol or drugs or other substance abuse. Sometimes it seems the only way to survive pain is to not feel anything.

But Job did something better. He stayed close to God. Even though he became angry and doubtful and frightened and sad, Job did not run away. Instead, he got closer to God. And God blessed Job for it.

Lord, help me to remember to come to
You when I am suffering. Amen. —ML

Fly Away

Oh, that I had wings like a dove;
then I would fly away and rest!
PSALM 55:6 NLT

Have you ever been so busy, you wished you could just sprout wings and fly away? Or maybe you have been driving in your car and wished you could just keep driving and driving until you were far, far away from the crazy, hectic schedule you had been trying to keep up with (and failing miserably at).

Sometimes the drastic solution of running away seems easier than actually dealing with the everyday hassles of your life, right? But in your heart, you know that running away wouldn't solve anything. Besides, in this day and age, with GPS locators and other gizmos, it's quite likely that if you tried to run, your troubles would be right there waiting for you at the end of the road!

It's better instead to recall to whom you belong and to call on the name of your Lord. In verse 17 we read, "Morning, noon, and night I cry out in my distress, and the LORD hears my voice." No matter what time of day it is, no matter if you are daydreaming about flying away or sitting with your hands clenching the steering wheel, God is there for you. Call on Him. Hand your anxiety over to Him. He will hear you. And He usually has some pretty good answers.

Thank You, Lord, for hearing me,
every time I need You. Amen. —ML

Listen to Wisdom

Better to hear the quiet words of a wise person than the shouts of a foolish king. Better to have wisdom than weapons of war, but one sinner can destroy much that is good.
ECCLESIASTES 9:17–18 NLT

The writer of Ecclesiastes told the story of a small town that was taken over by a great king and his army. A wise man, who had no money or power, knew how to save the town and spoke up. Because he was bold, and because people listened to him, the town was saved. It would be a lovely ending to the story to find out that the wise man was then made king and honored for his wisdom. Or even thanked. But that wasn't the case.

And that is often what happens in the world—those who are wise, but lack wealth or power or platform, don't get heard as much as those who do have money or can wield other kinds of power. This little story can remind you to do two things: (1) Keep your ears open for the quiet voices. Listen carefully to those who ask good questions and give intelligent, thoughtful answers. (2) When you have something useful to offer that could help solve a problem, don't be afraid to speak up. Pray and ask God for guidance, and then be patient and persistent as you seek to be heard.

*Lord God, help me to listen hard to
quiet voices of wisdom. Amen. —ML*

Gone Fishing

*As Jesus walked beside the Sea of Galilee, he saw
Simon and his brother Andrew casting a net into the lake,
for they were fishermen. "Come, follow me," Jesus said,
"and I will send you out to fish for people."*
MARK 1:16–17 NIV

Many people enjoy the refreshment and relaxation that comes with a day out fishing on a lake. Much of fishing involves quiet waiting or, for some, even napping.

For the fishermen of Galilee, fishing was a way of life, a job—not a vacation. But Jesus invited the fishermen of Galilee to go on a different kind of fishing trip—one that could easily last a lifetime. This kind of fishing might also involve a lot of quiet, patient waiting.

Jesus invited them to become fishers of people—to work to develop relationships with others, to love others, to serve others, and to tell others about the love of God. He asked them to be on His team—to take up the important duty of multiplying the kingdom of God.

And what did they do? They didn't even talk about it. They just left their nets and followed Jesus.

And what will you do?

*Jesus, my Lord and Savior, I want to help draw people
to You. Help me to know how to do this. Lead me to the
people who are waiting to hear about You. Amen. —ML*

Quiet Authority

"Be quiet!" Jesus said sternly. "Come out of him!"
Then the demon threw the man down before
them all and came out without injuring him.
LUKE 4:35 NIV

There were several instances in the Gospel accounts in which Jesus cast out demons. The surprising thing about these events, beyond the idea of hearing demons talk to Jesus, is that Jesus never performed elaborate ceremonies or sang chants or lit candles or rang chimes or did any other exciting activities in order to get those demons to come out. All He did was say, "Come out." And the demons obeyed Him.

In Luke 4, the people who witnessed this event were amazed and said, "What words these are! With authority and power he gives orders to impure spirits and they come out!" (v. 36).

Jesus didn't need a lot of words because He wielded complete power in every syllable. And we have access to this power. We can read His words and listen to His voice and obey Him. And we can also be amazed. Amazed at His power. Amazed that He can deliver it so quickly and so quietly. And amazed that the Lord of all was willing to come down, live among us, and show us His power every day.

Jesus, my Lord and King, I praise You for Your power
and authority. Lead me every day. Amen. —ML

The Lord's Portion

"You must present as the LORD's portion the best
and holiest part of everything given to you."
NUMBERS 18:29 NIV

The best of our work. The best of our wealth. The best of our days. The best of our nights. The best of our crops. The best of our productivity. The best of our talents. The best of our abilities. The best of our thoughts. The best of our dreams. The best of our words. The best of our time. The best of everything we have to offer.

That's what we are to give to the Lord. It is an honor to give this portion to the Lord, because it's an honor to have been given all that we have in the first place. Nothing we have would be available to us without God. There is nothing we make or do or say or produce or create that we can do apart from God. And nothing we do has any real worth unless it somehow contributes to the goodness of His kingdom.

But how often do we really save the best and the holiest to give back to God? How often do we think carefully about what we are devoting to the work of the kingdom?

Father God, forgive me when I don't save the best to give
to You. I know that I owe everything to You! Amen. —ML

Remain

"I am the vine; you are the branches.
If you remain in me and I in you, you will bear
much fruit; apart from me you can do nothing."
JOHN 15:5 NIV

Remaining doesn't seem like a hard thing to do. It's not even really an action—it's more like the lack of action. What does one have to do to remain? Stay. Don't move. Don't go away. Rest. Keep in one place. Go on existing. Live as you have been living.

Even though it doesn't sound like much, it really takes a lot to stay on a course and not waver. And it definitely takes a lot of persistence, endurance, courage, and faithfulness to stay with God. The world tries to pull you away through a thousand different distractions, temptations, and harassments. You'll be offered other ways of life that seem attractive. You'll be offered lifestyles that seem easier or more free. You might be tempted by wealth or power or glory.

But Jesus says if you remain—if you rest and breathe and exist in Him—then He will also be part of you. Like the branches of a vine are part of the vine, and the vine is part of the branches. Each part gathering fuel to live and grow from the same one source of all life.

Lord, let me rest in You so that I
can bring You glory. Amen. —ML

Rooted and Established

I pray that out of his glorious riches he may strengthen you with power through his Spirit in your inner being, so that Christ may dwell in your hearts through faith. And I pray that you, being rooted and established in love, may have power, together with all the Lord's holy people, to grasp how wide and long and high and deep is the love of Christ, and to know this love that surpasses knowledge—that you may be filled to the measure of all the fullness of God.

EPHESIANS 3:16-19 NIV

The little tomato plant was looking pretty sad. Its leaves were droopy. They were a pale shade of yellowish green, not the rich, deep green they should have been. The plant was short, just several inches off the ground. Here it was, late summer, and the poor tomato plant hadn't sprouted a single yellow blossom, much less an actual red, ripe tomato.

What had gone wrong? It could have been any number of things. Too little water. Too much. Too hot. Too cold.

Sometimes it's hard to know all the reasons why we haven't grown into people who behave like we should either. But one thing is sure in both the case of the plant's production and the case of our actions—our roots are too shallow and not well enough established.

Paul prayed that his fellow believers be rooted and established in love. And we should pray that for each other as well.

Lord, plant my heart in Yours. Amen. —ML

Your Faith

Then he said to her, "Daughter,
your faith has healed you. Go in peace."
LUKE 8:48 NIV

In Luke 7 and 8, Jesus made a very similar statement to two very different women. In chapter 7, Jesus' feet were bathed in the tears of the sinful woman who entered the Pharisee's house uninvited. Then in chapter 8, Jesus' cloak was touched by a woman who had been suffering from a long illness, and she was immediately healed.

In both cases, Jesus made a clear connection between the faith of the women and the fact that they received exactly what they needed. The sinful woman went away with forgiveness (vv. 48–50), and the ill woman went away with healing in her body.

Jesus told them they had been saved and healed, and then added, "Go in peace."

And they could go in peace, probably for the first time in a long time. The sinful woman could go on her way, free from the guilt and shame brought on by her life choices. She could choose to live a new life in Christ. And the woman with the bleeding disorder could go away free from health concerns and worries about paying doctors. She could live a new life as a clean, healthy woman—in both body and spirit.

Lord, may my faith be so great that I can always know
for certain that I may come to You with anything I need
and be answered and provided for and loved. Amen. —ML

Your Beauty

Your beauty should not come from outward adornment,
such as elaborate hairstyles and the wearing of gold
jewelry or fine clothes. Rather, it should be that of your
inner self, the unfading beauty of a gentle and quiet
spirit, which is of great worth in God's sight.
1 PETER 3:3–4 NIV

Recently, there has been a movement among women to "go naked." No, not to run around with no clothes on, but to go to work and go to school and go out and about on errands and take selfies with no makeup on one's face. Not a hint of blush. No foundation. No mascara. Not even a fine line of eyeliner. No glossy lips. Just bare skin and hopefully a smile.

Some women wouldn't dream of drinking their first cup of coffee, much less greeting anyone out in the world, without their "face" fully plastered on. Other women haven't bought makeup since they were in middle school and couldn't find a lipstick in their purses to save their lives.

Everyone is different when it comes to personal style and beauty regimes. But what the "go naked" proponents were trying to recognize is that every woman has beauty in who she is, not just how she looks.

And can't we all agree that true beauty comes from what's in a person's heart, not what's in a person's handbag?

Lord, help me to make sure my spirit is
beautiful to You every day. Amen. —ML

Always Be Prepared

But in your hearts revere Christ as Lord. Always be prepared to give an answer to everyone who asks you to give the reason for the hope that you have. But do this with gentleness and respect, keeping a clear conscience, so that those who speak maliciously against your good behavior in Christ may be ashamed of their slander.
1 PETER 3:15–16 NIV

Many Christians memorize this verse as an encouragement for evangelism. They focus on the idea of having your testimony ready and knowing exactly how you will talk to someone about the death and resurrection of Jesus, and how that has changed your life.

But if you look at these verses and the ones around them, you'll see that Peter is mainly talking about the whole concept of suffering for doing good, and how sometimes we have to suffer bad consequences, even when we feel like we've done the right thing.

So we can first be prepared by revering Christ—by honoring His example of sacrifice and trying to understand what that means. Then we can be prepared by knowing the reason we believe and cling to the hope of Jesus' resurrection. We can also be prepared by having right actions and thoughts, so that our minds can be free from guilt as we talk with people about living for Christ.

Which of these parts of preparation seem most problematic for you?

Lord, help me to prepare my heart to live for You. Amen. —ML

Soul Rest

Truly my soul finds rest in God;
my salvation comes from him.
PSALM 62:1 NIV

Have you ever tried to rest on a rock? At first, especially if the sun is shining, it can feel nice—the rock gets lovely and warm, and the firm surface feels good as you stretch out on it. But soon, your bones start to feel every hard edge of the boulder, and it no longer seems the least bit comfy.

Rocks don't make great mattresses, but they do make solid foundations. God is our "rock" and our "salvation" (v. 2). He is our unshakable fortress that no one can destroy. And this solid knowledge of our Lord and God makes a great place for our souls to find rest.

We will feel battered and beat up by what life throws at us sometimes. And in those times, we need the security of knowing our God will never change and that He is powerful enough to defeat any enemy—even death.

God, my Rock and my Redeemer, let my soul always
find a safe place to rest in You. Amen. —ML

Unsearchable

*Oh, the depth of the riches of the wisdom and
knowledge of God! How unsearchable his
judgments, and his paths beyond tracing out!*
ROMANS 11:33 NIV

Imagine that you look up a term on an online search engine,
and instead of giving you several results the page offers an
alert: "This word is unsearchable."

You'd be surprised, wouldn't you? In this digital age, it seems
like nothing is unsearchable or unknowable. The answer to any
question is right at our fingertips. All we have to do is ask our
phones or other electronic servants to go retrieve it.

But no one can know the mind of God. No one can advise
Him. And that's how it should be. If we could set limits on God—if
we could map out His construction—would He be God? Could
a limited being set eternity in the hearts of His people? Could a
mapped-out deity show us the way to eternal life?

*Lord, I want to know You more, even though I
realize I'll never know You fully here on this earth.
I want to be known by You. Amen. —ML*

In Every Way

*For this reason he had to be made like them, fully human
in every way, in order that he might become a merciful
and faithful high priest in service to God, and that he
might make atonement for the sins of the people.*

HEBREWS 2:17 NIV

You can't truly understand someone's suffering unless you experience it with them. You can try. You can read books about it. You can watch them go through it. You can get counseling on the subject. But until you've lived through it, until you've sat and cried through it and collapsed under the weight of it, you won't know the feeling of it. And until you know the feeling, until you know what it's cost a person, how can you know the price needed to be paid for atonement?

Jesus became like us—in every way—so that He could fulfill the job God had sent Him to do. To offer mercy and forgiveness. To make a worthy sacrifice. To atone for all our sins.

He became weak like us. Vulnerable like us. Heartbroken like us. Able to be tempted like us. And because He became like us, because He gave up so much for us, we can now live like Him.

*Lord, I don't know why You thought I was worth it,
but I'm glad You did. Amen.* —ML

Restoration

He restores my soul.
PSALM 23:3 NASB

The old table had layers and layers of stain and varnish on it. And somewhere in those layers were rings of a thousand glasses, set down and picked up and set down again. The antique table told the story of too many family dinners to count, of card-playing nights, and spousal fights.

There were impressions from zealously wielded forks. And nibbles from some family pet long forgotten. Chips flaked off from nervous, picking fingers. What stories could that table tell?

But to restore it to its former glory, all those layers of time and trouble had to be scraped away. The owner had to painstakingly remove every inch of the old to make the table new again. He had to get back to the original wood that someday, many years ago, a carpenter had cut and shaped and chiseled and smoothed.

God wants to remind us of who we are under all the years of hurts and stains and stories. He wants to take us back to when He created us so we can see the way He shaped us, see the purpose He placed in every part of us. See the work of His hands.

Will You let Him begin the restoration?

*Lord, I'd love for You to restore
my soul every day. Amen.* —ML

The Most Beautiful Gift

*For it is by grace you have been saved, through faith—
and this is not from yourselves, it is the gift of God.*
EPHESIANS 2:8 NIV

It's your birthday! You've heard the merry song, you've had that slice of gooey chocolate cake, and now there's a stack of gifts to open. Yay! There is this one package in the middle, though, that catches your eye. It's the biggest and most beautiful gift—and somehow you sense that it might be the most valuable. Yet you choose to toss it into the garbage without even opening it.

That thought makes us cringe, but isn't that what people do when they reject the gift of salvation through Christ? It is, after all, the biggest, most beautiful, and most valuable gift we will ever receive. The gift of salvation will bring peace and joy and laughter and love and life for all-time with our beloved Creator. But like any pretty package at a birthday gathering, we have to *receive* the gift.

Have you received the most beautiful present of a lifetime?

*Jesus, I acknowledge You as Lord of all, and I accept Your
gift of salvation. You alone have the power to forgive my
sins and make me all that I was meant to be. I choose
to follow You all the days of my life, and I'm looking
forward to eternity with You! Amen.* —AH

Bathed in Noise

He says, "Be still, and know that I am God; I will be exalted among the nations, I will be exalted in the earth."
PSALM 46:10 NIV

We live in an exceedingly high-speed, high-tech world, and we are bombarded with every kind of noisy gadget imaginable. But we don't often run from the clamor of it all. Instead we bathe in it. We are consumed by it. Dare we say—we worship it?

But what if we do choose to unplug for a while? Say, when it's time to eat, to sleep, to create, to work, to ponder, to have meaningful conversations with people—especially with God? Sounds so simple, and yet it's not all that easy, is it?

But we still can say no to techno when we need to, even if it feels impossible or unimaginable. We can choose to switch off, disconnect, and disengage from the gadgets and give our weary souls room for refreshment and restoration. How? Rest in God's loving embrace. Bask in His Word and His truths. Listen to His mighty and beautiful voice. . . .

Lord, please show me how to use technology at the right times. Help me to know when to switch it off and spend some "by still waters" time with You. I know I'll discover that gadget time will never be as glorious as God time. Amen. —AH

All Things Sublime

But we have this precious treasure [the good news about
salvation] in [unworthy] earthen vessels [of human frailty], so
that the grandeur and surpassing greatness of the power will be
[shown to be] from God [His sufficiency] and not from ourselves.
2 CORINTHIANS 4:7 AMP

There in the garden you spy a singular pink rosebud. Soon, it unwraps its blushing petal beauty before you until it is all blousy and beautiful and heady with scent.

God must have known such exquisite delight in creating that rose, that particular hue, that intoxicating perfume, knowing one day you would lean down and also delight in it. Perhaps even pluck it for your table. What joy!

God loves to create—you can tell. His masterpieces are sublime, and all that beauty and wonder and splendor creates awe in us.

When you create something, do you not feel God's happiness? Do you feel a special connection to Him? To create along with God is a kind of worship of Him. Those moments with our loving Lord will feed our souls. Embrace them all.

God, You are the Maker of all things sublime. I rejoice in
You and Your many marvels, and I love the way we can
create things of beauty together! Amen. —AH

Just Ask

If any of you lacks wisdom, you should ask God,
who gives generously to all without finding fault,
and it will be given to you.
JAMES 1:5 NIV

Some people have a wall full of impressive degrees to display. They can boast about their many accolades. But some of those people—as clever and brilliant as they are—don't seem to possess enough wisdom to choose the right way to go. The right way to live.

In the Old Testament, we find that (during a dream) Solomon asked God for wisdom, when he could have asked for anything. God was so pleased with Solomon's request that He gave the young man riches and honor, as well as wisdom. There is no guarantee, of course, that we will experience a windfall and accolades after we ask the Lord for wisdom, but we do know it pleases Him for us to sincerely ask for wisdom. And the Lord will fulfill His promise. Oh, to have good judgment in all things. It would make all of life so much calmer and more peaceful and livable!

Oh Lord Jesus, I find myself floundering around in life without much discernment, sometimes following what the world calls good advice. But I know many times the ways of the world are folly. Please give me Your wisdom, Lord! Amen. —AH

Granny's Pretty White Tablecloth

*"Come now, let us settle the matter," says the LORD. "Though
your sins are like scarlet, they shall be as white as snow;
though they are red as crimson, they shall be like wool."*
ISAIAH 1:18 NIV

You smooth out your grandmother's white linen tablecloth.
You set the tea table with all the antique dishes you've been
saving since forever. You fluff the cloth napkins, set out the bouquet of fragrant flowers, and set out the dainty tea cake. Perfect.
But—just when you sit down with your guest, you nervously knock
over your cup of hot, raspberry tea. The red fluid spreads faster
than lightning, and it makes what looks like a permanent blot
on your best tablecloth. Oh dear. Granny's gorgeous heirloom
has been defiled!

Isn't that just the way our sins feel in our spirit? We feel so
permanently stained, right? We're done. Hope is gone. And
yet, God says it isn't. Our lives can be redeemed. Our sins will
not only be forgiven when we ask, but the Lord promises that
our transgressions will become as white as snow. Yes, we can
sit back down at the table, relax our weary souls, and serve
that tea cake!

*Lord, thank You that when I fall, You pick me back up.
I praise You for Your unending love for me. Amen.* —AH

The Gift of Tears

*When Jesus saw her weeping, and the Jews who had come
along with her also weeping, he was deeply moved in spirit
and troubled. "Where have you laid him?" he asked.
"Come and see, Lord," they replied. Jesus wept.*
JOHN 11:33–35 NIV

If you ever used an old-fashioned pressure cooker, you know
that if you didn't use it right, it could explode. And not in a
funny cartoon way, but in a very dangerous way. So similar
to the way our spirits work. If we don't share life and laughter
with friends, if we don't have some "by still waters" moments
with the Savior, and if we don't let our tears flow when needed,
dangerous things can happen. Emotions build up like hot
steam, and we can reach a real crisis in our lives.

God gave us the ability to experience a wide range of
emotions, and shedding tears can express a number of them.
We shouldn't be ashamed of that moist stuff drizzling down
our cheeks. After all, when Jesus' friend Lazarus died, Jesus
cried. He not only wept with His friends over the loss, but
perhaps Jesus also shed tears because He understood well
the devastation that mankind endured when they separated
themselves from God's love.

Yes, Jesus did weep. So allow that sweet empathy and
understanding and tenderheartedness to bring you comfort
when you have need.

*Lord, thank You for all You've given me—
including the gift of tears! Amen. —AH*

Unfathomable Love

*Therefore confess your sins to each other and pray
for each other so that you may be healed. The prayer
of a righteous person is powerful and effective.*
JAMES 5:16 NIV

People have said, "What is the point of prayer if God is going to do what He wants anyway?"

But as we read through the stories in the Bible, we see that when humans approached God with a need, the Lord not only listened to the petition, but many times, He gave the people what they requested.

A skeptic might add, "But if God's will is perfect, then why would He change His mind to appease a feebleminded human who couldn't know how each alteration in events might affect the subsequent centuries?" Even though we don't understand such marvelous mysteries, God's reasoning appears to spring from His divine and unfathomable and transcendent love for us. Time and time again—whether in ancient times or modern times—He leans down as a Father does to his beloved child and listens intently to our pleas. Many times, He does alter the course of events for us. The mighty and supernatural ways of God are not easily understood, but there is one thing we can do—respond to Christ's love—heart and soul.

*Oh Lord, I don't fully understand You, but I love the way
You love. You hear my prayers and You allow me to have
what I need. I praise and thank You for that! Amen.* —AH

Watch Them Fly!

Worry weighs us down; a cheerful word picks us up.
PROVERBS 12:25 MSG

There's something sad and unnatural about a pretty and festive-colored kite resting flat on the ground. Why? Because we know the potential—the promise. The kite was meant for so much more than just lying there in the dirt. We can imagine its true purpose—to soar to great heights, to dip and sway and play with abandon. To fly, free and beautiful.

Worry weighs us down, and we become the pretty kite in the dirt, no longer knowing how to fly. No longer able to soar above the weary world. But a cheer-filled word can bring the steady currents of air, the running start, and the loft to someone's kite. No longer would we be sitting in the dirt—our colors getting faded in the baking sun, or our long vibrant streamers curling in a flimsy pile. We would become so much more. We could dip and sway and play—and know our purpose.

So offer the cheerful words to others—and with God's help, watch them fly!

Help me, Lord, to fly free and soar to the great heights that You envision for me. I want to be all that You created me to be. I'm ready for a launch. Together, may we soar! Amen. —AH

Streams in a Dry Land

"See, I am doing a new thing! Now it springs up;
do you not perceive it? I am making a way in
the wilderness and streams in the wasteland."
ISAIAH 43:19 NIV

When people think of a desert, they mostly conjure up images of a hot, barren, and lifeless landscape. But deserts can have many other attributes too—one being the potential for a sudden eruption of colorful plants. A profusion of wildflowers can transform what seems to be a dead terrain into an environment of stunning beauty. And then when you find a meandering stream through the desert, oh!—how welcome. That gurgling, burbling, cooling water brings such relief and joy.

God wants to make a way for us. He wants to lead us to a stream of goodness and mercy in this parched, thirsty land we call life. He is ready and willing to transform our dry days into something new, something full of truth, life, and colorful beauty!

Does your heart need relief and joy and spiritual refreshment? Drink from His brook and let His supernatural power renew every part of your being. He is there, waiting for you.

Holy Spirit, I do perceive something new springing up in my life, and I thank You with all my heart for bringing a refreshing stream into my wilderness! I love You, Lord. Amen. —AH

How Mighty You Are

"He speaks to the sun and it does not shine; he seals off the light of the stars. He alone stretches out the heavens and treads on the waves of the sea."
JOB 9:7–8 NIV

Sometimes the world seems to be a ball of anger that will soon spin itself into destruction. Evil is flourishing. Social media can go crazy within minutes. Friends who had always been so peace loving suddenly become divisive and mean-spirited.

Just when having a nervous breakdown seems like a plausible response, we can remember that God is still in control of the cosmos. Of our earth. Of our governments. Of our communities. Of every part of our lives, even the tiny details.

When we look at the heavens, we are once again reminded of how true that really is. When God speaks to the sun and asks it not to shine, it does just that. When the Lord speaks to the waves to cease, they do. And when the Father chooses to bring us to the end of the age, Christ will return.

So be of good courage—in the midst of a thousand troubles, we have one hope that will change the world forever!

Calm my heart, Lord, for I have been afraid of all that is happening in the world. Remind me daily of Your love and the promise of Your second coming! Amen. —AH

Breaking Free

*But he said to me, "My grace is sufficient for you,
for my power is made perfect in weakness." Therefore
I will boast all the more gladly about my weaknesses,
so that Christ's power may rest on me.*

2 Corinthians 12:9 niv

Check. Check. Check. We can make ourselves crazy with that one solitary word. When we succumb to perfectionism, it affects our joy, our relationships, our walk with Christ, our witness, our hope. Everything.

It is biblical to have a godly desire to be perfect like Christ and to follow Him closely, but perfectionism can be motivated by a worldly striving, which doesn't seek God in His supernatural power.

Perfectionism can go beyond doing our utmost for the Lord in gratitude for His mercy and grace; perfectionism is an obsession that fools us into thinking that if we can get every area of our lives in precise alignment, then we will indeed prove that we are worthy of taking up oxygen on this planet. And maybe even worthy of salvation—which we are not. Perfectionism will not lead us to lasting joy or a sound mind or a greater love for our Lord, because it is not a blessing but a concept conjured up by the enemy. Ask the Lord to free you of perfectionism. He can, and He will. His power is mighty and His grace is sufficient!

*Lord Jesus, please set me free from the treadmill of
perfectionism. May I remember that Your power
is made perfect in weakness. Amen.* —AH

Time for a Beauty Break

The heavens declare the glory of God;
the skies proclaim the work of his hands.

PSALM 19:1 NIV

First thing in the morning, is your head already down on the table, resting on your arms? Are you having some issues of exhaustion, and even that jolt of coffee doesn't help to get you revived? Or are you just depressed—totally burned out on the way this world is burning and churning? Had enough?

You need a beauty break—some powerful "let the heavens declare the glory of God" moments!

Yes, give yourself some time to notice a sunburst raining down light from the clouds, a field of wildflowers welcoming a chorus of honeybees, the breathy softness of snowflakes on your face, the wide world reflected in a tiny dewdrop, the ever-widening ripples and sighs on a pond, the birds on high flying free, and the crystalline stars strewn on a black satin night. Oh, and never forget to notice and be lead to those green, green pastures that have your name on them!

Take a walk with God, enjoy His presence, and find your song again!

Lord, I need a break from this world and its stress. May we always have plenty of time to walk and talk together in the wonderment of Your creation. In Jesus' name I pray. Amen. —AH

Cheap Candy

*When you run out of wood, the fire goes out; when the gossip
ends, the quarrel dies down. A quarrelsome person in a dispute is like kerosene thrown on a fire. Listening to gossip is like
eating cheap candy; do you want junk like that in your belly?*
PROVERBS 26:20–22 MSG

What happens when people with a sweet tooth discover a
big bowl of free candy? Well, things could get ugly, so
it's best if you just get out of their way! Because the first thing
they'll do is scrabble around in the bowl to confiscate anything
with chocolate or caramel. Then they go for the rest—the cheap,
artificially flavored hard candy. Yeah, it might be sort of pretty
on the outside, but in the end, everybody knows that it isn't
very satisfying.

This happens to be a good visual for gossiping. As Christians, we are surely learning to discern the good stuff from the
bad stuff in this life. We shouldn't want to gobble up the cheap
candy of gossip, nor should we be the ones divvying it out to
the crowd. It is junk to our spirits, and it will grieve the Holy
Spirit if we partake of it.

We'll live calmer, lovelier, more pleasurable lives if we
continue to enjoy what's real but leave the cheap talk behind.

*Lord, please watch over my heart that I might not
crave gossip, and watch over my mouth that I
won't be handing it out to the crowd! Amen. —AH*

Sweet Dreams

When you lie down, you will not be afraid;
when you lie down, your sleep will be sweet.
PROVERBS 3:24 NIV

Do you have pleasant bedtime memories of your mom or dad reading you a story, then tucking you in and whispering "sweet dreams" to you? How lovely those remembrances can be. Sometimes as adults it still might be nice to have someone tuck us in—maybe even God.

The world has become so scary that the fears of the day creep into the night—that is, they slither into our dreamscape world. Nightmares can be a pesky plague. We wake up night after night in a pool of sweat, glancing around in the dark, trying to recover from the scary images that seemed so alarmingly real just moments before.

But we *can* pray. Many people remember to pray for everyone and everything, except their sleep. God welcomes our requests, so ask Him. He cares about every part of our lives, our waking hours, our working hours, and even the hours in our dream world.

Dearest Lord, please teach me how to slow down and calm myself in the evening to prepare for bedtime. Please release me of fear and watch over me. May my sleep be deep and my dreams as sweet. In Jesus' name I pray. Amen. —AH

Beyond the Box

*"This is GOD's Message, the God who made earth, made it
livable and lasting, known everywhere as GOD: 'Call to me
and I will answer you. I'll tell you marvelous and wondrous
things that you could never figure out on your own.' "*
JEREMIAH 33:2–3 MSG

Humans have become container fanatics. We love boxes,
cabinets, storage facilities, cartons with sectional divides,
mini-organizers, and industrial shelving units for the ultimate
garage! In fact, whole stores are dedicated to this "everything
in its proper place" craze.

While we're at it, sometimes we like to put God in a box
too. It makes Christianity so much easier, doesn't it? We don't
have to think as much, pray as much, or believe as much.

The thing is, God cannot be stored in a spiritual box—He
is the mighty Creator of the universe!

Maybe we should let God be God. Then He may teach us
marvelous things we do not know, things that we cannot figure
out on our own. Are we listening to the Lord with faith? Have
we moved beyond the box?

*Lord Jesus, I admit sometimes it feels easier not to prayerfully
fathom the wonder of You. But since we will spend eternity
together I want to get to know You now and delight in all
that You have to teach me and show me. Amen. —AH*

Let's Dream Awhile

The LORD directs the steps of the godly.
He delights in every detail of their lives.
PSALM 37:23 NLT

On those sun-drenched, flower-festooned spring days made unforgettable by God Himself, do you ever rest back on a grassy hill and say, "It's me and You, God. . .let's dream awhile together. . .of new things to do, richer joys to know, and greater ways to enjoy Your creation"? How God longs for us to delight in Him and in all the wonderful things He's made for us! He takes pleasure in every detail of our lives because of His great love for us. What is keeping us from these days of heaven on earth?

Have we listened to the false ways of the world, the ugly whispers of the enemy, or the negative tapes playing in our heads? Have we been disobedient to God? Is there some sin we continue to cling to? Do we lack gratitude, or do we fail to praise God for who He is—for all His bounty, His forgiveness, and for His tender mercies?

There is a world of dreaming out there just waiting for us. A world of new adventures, of delights, of beauty and love and purpose meant for us. Just ask God.

Lord, whatever I'm doing that might grieve
Your Holy Spirit, please bring it to my attention.
I want to walk closely with You and experience the
fullness of Your joy! In Jesus' name I pray. Amen. —AH

When Our Earth Trembles

*God is our refuge and strength, an ever-present help in trouble.
Therefore we will not fear, though the earth give way and the
mountains fall into the heart of the sea, though its waters roar
and foam and the mountains quake with their surging.*
PSALM 46:1–3 NIV

Your day is smoothly running along. Items on your daily planner
are getting checked off. You have problems, yes, but you are
managing them as best you can. You have a strategy. You have a
routine. All hail to that mighty plan, because it gets you through.

Then the ground beneath your feet moves—a shattering
quake you never saw coming, and suddenly everything you
thought was safe, secure, steady is not any of those things. Our
personal earthquakes might be the worst possible news from
the doctor. It might be the severing of a beloved friendship. It
might be a spouse taking his own life. It might even be a real
natural disaster, such as a catastrophic flood that sweeps your
home away with all your earthly belongings.

How ferociously fast one's well-ordered life can come un-
done! But ordered and organized are only illusions in this
life. We desperately need God—not only when we face utter
disaster—but we need Him every day, every step, every breath.

*Lord, I need You desperately now. Be my refuge. Be my
strength. I see that I can do nothing without You. And please
help me to remember this lesson not only in bad times, but in
every kind of life moment. In Jesus' name I pray. Amen.* —AH

A Beautiful River of Song

My heart is confident in you, O God; my heart is confident. No wonder I can sing your praises! Wake up, my heart! Wake up, O lyre and harp! I will wake the dawn with my song.
PSALM 57:7–8 NLT

On a distant hill, the silvery tones of a flute drift effortlessly on the wind. The cathedral echoes with voices of the faithful, rising as one voice to the heavens, pure and sublime. The strains of music glorifying His name flow like a beautiful river before all mankind, and before God, which brings Him great delight.

Oh, how these sounds are easier to create when our heart is at rest in the Lord. When we luxuriate in the knowledge of whom we belong to. When our salvation is secure in Him. When our confidence is steady, not in our own abilities and talents and cleverness, but in what the Lord can do through us. Yes, no wonder we can now sing praises to Him.

So, wake up, my heart! Yes, wake up, piano, harp, and silvery flute! Let us all wake the dawn with our song! And may all the earth join in to praise His mighty and holy name!

Lord, I feel so confident in You and I love You so dearly, I want to wake up singing Your praises! Amen. —AH

Streams of Water

As the deer pants for streams of water,
so my soul pants for you, my God.
PSALM 42:1 NIV

How refreshing it must be for the deer—after running through the hills and meadows and forests—to finally come upon a cooling stream of water. They thirst and they are satisfied. So simple. So beautiful.

So is it when our souls pant for the Lord. We run through this life and we grow weary and thirsty and the Lord is right there for us, giving us what we long for.

But oh, how much harder it is for those who refuse the living water that Christ offers to our parched and withering souls. People may try and try and try to use the world's remedies for replenishment and refreshment, but their thirst will never be truly quenched. In fact, the more we drink of what the world has to offer, the thirstier and more dangerously dehydrated we get—as if we're drinking down salt water, instead of what is pure and cool and bracing.

May we all stop our running. Let us instead rest and commune with the Lord. Let us drink daily and deeply of His mercies. Of His forgiveness and grace. Of His wisdom. Of His enduring love. *Ahh.* Yes. My soul is filled. My soul is satisfied!

Oh Lord, I am so ready to be refreshed
in all that You have for me. Amen. —AH

Knowing the Heart of God

"You will keep in perfect and constant peace the one whose
mind is steadfast [that is, committed and focused on You—
in both inclination and character], because he trusts and
takes refuge in You [with hope and confident expectation]."
ISAIAH 26:3 AMP

Here's the scenario—you have a friend you've known since forever, right? She knows all about you, and you know all about her. You each know what the other one is thinking before the words are even spoken. The trust levels are through the roof. So if a bad report of some kind gets to you surrounding your beloved friend—perhaps some kind of gossip about her character—you don't jump to conclusions and think the worst. You don't freak out, thinking she is no longer worthy of your trust. You don't abandon your love for her. Why? Because you trust her as your dearest friend. Your relationship is strong. It's precious. It's enduring. It has weathered the worst storms. Yes, you might talk to her about it at some point, but the bottom line is—you know her heart.

When we know the heart of God—through His living Word and through fellowship—we will not be afraid. We will trust Him fully in all things, and we will be at peace.

Lord, I see our relationship as precious, and I want to know
You so well that I never question Your character. I want my
trust levels for You to go through the roof! Amen. —AH

The Big Red Marker

*And even as they did not like to retain God in their knowledge,
God gave them over to a reprobate mind, to do those things
which are not convenient; being filled with all unrighteousness. . .*
ROMANS 1:28–29 KJV

There are so many scriptures that make people squirm today,
maybe we should just remove them. "Well, or maybe just
delete the passages that offend *me*." Have you ever thought
something like this?

There wouldn't be much left of the Bible if we all had a
go at the big red marker—we wouldn't stop striking out verses
until we could live any way we wanted to and we could do it
all guilt-free.

But don't we have our logic backward? Shouldn't *we* as
God's willfully fallen creatures be wondering what offends our
Maker?

We live in a society that is spiraling more profoundly into
spiritual peril every day. We are now calling *good* evil and *evil*
good. We have exchanged the truth of the living Word of God
for the lies of the enemy. And in the midst of our defiance, we're
busy trying to make a deal with God! He is not impressed or
amused by our stubborn haughtiness. Obeying the Lord and His
precepts is the only way to live the purpose-filled and victorious
and beautiful life He meant for us!

*Lord, please bring our nation to a place
of repentance and redemption! Amen.* —AH

DAY 296

A Lullaby from God

*You made all the delicate, inner parts of my body and knit
them together in my mother's womb. Thank you for making
me so wonderfully complex! It is amazing to think about. Your
workmanship is marvelous—and how well I know it.*

PSALM 139:13–14 TLB

What delight when a mother feels that nudge inside, those
tiny feet pushing, a reminder of the precious little person
growing inside. Then in time, a mother holds her wee one, kissing
each finger, feeling the velvety softness of her skin, taking in the
aroma of bliss. She takes to singing a lullaby—a quiet song to
the clasping, gurgling, sighing, cooing, cuddling bundle. Such
a thrill and such wonder just to be near that baby—her angel,
her pearl. Once again she is overcome with love and a desire to
bring her child joy and offer the sweet infant every good thing.

Just imagine—God cares about us even more than that,
and He too has a desire not only to give us joy and every good
thing, but to draw near to us because He loves us. Amazing, isn't
it? So very lovely to ponder this truth, whenever we have need.

*Oh Lord, thank You for making me with such complexity
and for loving me so dearly. You are amazing, and Your
workmanship is marvelous to behold! Amen.* —AH

What Would She Look Like?

*If you preach, just preach God's Message, nothing else;
if you help, just help, don't take over; if you teach, stick to
your teaching; if you give encouraging guidance, be careful
that you don't get bossy; if you're put in charge, don't manip-
ulate; if you're called to give aid to people in distress, keep
your eyes open and be quick to respond; if you work with the
disadvantaged, don't let yourself get irritated with them or
depressed by them. Keep a smile on your face.*

ROMANS 12:6–8 MSG

Poise. Mmm. Sounds like the 1950s when a woman would float into a room with a book balanced on her head and, no matter how much she perspired in her nylon hosiery, she would sport a dignified expression! But there can be more to that smallish word—*poise*—especially if we were to consider using it in our spiritual lives.

In fact, what would a Christian woman of poise look like today? Perhaps she would be a woman with grace, self-control, inner beauty, humility, compassion, calm assurance in the Lord, and she'd choose to live the teachings of Romans 12:6–8. Maybe not without a few spiritual hiccups along the way, but this kind of woman would stand out in a crowd. You'd want to get to know her better, and you might even want her to be your dearest friend. So, is that kind of woman you?

*Holy Spirit, show me how to live
Romans 12:6–8! Amen. —AH*

My Gift of Time

As soon as the meal was finished, he insisted that the disciples get in the boat and go on ahead to the other side while he dismissed the people. With the crowd dispersed, he climbed the mountain so he could be by himself and pray. He stayed there alone, late into the night.
MATTHEW 14:22–23 MSG

The world whirls and whizzes by us like a mighty windstorm—so much so that sometimes it's hard to catch our breath in the midst of it. As we age, we gaze at that thing called time a bit more closely and come to see it as more precious than money. Perhaps we feel we can no longer be reckless or wasteful with time. Perhaps we divvy it out with more care. Or in our years of growing in wisdom, we've come to know more about what is truly a valuable use of our time—which might even mean more rest and less busyness.

When people celebrate our birthdays, maybe we should feel honored and truly loved when someone offers us their gift of time, since it is limited and valuable.

God also would enjoy our gift of time. When Jesus dwelled among us, He would often find a solitary place to talk to God. Jesus knew well that there was never a moment wasted when basking in His Father's loving presence.

Have you given God your gift of time today?

Lord, even when I think I'm too busy, help me to remember to honor You with my gift of time. Amen. —AH

May We Never Forget

*When GOD, your God, ushers you into the land he promised
through your ancestors Abraham, Isaac, and Jacob to give
you, you're going to walk into large, bustling cities you
didn't build, well-furnished houses you didn't buy, come upon
wells you didn't dig, vineyards and olive orchards you didn't
plant. When you take it all in and settle down, pleased and
content, make sure you don't forget how you got there—
GOD brought you out of slavery in Egypt.*
DEUTERONOMY 6:10–12 MSG

Oh, when life is good and rich and smooth as a chocolate milkshake, we can't help but breathe out a deep sigh of satisfaction. Why? Because we've entered a season of joy. When every day smells like spring and every moment feels blessed. Yes, it's time to do a merry little jig. And so we should. It is good and right to rejoice with all our heart!

But while in that dreamy, cloud-nine mode, may we never forget the Giver of all good things. May we never forget the One who helps us through the rough waters of life. The One who carried the burden of our sin and the One who cares for us in every area of our lives—Jesus Christ.

So, let us laugh. Let us love. Let us live. But may we never forget. . . .

*Lord, help me to remember all that
You've done for me. Amen. —AH*

The Seed Pearls of Peace

*And those who are peacemakers will plant
seeds of peace and reap a harvest of goodness.*
JAMES 3:18 TLB

Most women love bling and bangles and bracelets of one kind or the other. Perhaps emerald earrings for one's anniversary. A ruby pendant for one's birthday. Oh, and never forget that dazzle of diamonds—the one that will catch the light just so—for one's wedding engagement. Yes, let us enjoy those gemstones that God gave us to delight in, but wouldn't it be even more wonderful to be dripping in the seed pearls of peace?

Every day we choose whether our words and actions will be adorned in promoting goodwill toward men or will be festooned in discord and strife. One is as cheap and common as a bag full of rhinestone trinkets and the other is more beautiful to behold than the rarest of diamonds.

In the morning, after a trip to the jewelry box to accessorize and a quick check in the mirror, how are we dressed and fixed in our spirits? Are we bejeweled in kindness and amity and benevolence? If so, God promises us that we will plant seeds of peace and we will reap a harvest of goodness!

*Lord, please help me to be a peacemaker
and not a peace breaker. Amen.* —AH

Never Go Back

*He has removed our sins as far from
us as the east is from the west.*
PSALM 103:12 NLT

What a feeling—to take every bit of the junk in your life and just heave it and leave it at the city dump. You might even want to spin your car tires a bit as you drive away, since you're in such a celebratory mood. It's done, right? All that garbage, gone forever!

But then you glance back in the rearview mirror one last time—because maybe the freedom seems too wonderful to be true. Hmm. Was it really legal to leave it all there? Weren't you supposed to pay something or do something to get rid of all that junk? Or maybe you left a thing or two behind that you might come to miss. Could you have been wrong about that one particular item after all? Maybe it was more treasure than trash.

Then, on a whim or perhaps an enticement from the enemy, you turn around and go back to the dump. And for whatever reason, you start picking through that trash again!

Is that what we do with sin once it's been left at the foot of the cross and forgiven? Too often we refuse God's grace because it is all too wonderful to be true. But it is true. Embrace the grace that God offers us through Christ and never go back to that dump again!

*Lord God, I accept Your mercy, grace, and forgiveness. Help
me to never look back! In Jesus' name I pray. Amen.* —AH

Better Than Tea!

"They will not be sinners, full of lies and deceit.
They will live quietly, in peace, and lie down
in safety, and no one will make them afraid."
ZEPHANIAH 3:13 TLB

Society has lots of tips on how to de-stress—all the way from taking a leisurely stroll to sipping on a cup of lavender tea. Both are good things, but what about an honorable and authentic way of living? Can such a thing bring peace?

Well, if you've ever told a lie, you know they are wily little rascals. They multiply faster than rabbits, they are stickier than glue, and they will always follow you around like a trail of used toilet paper on your shoe. Not a good look! And certainly not a good way to live.

Yes, lies bring on a feeling of instability and confusion and fear as you try to keep up with them all, wriggle out of them, defend them, and then face them when you're caught. On the other hand, truth brings on good deep sleep. It brings on refreshment in the morning.

Yes, drink the tea, but offer people the gift of an honest life too. They will love you for it. It will bring God joy, and it will bring you peace.

Lord, help me to live a life of integrity and truth. Amen. —AH

That Golden Goodness

Kind words are like honey—enjoyable and healthful.
PROVERBS 16:24 TLB

*C*ruel words can hang in the air like a foul-smelling and toxic vapor. What we don't realize in the heat of the moment is that the hurtful words can also damage the speaker of them too. These harsh words have the potential to stain the spirit and destroy relationships. Yes, afterward, there might be forgiveness all around, but the "forgetting" might take many years, if it ever comes at all. Yes, being reckless and ruthless with what escapes our mouths is not the way of heaven.

On the other hand, kind words are like a honeycomb, dripping with golden goodness that not only bolsters us with healthful energy but soothes and uplifts one's spirit. And the good news is that this kindness heartens the giver as well as the receiver. And that glorious ripple effect goes on and on and on, perhaps never ending.

A smile. A good deed. A comforting word of encouragement. Let this be the prayer of our hearts that we withhold no good thing and kind word from those who cross our paths! Now that's the way of heaven!

Lord Jesus, may the words that pour out of my mouth always be pleasing to You. May they be full of truth as well as kindness, and may they bring health and healing to all. Amen. —AH

From the Biggest to the Smallest

When the wine was gone, Jesus' mother said to him,
"They have no more wine." "Woman, why do you involve
me?" Jesus replied. "My hour has not yet come." His
mother said to the servants, "Do whatever he tells you."
JOHN 2:3–5 NIV

God cares more about sweeping changes than personal epiphanies. He cares more about long-term covenants than daily needs. He's better at universal love than intimate fellowship. In other words, He's too big and too busy for me.

Have you ever had thoughts like these?

Well, the story of Jesus and the wedding at Cana blows those ideas right out of the water. Read the whole passage from John and discover how Jesus dealt with the request from His mother—that even though changing water into wine was not a miracle Jesus had planned on performing that day at the wedding, He followed through anyway.

Why? Even though the scriptures don't give us a lot of details, a few reasons might be that Jesus loved His mother, that He chose to give us a glimpse of His glory, which helped the disciples to believe in Him, and that He wanted us all to know how much He cares for us—from the biggest problem we're facing today to the smallest needs of a couple on their wedding day!

Lord, thank You for caring about all the areas of
my life from the biggest to the smallest. Amen. —AH

Look a Little Deeper

*When he saw the crowds, he had compassion
on them, because they were harassed and
helpless, like sheep without a shepherd.*
MATTHEW 9:36 NIV

You've had a good day until you run into "her." Yeah, every time you see her, she comes off like a total crab. In fact, you've decided she *is* a crab—the kind that wants to pinch your nose clean off—and you want to run. But this time, you're stuck, and you have to deal with her whether you like it or not. But then suddenly, you're close enough to see into her eyes, deeply—almost into her soul—and you discover what you've never seen before. You see her pain. God has now given you a window into her heart, and if you're willing, there's also a teachable moment.

The Lord has compassion on His people, and He wants us to have compassion too. Next time we write somebody off as a crab, let us look a little deeper—through God's eyes. We might see her past, her sadness, and that tiredness that goes to the bone. We might even see that, with the Lord's help, we can rise up with compassion and make her day just a little bit better.

*Dearest Lord Jesus, teach me how to see all the facets
of a person, not just the facade, and please let me be
merciful as You have shown me mercy. Amen.* —AH

That First Stone

When they kept on questioning him, he straightened up and said to them, "Let any one of you who is without sin be the first to throw a stone at her."

JOHN 8:7 NIV

It's easy to hastily read through the Lord's response to the crowd that was ready to stone the adulterous woman—because we think it doesn't relate to us. After all, we would *never* throw a rock at anyone!

Certainly we wouldn't cast a *real* stone, but have we ever hurled a snobbish look of condemnation, a judgmental quip, or a morsel of gossip about someone's alleged transgression? These kinds of sharp stones can be painful too, leading to all kinds of trouble—despair, depression, divorce, abandonment of one's faith, and sometimes even suicide.

Christ's response to the woman caught in adultery was one of wisdom, compassion, forgiveness, and an appeal for her to leave her sin behind.

So yes, we are not to condone sin, and we are called to speak the truth in love, but haughty or mean-spirited or self-righteous commentaries have no place in our Christian walk. If in doubt over a situation, pray for wisdom. God is faithful.

Lord, help me to remember to adopt Your holy response to sin—that I can love the person who is sinning without applauding her sin. Amen. —AH

Our Real Struggle

For our struggle is not against flesh and blood,
but against the rulers, against the authorities,
against the powers of this dark world and against
the spiritual forces of evil in the heavenly realms.

EPHESIANS 6:12 NIV

You're taking the most delicious stroll along a lush garden path when you suddenly walk smack-dab into the center of a spider's web. Instantly you recoil from the sticky horror, knowing you may now have a spider stuck in your hair! Or perhaps you're at home sipping a cup of tea, minding your own business, when a spider—the size of a forklift—clambers across the floor right next to your shoe. You know what to do with that shoe, right?

Maybe this peril is a little funny, but there are far greater dangers lurking about that threaten your very soul. The dangers are the powers of this dark world and the spiritual forces of evil in the heavenly realms. As Christians, this scripture shouldn't paralyze us with fear, but we should be aware of what is going on around us. That way, we might be armed and ready for battle, whether the enemy comes at us full force or slyly creeps in when we least expect it.

Yes, may we always be armed with the Word of God and the mighty power of prayer!

Lord, keep me safe from all harm and all evil.
In Jesus' holy name I pray. Amen. —AH

The Finest Treasure

*That is the plan I follow, too. I try to please everyone in
everything I do, not doing what I like or what is best for me
but what is best for them, so that they may be saved.*
1 CORINTHIANS 10:33 TLB

The world says, "I am gonna do it my way, and I intend to
please the three most important people in the world—me,
myself, and I!"

But the apostle Paul's letter to the Corinthians encourages
a very different mind-set. He explains that he wants to please
everyone in all that he does. Paul does not demand to do
things his way. He's not constantly manipulating things to his
own advantage, but he instead concentrates on the needs and
desires of others for the sake of the Gospel—that he might help
win many to Christ.

This kind of generosity of spirit and self-sacrifice and passion
for the Gospel isn't all that common in today's society, but if done
to the glory of God and for His purposes, it is a most peaceful
way to live. This way of living won't promise us a plethora of
earthly pleasures, but on the other hand, isn't peace in Christ
the finest treasure and greatest pleasure of them all?

*Holy Spirit, give me the courage to live Your way and to think
of others first. And please allow this giving nature to help
show people the way to Your saving grace. Amen. —AH*

Something Glorious

"And do not fear those who kill the body but cannot kill the soul. But rather fear Him who is able to destroy both soul and body in hell."

MATTHEW 10:28 NKJV

We hear a lot about how toxic the environment is getting—how the dangers of every kind of man-made chemical are polluting the world. And no doubt we do have a mess to clean up.

But earth's greatest calamity is the toxic waste we allow into our spirits. And some of that may come in the form of friends, coworkers, and even family members who cause us to stumble and fall in our walk with the Lord.

Does that friend entice you into doing things you know are wrong? When you are in the midst of certain crowds or attending certain parties, do you realize that you are not quite the person God desires you to be?

Yes, we need to clean up the earth, since God wants us to be good stewards of all that He's gifted us with, but the ultimate priority—as the Gospel of Matthew reminds us—is to keep watch over our souls. To make sure our spirits don't become a toxic landscape but instead bloom into something glorious, something beautiful.

Holy Spirit, guide me in all my choices so that my life is everything You meant it to be. Amen. —AH

A Little Tea Party Time

Finally, all of you be of one mind, having compassion for one another; love as brothers, be tenderhearted, be courteous.
1 PETER 3:8 NKJV

Have you ever attended a real, old-fashioned tea party? They are not quite like anything else. You gather with some ladies who are dressed up—maybe even wearing hats!—and you enjoy fresh-cut flowers, crisp linen napkins, and maybe even some beautiful live music. You dine on sweets and savories and pots of fragrant teas. One of the other delights is the pleasant dialogue. Tea parties are known for their courteous, welcoming, and good-humored conversations that will bring joy and comfort to everyone attending. Sound heavenly?

Aah, yes, wouldn't this world be a better place if we had a little less vitriol and a little more tea party time? Fewer tempers flared and more sisterly love? Less hurtfulness and sarcasm and more compassion, tenderheartedness, and courteousness?

Maybe hosting a tea party event would be something that would set more hearts to hoping and more faces to smiling. Give it a try. And never forget to invite the Lord to your wonderful event!

Dearest Lord Jesus, we need a little more sisterly love in this weary old world. Teach me the art of hospitality and help me to be an ambassador of Your goodness and mercy. Amen. —AH

The Ragged Edge

But my eyes are fixed on you, Sovereign LORD; in you I take refuge—do not give me over to death. Keep me safe from the traps set by evildoers, from the snares they have laid for me. Let the wicked fall into their own nets, while I pass by in safety.

PSALM 141:8–10 NIV

Do you ever feel like you're on the ragged edge of some peril and you see no safe haven or sanctuary in sight? Perhaps you're chronically ill, or you've been abandoned, or maybe your good deeds are met with skepticism and your love with a shrug. Perhaps loneliness or some mental anguish has become an unbearable way of life. Maybe an addiction or a fear of the future is slowly killing you.

This is such a good time to cry out to God, like David did in the Psalms. The Almighty has known these kinds of desperate pleas throughout the ages. He is all-powerful enough to handle it, and He's loving enough to help you all the way through your troubles, whatever they may be.

When you sense yourself tottering on the edge of an abyss, run for your life into the arms of the Lord. He is ready. He is able.

Almighty God, I am on the ragged edge.
I need You today more than ever. Please rescue me!
In Jesus' name I pray. Amen. —AH

Trusting God with Every Season

*There is a time for everything, and a
season for every activity under the heavens.*
ECCLESIASTES 3:1 NIV

Life surprises us with little daily adjustments—and some Tyrannosaurus rex–sized transitions. Yes, some life changes are giddy and glorious fun—like your big wedding day. Or cuddling your newborn baby. Or heading off to college. Or starting the job of your dreams. Good stuff.

But what about the other life shifts that you don't get to choose? Like being forced into retirement? Or the emotional pangs of empty nest? Or downsizing into assisted living?

Those who aren't going through any hard seasons might say, "Well, you should embrace every new life era. Think of each interlude and change as a glorious new adventure!"

Yeah, right.

But do we trust God with *everything* in our lives or not? In the earthly seasons of summer, fall, winter, and spring, each have their benefits and perks as well as their obstacles and disadvantages—just as do the seasons of our lives. And just as we trust God for rain in the spring and harvest time in summer, we must trust Him with every phase and transition and moment of our lives.

*Lord, I accept whatever comes—even this new path
You've set me on. But I can't do this new season alone.
Please guide me and be with me every step of the way.
In Jesus' name I pray. Amen.* —AH

Well and Usable!

"Physical training is good, but training for godliness is much better, promising benefits in this life and in the life to come."
1 TIMOTHY 4:8 NLT

It's easy to rephrase the scripture in 1 Timothy to read, "Godliness is the only thing to strive for; keeping your body in shape isn't necessary." That isn't what the verse says, but it's tempting to think otherwise, especially when we're in the middle of gobbling down a third helping of chocolate cake, or when we feel no motivation to exercise, or when we're playing the role of a binge-watching couch potato!

Make no mistake, training for godliness is indeed far better than physical training—in that the former promises immeasurable benefits in this life and in the life to come. How true and great that is! However—when we are rested, fueled with healthy foods, and in good shape, God is able to use us more easily than if we are tired and grouchy, overweight, out of shape, and falling victim to various addictions. We know these truths in our hearts, but sometimes those same convictions don't make it to the gym or to the grocery store when making choices.

Lord, help me to make good choices when it comes to diet, exercise, and proper rest. I want my body to be well and usable for Your holy purposes. Amen. —AH

A Zigzag World

For we know that when this earthly tent we live in is taken down (that is, when we die and leave this earthly body), we will have a house in heaven, an eternal body made for us by God himself and not by human hands.

2 CORINTHIANS 5:1 NLT

Do you ever feel like when you're busy going zig, everybody else is going zag? As if the whole world has a code and they forgot to tell you what it is? Maybe you feel alone, left out, or that you don't fit in anywhere. You can't seem to find your groove. Well, everyone has felt these earthly pangs.

But the good news is that we don't need to fit into this life perfectly. In fact, we shouldn't be entirely in sync here. This world is deeply fallen, and we were created for greater things. To love God and to be loved by Him. To fly free of the bonds of sin through Christ. To let go of this feeble and dying human shell of ours and exchange it for an eternal body made by God Himself!

So the next time you don't feel all that comfortable in your skin, take heart. There is so much more to come!

Lord, thank You that as a Christian I can look forward to Your house in heaven and an eternal body made for me by You! Praise You for this promise, this miracle! Amen. —AH

God Loves Us Still

But you, O Lord, are a God of compassion and mercy, slow to get angry and filled with unfailing love and faithfulness.
PSALM 86:15 NLT

Mankind has transgressed in every way they can—we are, after all, very creative when it comes to sin. We have reveled in all the world has to offer. We have not only offended God by disobeying Him, but at times we have been bold and haughty and without shame while we're doing it! Not just once. But over and over and over until it really would be quite humorous—except there isn't anything funny about sin.

We humans could easily become crushed under the weight of our own sin and its many consequences; we could even fall into despair and give up on doing what is right altogether. But that attitude is not of God either. We might think we've sinned too much and gone so far that no one can save us, not even God. So, we might be tempted to hide as Adam and Eve did. But the truth is, when we fall so far that we feel there is nothing left in us to love—God loves us still.

Run toward Christ with a repentant heart. The Lord is there, full of compassion and mercy, waiting for your return.

I am so grateful, Lord, that You will forgive me and love me still. Amen. —AH

You're Not Alone

"Never will I leave you; never will I forsake you."
HEBREWS 13:5 NIV

Be honest. Have you ever been caught looking through those online "then and now" photos of celebrities? Or have you ever secretly rejoiced when you found out that a friend suffers with the same travail or ailment as you? Why do we resort to such behaviors and thoughts? Part of the reason might come from our fallen nature, but another part might be that when we see others who look as ragged as we sometimes feel—especially celebrities who have an arsenal of youthful secrets at their disposal—we somehow feel less alone in the world. Or when we see that our friends suddenly know what it's like to suffer as we have, we feel strangely heartened—that we all have a common bond after all. That we all are indeed in this together.

But there is no need to feel alone or abandoned like this. We have God. He has made us this promise: "I will never leave you or forsake you." We should take Him at His word. When we feel desperately lonesome in the world and we are tempted to turn to the oddest things to make us feel less so, remember the powerful words of God Almighty when He says, "I will never leave you or forsake you." His words are real. His words are for you.

Oh Lord, please let me learn to lean on You for everything, including in those moments when I feel alone and afraid. Amen. —AH

The Choice of Life

*"Today I have given you the choice between life and death,
between blessings and curses. Now I call on heaven and
earth to witness the choice you make. Oh, that you would
choose life, so that you and your descendants might live!"*
DEUTERONOMY 30:19 NLT

Every day we have choices to make. Smallish ones: oatmeal
or that jelly donut? Shortcut or scenic route? Stilettos or
comfy clodhoppers? Medium-sized choices might include university or community college, vacation or volunteer, or apartment
or house. But the biggest choices we will ever make in this life
are connected to our spiritual lives. Do we choose the way of
God, or do we choose the aspirations and temptations and idle
imaginings that are connected to this mixed-up world? Do we
choose death or life?

The Word of God tells us plainly that we have choices and
they do matter.

What shall you choose on this day? All of heaven is watching. More importantly, God is watching.

God is hoping you will choose His way—the way of salvation in Christ. Nothing else on earth will bring peace like
going with God.

*Oh Lord, in every deed and thought, I know I can choose
good or bad, death or life. Too often I make the wrong choices.
Please show me the way of Your light and love and life!
In Jesus' name I pray. Amen. —AH*

Oh, How He Loves Us

"See, I have engraved you on the palms of my hands."
Isaiah 49:16 NIV

There's a big oak tree that spreads its branches like arms ready to embrace. The tree is sometimes drenched in sunlight but always filled with lovely memories. No matter how much time passes, you can still return and read the markings that came from ardent hearts and youthful hands. There in the trunk is the engraving "Charlie loves Franny."

You sit a spell on the old swing tied to the sturdy branch, then suddenly you push off, which makes laughter spill from your lips. You are flying and you are free. Then you slow to take in the whispers of the past. Sweet words tumble into your heart, like a basket of gems poured into your lap. *Aah*, the beauty of such joy. The glory of such endearing and enduring love.

God's love for you is also endearing and enduring. Shall you not sit a spell with the Lord and bask in His divine love? No matter how far you've run away, you can return and still see the markings "God loves _____." Your name is there, carved in the heart of the Almighty. Won't you sit under the tree a spell? Perhaps take to swinging to new heights? Maybe have a heart-to-heart with the One who loves you more than you could ever imagine? *Aah*, such joy!

Oh Lord, Your love fills my soul and
satisfies like nothing else. Amen. —AH

A Sign among You

*". . .to serve as a sign among you. In the future, when
your children ask you, 'What do these stones mean?'
tell them that the flow of the Jordan was cut off before
the ark of the covenant of the LORD. When it crossed
the Jordan, the waters of the Jordan were cut off. These
stones are to be a memorial to the people of Israel forever."*
JOSHUA 4:6–7 NIV

God does miracles in our lives. Some little. Some big. It can be so easy on rough days and on smooth days to forget about all the miracles our God has done for us and continues to do for us. The Israelites became very forgetful about their rich heritage of miracles, and the same malady can happen to us.

Perhaps when God does something special in our lives we can create a remembrance of some kind. Keep a journal. Let your kids create a craft that will commemorate what God is doing in your lives as a family. Hang a picture as a reminder. Create a tradition that is a tribute to God. Ask the Lord for ideas on how you can uniquely remember all that He has done for you.

May we never forget all the Lord does in our lives. May we celebrate and commemorate to His glory. May we never forget His works and His miracles. His sacrifice and His forgiveness. His mercy and grace. His love.

*Lord, may I always remember Your
miracles and gifts to me. Amen. —AH*

Usable

*"Salt is good for seasoning. But if it loses its flavor,
how do you make it salty again? Flavorless salt is good
neither for the soil nor for the manure pile. It is thrown away.
Anyone with ears to hear should listen and understand!"*
LUKE 14:34–35 NLT

Have you ever given a few twists to a salt grinder—releasing some of that gourmet pink salt on your spaghetti—only to discover that you needed to give it a few more twists? And then a few more? Hmm. No matter how much salt you dump on your pasta, your taste buds still come up unsatisfied. What happened? The salt has obviously lost its saltiness—the very essence of what makes it usable is now gone.

As Christians, we are to be salt and light in this spiritually hungry world. When something is holding us back from being usable for the cause of Christ—whether it's an unwholesome friendship or an exaltation of material possessions or a pursuit of selfish aspirations—it's time to pause and pray. We don't want our witness to become as worthless as that tasteless salt, and we don't want our own spiritual well-being to be hindered— because to be used by God and work closely with Him means we have chosen a life rich in purpose and contentment and joy.

*Oh Lord, help me to be real salt and light in
this spiritually hungry world! Amen. —AH*

Peacefully Simple

If we confess our sins, he is faithful and just and will forgive us our sins and purify us from all unrighteousness.
1 JOHN 1:9 NIV

You tell your boy to dump out what he has in his pockets, and with grimy fingers he sets out a shiny new quarter, a rock that looks like a heart—which melts your heart when he gives it to you as a gift—and a still-live frog that looks as though it has known better days.

But suddenly your boy admits that he stole the quarter from his sister's piggy bank, and he offers you a genuine expression of regret. You forgive him and turn it into a teachable moment by having him return the money with an apology. He is then set free to head out on his merry adventures again.

Wouldn't it be wonderful if the acts of repentance and forgiveness were that simple when we come before God? Well, the good news is, it is. Even though we should take sin seriously and we should expect some consequences from it, we should also know that if we confess our sin, Jesus is faithful to forgive us. And with repentance comes freedom, and with that freedom comes peace.

Lord, I have sinned, and I am so deeply sorry. Please forgive me, and help me to sin no more. Amen. —AH

Through All the Ages

Panic and pitfall (traps, danger) have come on us, devastation and destruction. My eyes overflow with streams of tears because of the destruction of the daughter of my people (Jerusalem).
LAMENTATIONS 3:47–48 AMP

These days our world lives amid many terrors—earthquakes, terrorist attacks, volcanic eruptions, wars, sex trafficking, tsunamis, health crises, nuclear threats, wildfires, not to mention rage, dissention, and vengeful language, even among friends. We live on constant alert for the next crisis. Our earth seems to be spinning out of control. How can we keep living like this?

As we see in Lamentations, mankind has experienced terrors in ancient times, and we have known them through all the ages, whether they are natural disasters or man-made. What people were supposed to do back then is the same thing we must do now.

Trust God. Love God. And let that love pour out onto each other. Does that sound too simple, too naive, too unrealistic? It is impossible without God's supernatural help.

Now is the time. The hour has come. Embrace the peace that Christ offers, and then pass it on.

In a world full of dangers and despair, You are the only one who can help us. We need You now, Lord! Amen. —AH

It's Official!

Be cheerful no matter what; pray all the time;
thank God no matter what happens. This is the way
God wants you who belong to Christ Jesus to live.
1 THESSALONIANS 5:16–18 MSG

Have you ever had a really bad day and thought *Well, it's official—I am not qualified to be a human being!*

Everyone is acquainted with that moment when you can no longer keep up with life using your own wits and strength. If people tell you otherwise, they're lying.

Then what in the world can a body do? Well, say you get a big pay cut at work? Pray. You fall back into an old sin? Pray. You have vengeful thoughts? Pray. You want to thank God for helping you out of a tough spot? Pray. Someone has been gossiping about you? Pray. Got good news from a long-awaited blood test? Pray. Want to share the beauty of the day with the One who made it? Pray. The Word says to talk to God all the time. And for good reason. It works. God is listening. God is good. God cares. And yes, miracles do happen.

It's official. With His divine help, you can make this day work!

Oh Lord, I love You and I trust You with all areas
of my life. I come to You now with all my needs,
praises, and concerns. Amen. —AH

His Tears Mingle with Ours

*He was despised and rejected—a man of sorrows, acquainted
with deepest grief. We turned our backs on him and looked
the other way. He was despised, and we did not care.*

ISAIAH 53:3 NLT

What was your most horrible moment? What did that day look like? Remember the pain of it. Then cover that moment with the knowledge that Christ—who was called a man of sorrows—endured horrors not only beyond what we have personally suffered, but beyond our imaginings.

Think of it. Jesus came to walk among us, to redeem us, to be our friend, but many who loved Him abandoned Him when He needed them the most. Then Christ not only willingly died a cruel death, but in a supernatural event we cannot fathom, He took on the weight of our sin. How excruciating that must have been on His spirit! But Jesus brought the ultimate triumph out of that suffering—death transformed into life!

When we hurt as Christians, may we always be encouraged by knowing that Christ truly knows our pain. Ever near, His tears mingle with ours and His heart longs for the day when we will be free of this earthly life and all its many travails—when we will live His promise of love and peace and joy for all time!

*Jesus, when I am consumed by sorrow, remind me of Your
sacrifice and Your promise of heaven. Amen. —AH*

A Chance to Grow

Dear brothers and sisters, when troubles of any kind come your way, consider it an opportunity for great joy. For you know that when your faith is tested, your endurance has a chance to grow. So let it grow, for when your endurance is fully developed, you will be perfect and complete, needing nothing.

JAMES 1:2–4 NLT

The storms have come again, and the intense force of the wind batters your windows enough to scare the willies out of you. Meanwhile, the trees outside can do one of two things—either topple over or let their roots grow deeper and stronger to hold them up in future blasts.

Uh-oh. That sounds like a spiritual lesson coming on, and it sounds painful. But unless our faith is tested, unless we let our troubles make us grow stronger in the Lord, we will indeed topple over time and time again in the hot and howling winds of this world. A tree lying on its side with its roots exposed is a sad and sorry sight. But on the other hand, what a joyful sight is a tree with sturdy branches spread broadly because the roots have gone deep! How useful. How beautiful!

Holy Spirit, help my endurance to develop fully so that I will be perfect and complete, needing nothing. Amen. —AH

Giving Us Sanctuary

"O Jerusalem, Jerusalem, the city that kills the prophets and stones God's messengers! How often I have wanted to gather your children together as a hen protects her chicks beneath her wings, but you wouldn't let me."

MATTHEW 23:37 NLT

You tell your kids to do something and they always jump to it, right? And when there is danger, they listen even more closely to your every instruction. Hmm. There is now a pregnant pause, because you want those statements to be true, but alas. . .

You then find yourself grieving over your kids as Jesus grieved over Jerusalem. Oh, how you long to gather your dear ones under your sheltering arms like a hen does her chicks, but your children—young and older alike—sometimes scatter recklessly into a world of predators, which includes the enemy himself.

In Matthew 23:37, you can clearly see the heart of God. You can see that His desire is to love us, guide us, and give us sanctuary. *Aah,* yes. Doesn't that sound like just the thing for a weary soul?

What is your choice today? Will you abide in Him?

Oh Lord Jesus, I am so sorry that oftentimes I flee from You instead of resting under Your sheltering wings. Show me how to trust You, obey You, love You, and allow You to be my holy protector. Amen. —AH

The More Family

*I am not saying this because I am in need, for I have learned
to be content whatever the circumstances. I know what it is
to be in need, and I know what it is to have plenty. I have
learned the secret of being content in any and every situation,
whether well fed or hungry, whether living in plenty or in
want. I can do all this through him who gives me strength.*
PHILIPPIANS 4:11–13 NIV

Most of humanity wants more. More in their bank account.
More stuff in their house. More cars in their garage. More
stamps on their passport. On and on and on.

Have you ever said, "I'm content. I want to keep working
for God, but I no longer need to strive for more stuff"? Who has
said those words and meant them for more than five minutes?
If you have, it will be like the passage in Philippians when Paul
talks about learning to be content in every situation, whether in
plenty or in want, whether well fed or hungry.

How is this achievable? The verse goes on to say, "I can
do all this through him who gives me strength." So with God's
help, this way of life is *more* than possible.

*Lord, I am always begging for more than I need.
Show me how to be content in all things. If I'm going
to have more, let it be in the living of life for You and
not the gathering of things for myself. Amen.* —AH

Breathe on Us

*"The Spirit of God has made me;
the breath of the Almighty gives me life."*
JOB 33:4 NIV

For some time now, Lord, it's as if a foul and frightful wind has blown its way across our nation, and it has become so choking and toxic that it's making people ill, even in their minds and spirits. Their souls are aching for something fresh and real and good. They are longing for You, and they don't even know it.

Oh Almighty God, we are driven to our knees as we cry out to You. We admit that we are helpless without You. We are lost and hurting and in great need of a miracle. Please breathe on us, Lord. Let Your holy breath purify and revive our land. May it bring us new life. May it enlighten us with clear understanding. Show us Your divine truths. Forgive us for our sins for we have fallen profoundly by calling *good* evil and *evil* good. We are not ashamed, but we should be for the way we have polluted our souls, far beyond the way we have soiled Your creation. Deliver us and redeem us. Thank You, Lord, for Your tender mercy, which endures forever.

Lord, make us into a Christian nation that takes to heart the words "In God we trust." In Jesus' name I pray. Amen. —AH

Season of Gold

And people should eat and drink and enjoy the
fruits of their labor, for these are gifts from God.
ECCLESIASTES 3:13 NLT

The day is as bright and crisp as a freshly picked apple. The leaves on the trees—now bedazzled with autumn jewels—glow and glimmer in the cooling breeze. You've worked so hard, and now it's time to celebrate the harvest. It's time to take pleasure in the fruits of your labor with family and friends all around. Embrace the moment. Enjoy the day. For these are gifts from God!

Then a holy hush sweeps around your table, and you bow your head to thank Him for His many blessings. You pass the heaping bowls of steaming stew, the bread hot from the oven, and the homemade pies. You toast. You sing. You laugh. You fall in love with the season all over again. These are the days—the days of autumn gold—for the making of memories, for the mellowing of hearts, and for the worshipping of our glorious God.

Yes, your heart swells with joy so much that your spirit can hardly contain it. Praise God from whom all blessings flow!

Oh Lord, thank You for this season of autumn gold. Thank You for Your bounty, Your beauty, Your blessings! Amen. —AH

Close beside Me

Even when I walk through the darkest valley,
I will not be afraid, for you are close beside me.
Your rod and your staff protect and comfort me.
PSALM 23:4 NLT

You find lovely woods filled with ferns and wildflowers and quiet mysteries. You decide to take a stroll, even though you know the sun is waning. But the shadows come even more quickly than expected, and a storm comes out of nowhere. You head back, but suddenly no path looks like the right one. Very soon, you know you will be truly lost, soaked through, and chilled to the bone.

Deep tremors run through you as you cry up to the heavens, "Please help me, God! I am scared and all alone. Where do I turn? What do I do now?" Then you hear that still, small voice, "I am close beside you. Do not fear."

After a moment or two, the faintest light glimmers through the trees, one you hadn't seen before in your panic. After a few more steps, you reach a clearing, and you see that it is the lights from a local farmhouse. They are the lights of your deliverance.

Oh Lord, so many times I am too busy to listen to You
until there is a life crisis. Please quiet me so that I can
always hear Your voice. I thank You that You have
promised to stay close beside me through all life's
mountaintop moments and darkest valleys. Amen. —AH

My Cup Overflows!

*You prepare a feast for me in the presence of
my enemies. You honor me by anointing my
head with oil. My cup overflows with blessings.*
PSALM 23:5 NLT

You arrive at the big tea party late since you didn't think it
was all that necessary to get there on time. You show up a
bit shabby too—with mud-coated shoes and hair that's coiffed
like a plucked chicken. You also chose not to bring a thank-you
gift for the hostess, since you thought the event was really about
getting, not giving.

That social situation should make us cringe. But in our
spiritual journey, we all arrive at the Lord's table in the same
way—late, mire-coated, and ungrateful. But the Lord honors
us with blessings anyway—blessings we don't deserve. He
fills our cup to the brim with mercy, love, forgiveness, comfort,
redemption, and fellowship. And that is not to mention all the
other pleasures and gifts, such as the wonder of His creation,
marriage, friendship, and satisfying work.

Oh, how we are loved beyond measure, and how humbled
we are by all these undeserved offerings.

Have you thanked the Lord today for all His good gifts?

*Lord, my cup overflows with blessings.
I thank You and praise You! Amen.* —AH

Doing Life Your Way

*Don't be impressed with your own wisdom. Instead, fear the
LORD and turn away from evil. Then you will have healing for
your body and strength for your bones.*
PROVERBS 3:7–8 NLT

The healthcare industry is a mega money-making business.
There are thousands of ways to spend your cash on various
attempts at getting well. Doctors, hospitals, drugs, alternative
medicine. Some methods work. Some don't. But one way to stay
on the healthiest path in mind, body, and spirit is to flee from evil.

Hmm. On first blush, that sounds more than doable. Why
would a sweet-tempered, cookie-baking, soccer mom want to
pursue evil anyway? But many people want to use their own
wisdom to navigate life. They don't want to respect God. They
want to define good and bad behavior by their own personal
ethics scales. But anything that is not God's way is rebellion—
and disobeying God is evil.

Oh.

Sound kind of harsh? Maybe, but there is also love and
beauty and comfort connected to God's truth. There is freedom
and healing in doing life the Lord's way—and with His supernatural help, His way really is doable.

*Lord, guide me in all things that I might know
Your healing and strength! Amen. —AH*

The Stuff of Poetry

*"Come now, let's settle this," says the LORD. "Though your sins
are like scarlet, I will make them as white as snow. Though
they are red like crimson, I will make them as white as wool."*
ISAIAH 1:18 NLT

Let us write an ode to that beautiful event—when you rush
out to experience the breathless wonder and giddy delight
of that first snowfall. Those bits of feathery lace tickle your face,
as well as your fancy. It's only a matter of time before the snow
angels arrive, the snow ice cream gets made, and the snowball
fights ensue. *Aah*, yes—all things snow. It's the stuff of poetry.

And even more wonderful is the way that drape of frosty
white can cover up our world of grimy streets and junk and
debris. Every winter's first snowfall gives us a hope-filled and
magnificent reminder of that scripture, "Though your sins are
like scarlet, I will make them as white as snow."

Our Lord is so gracious. He came to redress our hearts in
the fresh finery of forgiveness and to make us beautiful again.
Shall we let Him?

*Jesus, I confess my sins to You. As You promise in Your Word,
please make them as white as snow. Amen. —AH*

Big Heart–Big Smiles

*Make sure you don't take things for granted and go slack
in working for the common good; share what you have with
others. God takes particular pleasure in acts of worship—a
different kind of "sacrifice"—that take place in kitchen and
workplace and on the streets.*

HEBREWS 13:16 MSG

People love a good report after they get checked out by the
heart doctor. They also love to feel good deep down in
their hearts too. That last one is easy. Hebrews tells us how. . .

You happen upon an older woman who is stumbling across
a busy street, and after offering her a steadying hand, you help
her find her way. A young mother puts some bread and essentials
back on the counter in the checkout line because she can't afford
them, so you discreetly hand her the money to pay for the extras.
You know your elderly neighbor has just had surgery, and you
take him a few meals to get him by as he recovers.

These acts of kindness can also be acts of worship. They
bring God pleasure. They make our hearts big and our smiles
even bigger. Yes, do good and share what you have. So simple.
So beautiful.

*Dear Lord, show me how to love others as You love them.
Give me a heart as big as Your heart. Amen. —AH*

Real and Deep and Good

The LORD gives strength to his people;
the LORD blesses his people with peace.
PSALM 29:11 NIV

The kids are on summer break and their bickering levels are making you want to hide in the closet—a closet in someone else's house! You turn on the TV and then you switch it off because you can't bear to hear about more riots or media lies or wars or violent rhetoric—or even about the celebrities who are always at each other's throats over yet another affair! You've had it. Peace in the world seems to be as shaky and elusive as a shadow.

You want to holler to the sky, "Lord, have mercy on us all!"

He hears you. Christ does bless His people with peace. He is, after all, the Prince of Peace! Not the brand of peace the world gives, but *His* peace. The kind of peace that springs from our souls and shows on our faces. The kind of peace that cannot be understood in human terms but is nevertheless so real and deep and good that people will ask, "How can you be so settled in such an unsettled world?" Be sure and tell them!

Lord, I am grateful for Your peace, for it is a gift like no other. It permeates me so profoundly that people notice. Show me how to tell them about You, Lord. Amen. —AH

Distilling One's Life

And without faith it is impossible to please God,
because anyone who comes to him must believe that he
exists and that he rewards those who earnestly seek him.
HEBREWS 11:6 NIV

No one really likes to think about one's last hours on earth. It's simply not a pleasant topic to think about or chat about, so people tend to avoid it altogether by staying busy with all manner of life stuff. But dying is a subject everyone must face someday. And when we reach the end of our days, what will become most important?

It won't be all those petty arguments we felt we had to win. Or all those accolades and money and toys we gathered in. Yes, a thousand and one things that we thought were vital will suddenly seem trivial and a colossal waste of energy and time.

What will become significant is how much we loved others. How much we gave of ourselves. And most importantly, did we seek and follow Christ? Did we keep the faith? Did we tell others about His mercy and grace? Now these are the elements of life that make living full of purpose and dying full of hope!

Lord, help me to remember what is important and
what is unimportant in Your kingdom. Amen. —AH

No Matter What!

Even though I walk through the darkest valley,
I will fear no evil, for you are with me;
your rod and your staff, they comfort me.
PSALM 23:4 NIV

If you're a mom, you've most likely known that moment of panic when a child slips away from you in a crowded place. Rattled with fear, you scan your surroundings and search, but you don't see her anywhere. You pray. You try not to panic, but it's useless. You're already wild with terror, thinking of every possible scenario. You ask people to help you search for her. And you pray some more. Your heart didn't know it could beat so hard and fast.

And then you hear the most comforting words imaginable on the loudspeaker about a lost child being found! Soon your lost little darling is running into your arms. No hug ever felt so good. You weep for joy. You thank God.

Those kinds of days can be scary and dark. Those kinds of days we may fear every kind of evil. But know that even then you can trust God. You can cry out to Him. You can be comforted. No matter the dark hour. No matter the evil. No matter what.

God is there.

Oh Lord, thank You that You are always there for me,
night and day. No matter what. Amen. —AH

DAY 338

What We Don't Deserve

*He generously poured out the Spirit upon us through Jesus
Christ our Savior. Because of his grace he made us right in his
sight and gave us confidence that we will inherit eternal life.*

TITUS 3:6–7 NLT

Dear old Uncle Charlie has passed on, and after attending
his funeral, you discover that he was much richer than
anyone ever knew. *And* he has left a large portion of his wealth
to you! Oh wow.

You are shocked. You are happy. But after the money is
sitting in your bank account, you are anxious and shadowed
with guilt. Why?

No matter how much time you spent with Uncle Charlie or
how much you loved him, you still feel undeserving. It's easy to
think, *I didn't earn this, so I can't accept this or ever enjoy this.*

Way too often that is how we feel about Christ's grace—His
gift of salvation and our eternal inheritance in the kingdom of
God. But grace is by definition a gift of kindness that is unearned.
Even though we certainly don't deserve Christ's gifts, we can
indeed accept them and enjoy them to the fullest measure!

*Lord, I thank You for Your gift of salvation and eternal life.
I love You so dearly for all You've done for me! Amen.* —AH

A Driven and Jittery Bunch

There remains therefore a rest for the people of God.
For he who has entered His rest has himself also
ceased from his works as God did from His.
HEBREWS 4:9–10 NKJV

We humans are a jittery bunch. We work until we are too exhausted to sleep. We worry until we are too wired to work. We do three things on our to-do list and then add thirty more. We race around with vital tasks only to later call them a waste of time. Basically, when it comes to time—like in everything else—we are a mess!

Wouldn't it be wonderful to rest—truly rest and not be so driven and jittery? To have a day to reflect, to pray, to eat simply, to play, to laugh, to nap, to soak in a bubble bath, to stroll, to sit on the porch swing a spell, and to let the Lord speak to us through His Word?

We do have that opportunity. That special day. It's been given to us, and we're expected to use it. It's called the Sabbath. God rested after making His creation, and He expects us to do the same after our weekly labor. Shall we not partake of this very pleasant and very necessary cup?

Lord, teach me how to relax and refresh on Sunday,
and not use Your holy day to play catch-up
with all my labors. Amen. —AH

Every Season under Heaven

*There is a time for everything, and a
season for every activity under the heavens.*
ECCLESIASTES 3:1 NIV

Embracing every season of life isn't always easy, especially as one grows older. People find themselves saying, "I want all the good years back. I want to look young and pretty again. I want to be able to control my life again, or at least to be able to control my bladder!"

Growing old is part of living in this fallen world. Aching joints and memory loss and the deterioration of one's reflection are far from pleasant. Most of the time, it's no laughing matter. Even when we eat right and exercise, time will win in the end. We just can't go on forever trying to force a spring life into an autumn season. Wow, that sounds depressing. What can be done?

Find comfort in God's truths. With the Lord's help, we can embrace all the various seasons of our lives. He promises to give us His strength no matter what comes. Know that He will never forsake us. Ever. And when the time comes for us to enjoy the beauties of heaven, know that He awaits your arrival with open arms.

*Lord, thank You that I can come to You,
no matter the season of my life. Amen.* —AH

Who Do You Worship?

"Worthy are You, our Lord and God, to receive
the glory and the honor and the power; for You
created all things, and because of Your will they
exist, and were created and brought into being."
REVELATION 4:11 AMP

Want that deep-down feeling of well-being? Absolutely. Want joy and peace so real you can't stop smiling? Sure! Then worship the living God, for He is the only one who deserves our praise. It is God who brought everything into existence—including you. To praise Him is to be humble and good and wise.

The enemy—Satan—wants us to worship anything and everything but the living God. We are subtly and not-so-subtly encouraged through every dark means possible to offer our reverence and adoration and love to something or someone else. So, who do you worship? Other gods? False prophets that the Bible warns against? Nature? Cash? Power? Celebrity? Beauty? A life of pleasure? Yourself?

According to Isaiah 9:6 (NKJV), "His name will be called Wonderful, Counselor, Mighty God, Everlasting Father, Prince of Peace." May we never allow pride to blind us from the truth—God is God, and He alone is worthy of glory and honor and praise!

Oh Lord, I worship and adore You. You are
indeed worthy of my worship! Amen. —AH

Love Our Enemies?

*"You have heard the law that says, 'Love your neighbor'
and hate your enemy. But I say, love your enemies!
Pray for those who persecute you! In that way, you will
be acting as true children of your Father in heaven.
For he gives his sunlight to both the evil and the good,
and he sends rain on the just and the unjust alike."*
MATTHEW 5:43–45 NLT

Oh no, it's *that* woman again—the one who gives you the hives when you just hear her stilettoes clattering down the hallway toward your office. The woman you secretly named Komodo. You know that soon every bit of your Christianity is going to be stretched to its limits. The moment arrives when the dragon lady walks into the room, and her fiery, reptilian gaze drifts over to you. Then you do what you always do—you choke on your saliva.

Wait, did someone say we are to love our enemies? Even pray for them? Oh dear. Maybe that's simply asking too much of us feeble humans. But then anyone can love the lovable. Christ asks us to take love a step further, and yes, to do what seems impossible. If we want to live a peace-filled life that pleases our Lord, then with His supernatural help we can learn how to love people who are unlovable—and yes, even the dragons.

*Holy Spirit, teach me how to love all
people as You love them. Amen. —AH*

The Puzzle

And do not be conformed to this world [any longer with its superficial values and customs], but be transformed and progressively changed [as you mature spiritually] by the renewing of your mind [focusing on godly values and ethical attitudes], so that you may prove [for yourselves] what the will of God is, that which is good and acceptable and perfect [in His plan and purpose for you].

ROMANS 12:2 AMP

Have you ever gotten so frustrated with a jigsaw puzzle that you started to try to make the pieces fit where they didn't belong? You think, *I will just give this corner a mash with my thumb. Hmm. Guess I need to pound it a bit. Okay, maybe I need a hammer!* But then you realize that your box is also full of stray random pieces that were never meant to fit. Oh dear.

Isn't that what we try to do with our lives in today's culture? We get so caught up in the way the world is doing everything, we forget about God's way. But in the end, when a Christian tries to fit into a worldly mind-set, it's going to be like those puzzle pieces.

Maybe God has a different picture for your life—a more beautiful one. Ask Him, and He will tell you all about His plan and purpose for you. And you can be assured, every piece will fit right!

Holy Spirit, show me Your good and perfect will for my life. Amen. —AH

Every Little Detail

The LORD directs the steps of the godly.
He delights in every detail of their lives.
PSALM 37:23 NLT

Your dear friend, Rita, invites you to lunch, and it's the usual. You hug. You laugh. You cry a little. You share your hearts. But sometimes when you offer too much of your life, you can see that glazing-over thing in her eyes. She wants to listen, bless her heart, but alas, even dear Rita is human and can't last all day with the minutiae of your life without falling into a coma. So, you suddenly find that your friend is changing the subject and even talking about leaving the café early!

You find yourself secretly sighing and wishing you had a friend who really, truly cared about every little thing concerning your life.

You do indeed have a dear friend just like that. The Lord makes it clear in His Word that He cares about all the big stuff in our world, the little stuff, and everything in between.

So find comfort in the friendship of Jesus. Talk to Him. He is ever listening, ever caring, ever loving.

Lord, thank You that You care for me so tenderly and delight in all the details of my life. I love You too! Amen. —AH

When Even the Day Goes Dark

"When you go through deep waters, I will be with you.
When you go through rivers of difficulty, you will not
drown. When you walk through the fire of oppression,
you will not be burned up; the flames will not consume you."

ISAIAH 43:2 NLT

You wake up in bed startled and frightened. You realize you're lying there in a pool of sweat after some horrific nightmare. And then the ugly truth hits you: it wasn't just a dream—it's real. It might be the sudden death of a loved one. Or the loss of your home and all your possessions. Or the severing of a lifelong friendship. Or false accusations that ruin your career and reputation. Our fallen world along with the enemy of our souls are capable of creating every kind of evil mischief.

Yes, even when the day goes dark with misery, God is there. No matter how deep the waters of difficulty are, no matter how hot the fires of oppression, with God's help, you will not be consumed. You will prevail. Take heart. Know.

Oh Lord, I am falling into fear and despair.
Please help me deal with all my travails. They are
too much for me. You are the only one who can
rescue me! In Jesus' name I pray. Amen. —AH

Joy in All the Little Gifts

*Praise the LORD from the earth, you creatures of the ocean
depths, fire and hail, snow and clouds, wind and weather that
obey him, mountains and all hills, fruit trees and all cedars, wild
animals and all livestock, small scurrying animals and birds.*
PSALM 148:7–10 NLT

God has given us such a vast creation, it's impossible to take it
all in. So much to explore, to delight in, and to praise Him for!
But some days we can play it small and concentrate on the
smaller blessings that God has gifted us with. Have you ever
taken the time to study a snowflake under a microscope or a
spider's web glistening with dew? How about the tiny wildflowers
peeking out from a cluster of rocks? Have you noticed the mega
cuteness of a duckling or a lamb or a newborn bunny? Have you
ever swooned while biting into a lush sweet apricot or sighed
over a cooling breeze on a hot day? Never forget the spray of
colors as the sun gives its last hurrah for the day or the chorus of
the bugs and the songs of the night birds. So much to experience
and take pleasure in. Where shall we begin?

*Oh Lord God Almighty, I praise You and thank You for
Your splendiferous handiwork. What masterpieces of
ingenuity and creativity and beauty they are. I am
in perfect awe of all You do! Amen. —AH*

That Peaceful Kind of Living

If it is possible, as far as it depends on you,
live at peace with everyone.
ROMANS 12:18 NIV

The kids are screaming at each other. After calming them down, you try to relax by reading some social media posts only to discover a bickering bonanza escalating out of control—and among your dearest friends! Your church is suddenly on the brink of a split over things that are beyond petty, and the evening news greets you with stories of war and violence and hatred like you've never seen before. You too feel like you're on the brink of something—and you're praying it's not a nervous breakdown.

Maybe you could put on some classical music, have a warm slice of chicken pot pie, and then take a nap. Those are all good things, but not the big answer. What does Christ say about peace? If possible, the Lord would like us to live in harmony.

So, what have you personally done to be a peacemaker in your home, your church, your workplace, your neighborhood, and your world? If you want to experience some serious, peaceful kind of living, it needs to begin with you—and all of us.

Lord, show me how to be an instrument of Your peace. Our world needs You now, and I need You too! Amen. —AH

Gifts of the Heart

We have different gifts, according to the grace given to each of us. If your gift is prophesying, then prophesy in accordance with your faith; if it is serving, then serve; if it is teaching, then teach; if it is to encourage, then give encouragement; if it is giving, then give generously; if it is to lead, do it diligently; if it is to show mercy, do it cheerfully.

ROMANS 12:6–8 NIV

It's the big day—your birthday—and after eating a gooey wad of three-layered cake, you open several impressive-looking gifts. Wow, such generous gifts and wisely chosen too—everything you needed, in fact. You've never been so happy. Then you promptly take all those pretty gifts and stuff them into the attic where they will collect dust and never be seen again.

Wait. Something isn't right here.

That is not at all what you would do with those valuable and much-loved presents. You would use them. Enjoy them. Share them. God gives all of us gifts from His heart, and if we don't use the many talents and abilities He's given us, that attic scenario shows us just how we are treating His generosity.

So, use the gifts. Enjoy the gifts. Share the gifts. The world will be a better place because of them!

Lord, I thank You for the many talents and skills You've given me. Please show me how to use them for Your purpose and glory. Amen. —AH

A Carefree Life

So be content with who you are, and don't put on airs.
God's strong hand is on you; he'll promote you at the right
time. Live carefree before God; he is most careful with you.
1 PETER 5:6–7 MSG

The pig says to the giraffe, "I've always wanted to be a long-necked giraffe. . .an animal that is tall, slim, and can eat all the time." So the pig tries on a giraffe costume, and she gives it a go. But all the pigs are flopping around in the mud, chortling. Why? Because a pig can't be a giraffe. She's a pig.

And that is how ridiculous it is to put on airs before man and God—to be what we are not—not to mention how unmercifully and unnecessarily stressful it is. This is just one good example of the ways we give up living carefree with God. We traumatize ourselves over our "look," our social standing, our long-ago forgiven sins, our dreams and goals, our bills and bank accounts—and so it goes on and on and on.

Remember as a Christian, God's strong hand is on you. He is most careful with you because He loves you so dearly. Relax and let God help you to simply "be."

Lord, show me how to live a carefree life, knowing
You have everything under control. Amen. —AH

A Few Good Friends

The man of too many friends [chosen indiscriminately] will be broken in pieces and come to ruin, but there is a [true, loving] friend who [is reliable and] sticks closer than a brother.
PROVERBS 18:24 AMP

Life is better when you have a good friend to share it with. God gave mankind the gift of friendship—that way we can help, comfort, encourage, support, challenge, inspire, and love each other through our lives.

So if having a bosom buddy is so important to a good life, how does one go about making a few good ones? Ask God for help. Tell Him to send you a few good friends. And then ask Him to teach you how to be a loyal and kind companion in return. It's easier to gather in friends than to maintain them long-term. It's easier to have a lot of friendly acquaintances than to have a couple of "serious" friends you can call during a two a.m. crisis. That more serious kind of friend is like family—sticking to you like a sister. She is pure gold and a keeper. When it comes to friendship skills, are you a keeper too?

Oh Lord, my friends have come and gone over the years. I need You to show me how to make godly friends and how to be a godly friend in return. In Jesus' name I pray. Amen. —AH

Glorious Reminder of All Things New

So we have stopped evaluating others from a human point of view. At one time we thought of Christ merely from a human point of view. How differently we know him now! This means that anyone who belongs to Christ has become a new person. The old life is gone; a new life has begun!
2 CORINTHIANS 5:16–17 NLT

Spring brings out the muse in us all. We want to write and sing about the blossoming flowers, the vibrant green shoots pushing their way up out of the brambles, and the baby animals being birthed in little burrows. The bright warming sun makes us want to leap for joy—even if only in our hearts. Yes, spring, that sweet season of surprises—when smiles come more easily after the long winter and hope flows like the melting snow.

Oh, and what a boisterous and beautiful reminder of all things new, including the way Christ can change us into new people. We can be released of that old, sullied winter coat and burst forth with a new spiritual covering. Dressed for the promise of eternity!

*Praise You, God, from whom all blessings flow—
including spring and the reminder of all things new!
In Jesus' name I pray. Amen. —AH*

Love Has Arrived!

"For God so [greatly] loved and dearly prized the world,
that He [even] gave His [One and] only begotten Son,
so that whoever believes and trusts in Him [as Savior]
shall not perish, but have eternal life.
JOHN 3:16 AMP

The nurse hands you your wriggling, cooing newborn baby, and the moment he wraps his finger around yours, you're a goner. You tear up and your heart feels like it will squeeze with such intense joy, you think you might just die of too much love. How can it be? How can an ordinary person feel such extraordinary emotions? Unfathomable. And over-the-top glorious. It's a big beautiful case of baby love, and you've got it bad.

Hard to imagine, but God loves you even more than you love that precious newborn. He loves you so greatly that He sent His only Son to rescue you from this lost and heartbroken world. He came for all of us, but He also came just for you. Imagine.

Yes, love is here because God has arrived. His name is Jesus. So, take heart. Embrace the living Christ and all He's done for you.

Oh Lord Jesus, thank You for loving me more
than I could hope for or imagine—more than
I deserve. I love You too! Amen. —AH

I Choose Love!

*Get rid of all bitterness, rage, anger, harsh words,
and slander, as well as all types of evil behavior. Instead,
be kind to each other, tenderhearted, forgiving one another,
just as God through Christ has forgiven you.*
EPHESIANS 4:31–32 NLT

At times loving humanity is far from easy, but with God's help, it is possible. Hate, on the other hand, comes naturally to us in this sinful world. But hate has tremendous consequences. There is a vast ripple effect across the world, and the damage to our own souls and health is devastating.

We shouldn't love the evil deeds of mankind, but just as God forgave you and me, offering forgiveness to the sinner is wisdom. Yes, with Christ's love comes healing in the mind, body, and spirit, and that ripple effect of His redeeming love will also help heal the nations.

Shall we then choose love? That phrase will become a beautiful thing as we live it out daily, and it will also look good monogrammed on the front of a hat—I Choose Love!

*Lord, I admit that when I see the evil deeds committed through-
out the world and even in our own country, I am tempted to
hate certain people and groups. Show me how to hate wicked
behavior without hating those who promote it. Amen.* —AH

Remarkable Secrets

"Ask me and I will tell you remarkable secrets
you do not know about things to come."
JEREMIAH 33:3 NLT

You only tell secrets to your very closest friends, those whom you love and whom you trust with the information. And you don't tell a friend anything sensitive or too close to the heart while she's on the run or when she doesn't seem all that interested. You wait.

In the Old Testament, God told Jeremiah that if he asked, God would tell him remarkable secrets. We might think that those kinds of miraculous happenings between the Lord and His people could only happen during ancient times or epic events. But God never changes, and so He also reaches out to us with invitations of intimacy, as He did with Jeremiah.

God welcomes us to commune with Him. To share our lives with Him. To embark on that glorious and supernatural adventure called prayer. Spend time with the Lord, give Him the firstfruits of your day, the best part of your time. Show Him how much you love Him and that you not only trust Him, but that He can trust you to be faithful. Ask Him to share the secrets of His kingdom with you. And then wait respectfully, earnestly, and eagerly for His replies.

Father in heaven, I know I come to You steadily with my
requests. But I also want to spend time with You as my
Redeemer and my friend. In Jesus' name I pray. Amen. —AH

Too Frazzled to Dazzle

*Three different times I begged the Lord to take it away.
Each time he said, "My grace is all you need. My power
works best in weakness." So now I am glad to boast about
my weaknesses, so that the power of Christ can work through
me. That's why I take pleasure in my weaknesses, and in the
insults, hardships, persecutions, and troubles that I suffer for
Christ. For when I am weak, then I am strong.*

2 Corinthians 12:8–10 nlt

Do you wake up so frazzled some mornings that you can't even out-dazzle a paper bag?

Your boss thinks you're an idiot, and your coworkers make fun of you because they know you follow Christ. You can't seem to ever pay off your credit card, and if that's not enough, your big toe is throbbing with something called gout! You are drained body and soul. You don't just need a soft mattress for a nap—you need a cave to hibernate in!

There's good news for everyone who finds themselves weak and worn out.

Christ's power is made perfect in our weaknesses. What a biblical paradox! We can even take pleasure in these hardships, knowing it is not about us. This really takes off the pressure. After all, God is the one who created this world, so He is the only one who can truly dazzle it with His power and presence!

*Lord, help me to always remember that when
I am weak, then I am strong. Amen. —AH*

Do You Love Me?

The third time he said to him, "Simon son of John, do you love me?" Peter was hurt because Jesus asked him the third time, "Do you love me?" He said, "Lord, you know all things; you know that I love you." Jesus said, "Feed my sheep."
JOHN 21:17 NIV

You said you fully understood the plan of salvation. Great. You acknowledged your sin. You asked God to forgive you. You accepted Christ as the Lord and Savior of your life. Wonderful! This is the most important decision you'll ever make. But one more thing—did you tell Jesus, "I love You"?

Perhaps you thought those words of love were assumed. Or maybe it's easier to love a child, a husband, a beloved pet, a teacher, or a friend than the Creator of the universe. And yet, Christ asks not only Peter, but He asks us, "Do you love me?"

How have you responded? Have you told the Lord how much you appreciate all that He has done for you? His sacrifice? His promise of life eternal? His daily provisions? Have you said those simple but profound words—*I love You*? After all, since God is the author of love, why wouldn't He desire it in return?

Lord, You are my most beloved friend, and with all my heart and soul, I love You! Amen. —AH

Mercy Remembered

*"Therefore, I tell you, her many sins have been
forgiven—as her great love has shown.
But whoever has been forgiven little loves little."*
LUKE 7:47 NIV

If we could make a list of all our mistakes through the years—all
the miscellaneous transgressions, little white lies, some big
black lies, questionable mischief, dark thoughts, selfish deeds,
etc.—we'd be put at risk for carpal tunnel syndrome!

You might think, *But I'm forgiven now. I don't need to ever
revisit all that junk again, right?* Yes! We don't need to keep
asking forgiveness for the same sin over and over and over.
But to remember where we've been and how far we've come
with the power of the Holy Spirit, and how much has been
forgiven by the mercy and goodness of Christ, is a good thing.
If we know we've been guilty, we also know we have a lot to
be thankful for.

Jesus said, "Whoever has been forgiven little loves little."
Does that mean we should go sin up a storm so we can be
forgiven much and love even more? Never. But most likely our
list of sins is already pretty extensive, so a deeply thankful heart
for all the forgiveness would not only be pleasing to the Lord;
it would be healing to our souls.

*Thank You, Lord, for forgiving my many transgressions.
Your mercy and compassion never fail! Amen.* —AH

By Still Waters

*The LORD is my shepherd; I have all that I need. He lets
me rest in green meadows; he leads me beside peaceful
streams. He renews my strength. He guides me along
right paths, bringing honor to his name.*
PSALM 23:1–3 NLT

There is this "by still waters" kind of place. It's a special spot where you can go and walk for a while and sit for a while, far from this maddening, crazy world—where there is no turmoil, no tears, and no fear.

Jesus is with you, and you know in your soul that life is at its best when He is by your side. You take hold of His hand, and you let Him lead you to a green meadow radiant with the sun and then by a pretty stream that is burbling its way down the hillside. You share your heart and your life with Him. You come to trust Him and love Him like no other. *Aah*, yes, you can hear yourself breathe in this place, and little by little, your strength is renewed.

For a lifetime of those heavenly "by still waters" moments—just follow the Shepherd.

*Lord, when I am with You, I have all that I need.
Stay ever by my side. Amen.* —AH

Big, Bold, and Beautiful

You can make many plans,
but the LORD's purpose will prevail.
PROVERBS 19:21 NLT

Mankind loves to make plans. We scribble notes all day long on our to-do lists. We attend seminars on how to reach goals better and faster. Plans are good. Otherwise we'd be adrift in life. And good and godly goals can wake us up with a smile and put us to sleep with satisfaction.

But do we ask God about the plans He has for us? Or do we create elaborate and detailed goals to hand to the Lord only for His stamp of approval? No matter how elegant and clever and godly our dreams, we need to make sure they are in alignment with what the Lord would want for us.

Hmm. Sound too constraining? Too boring? Never. Not when you're allowing the Creator of the universe—the one who designed the sun, moon, and stars—to help you design your dreams. They will be bigger, bolder, and more beautiful than anything you could imagine.

Allow God to join you in the planning phase of all your days. You'll never regret it. Ever.

Oh Lord, I'm sorry that too many times I get ahead of
You and just go my own way. I have failed too many
times doing it my way. Teach me how to rely on You
for everything, including my future! Amen. —AH

More Love Than Lectures

*Anxious hearts are very heavy,
but a word of encouragement does wonders!*
PROVERBS 12:25 TLB

Even as Christians, sometimes we can be unexpectedly slammed with bouts of depression, sickness, and grief. Has your heart ever been so utterly weary that you could barely get out of bed in the morning? You are not alone.

During those times, what would be the most helpful thing someone could do for you? What would be the salve that might start your healing? Probably not a lecture. And probably not an exhaustive list of personal experiences meant to prove that what you're going through isn't heartbreaking enough to merit a listening ear and a kind word. Yikes!

According to Proverbs 12:25, encouragement will do wonders for a heavy heart. Yes, it will spread as smoothly as Irish butter on biscuits straight from the oven. And it will go down just fine.

When people are going through difficult patches, don't we want to be the ones to support and inspire too? Wouldn't we all sleep better—more soundly, more sweetly—knowing how we listened and encouraged someone through life's hardest times?

*God, help me to remember to give my family and friends
more love than lectures. Help me to arrive with the elixir of
encouragement! In Jesus' holy name I pray. Amen. —AH*

What Appears Impossible

Looking at them, Jesus said, "With people [as far as it depends on them] it is impossible, but not with God; for all things are possible with God."
MARK 10:27 AMP

The world can be like a dark and miserable scene from Charles Dickens's *Bleak House*. Unattainable dreams. Irreparable relationships. Irresolvable problems. Unworkable jobs. Uncontrollable kids. Inconsolable grief. Some days it can feel like a never-ending black flood of the "impossibles."

Yes, many times this fallen existence appears to be hopeless. But when the world confounds us, God can unravel the mysteries. When the world is steeped in hate, God can cover it with His love. When the world hands us sorrow, God can bring comfort and healing. When the world laughs at our God-given dreams, He can find a way. And most importantly, because of Christ's work on the cross, what appears unredeemable can be redeemed. The Lord can replace hopelessness with grace, forgiveness, and eternal life!

Yes, with God's supernatural power, He can move mountains, because He is the one who made those mountains. If He can speak something into existence, then He has power over it, to move it, to free it, to make it all that it needs to be. And He has the power to help you. That is the kind of God we worship. Trust Him now. Trust Him always. . . .

Thank You, Lord, that You are the God of possibility! I will put my trust in You. In Jesus' name I pray. Amen. —AH

Pray Like You Mean It

*Therefore, confess your sins to one another [your false steps,
your offenses], and pray for one another, that you may be
healed and restored. The heartfelt and persistent prayer of
a righteous man (believer) can accomplish much [when put
into action and made effective by God—it is dynamic
and can have tremendous power].*

JAMES 5:16 AMP

When a friend says casually, "I'll be praying for you," you'd
like to think well of her, but in your heart of hearts, you
can't help but wonder, *Will you really pray for me? For real?*
Or has that phrase become too much like the greeting "How
ya doing?" which no longer seems to need a reply because it
is just considered to be something nice to say?

But when the Lord asks us to pray for each other, He wants
us to pray like we mean it. After all, James tells us that the earnest
and persistent prayer of a believer can have tremendous power!
It is dynamic! Prayer can change the course of human history,
and it can change a life forever. . . .

*Lord, please show me how to pray with all my heart.
Help me to have true compassion for people and their needs,
and may that heartfelt spirit be reflected in all my prayers.
Thank You for hearing me, Jesus. Amen. —AH*

With You or At You

*Always be humble and gentle. Be patient
with each other, making allowance for
each other's faults because of your love.*
EPHESIANS 4:2 NLT

Your little party watches a snarky video, and people howl with laughter. Well, not everyone is laughing. Some people are cringing. And some people leave the room hurt.

Was the video a bit callous in the way it targeted certain individuals or groups? Humor can be healing and helpful, and a merry heart is good medicine, but laughing *at* someone is not the same thing as laughing *with* them.

All our humor, all our words and actions, should be filtered through Ephesians 4:2. We always expect people to treat us with dignity and gentleness and grace, so isn't that just how we should treat others? Matthew 7:12 (NIV) reads, "So in everything, do to others what you would have them do to you, for this sums up the Law and the Prophets." But the Golden Rule seems to be a long forgotten way to live. With the Lord's help, though, it can be revived in our daily lives, so that even one's humor can be helpful and healing and can glorify God.

As Christians, may we show the world how to live and love and, yes, how to laugh!

*Lord, may I be kind and gentle and patient
to all my fellow sojourners. Amen.* —AH

Where Clocks Mean Nothing

But you must not forget this one thing, dear friends:
A day is like a thousand years to the Lord,
and a thousand years is like a day.
2 PETER 3:8 NLT

Stress comes in many forms, and some of it is related to time. There is simply not enough of it. We leave some conversations half-finished. The pretty craft projects we promise to finish are still in the bottom drawer—somewhere! The piles of dirty clothes and dishes never seem to diminish. We wonder when we can sit down and have a good cry. Or a good belly laugh. Nope. You checked your schedule. You're officially too busy for either one.

But time from God's point of view is very different from our vantage point. When time goes on forever, nothing needs to be rushed. There will always be time for everything under the sun. We have so much to look forward to—time with no end—free from our messy, aging, fragile, corroding bodies!

When we face suffering of any kind in this life, take heart. God has overcome it all. He has the victory, even over the constraints of time. We will be escorted into a kingdom where clocks mean nothing but love means everything!

I thank You, God, that heaven awaits me,
where we can be together for all time! Amen. —AH

An Affair of the Heart

But God showed his great love for us by sending
Christ to die for us while we were still sinners.
ROMANS 5:8 NLT

Some people think the Bible is more or less a book of rules on how to live a better life. But the Bible is so much more than that! It is also a book of living words, inspired by God Himself and offered as a gift to us—His beloved. Yes, it shows us how we can be made right with God again through Christ. It reveals the essence of what we were meant to be and how we're to live.

But the Bible is also a love story—revealing God's love affair of the heart with all mankind. Not just a sweeping, faraway, impersonal condescension to humans, but an intimate and dear love affair of the heart—with each of us—with you.

So, how much does God love us? Enough to be born from a woman like all of us. To grow up in a family. Breathe our air. Sip our soup. Laugh and eat and learn and play. To not only *know* our pain but to *feel* it. And ultimately, He loved us enough to die for all of us. Such love. Can we even take it in? Probably not.

But we can say yes to it.

I say yes, Lord! May You and I live a life of love
together, until You take me home. Amen. —AH

A Love Note from the Authors

Marian and I sincerely hope you have been inspired, challenged, and comforted by the devotions in *By Still Waters*. The creation of this book was a remarkable journey, to say the least. We had profound and intimate moments when we felt the Savior drawing very near to us. We had moments when we felt the sting of the enemy as we encountered discouragements and illnesses during the many months of writing. But never did we lose hope. The Lord sustained us, nourished us, and loved us right to the finish line. And He will always do the same for you.

Yours in Christ,
Anita Higman & Marian Leslie

We leave you now with a beloved blessing from the book of Numbers.

"May the LORD bless you
and protect you.
May the LORD smile on you
and be gracious to you.
May the LORD show you his favor
and give you his peace."
NUMBERS 6:24–26 NLT

About the Authors

Bestselling and award-winning author **Anita Higman** has fifty books published. She's been a Barnes & Noble "Author of the Month" for Houston and has a BA in the combined fields of speech communication, psychology, and art. A few of Anita's favorite things are fairy-tale castles, steampunk clothes, traveling through Europe, exotic teas like orchid and heather, romantic movies, and laughing with her friends. Feel free to drop by Anita's website at anitahigman.com or connect with her on her Facebook Reader Page at www.facebook.com/AuthorAnitaHigman. She would love to hear from you!

Marian Leslie is a freelance writer and editor from Ohio who loves most animals (but not rodents of any size, unusual or otherwise), most food (but not sushi), and all the books of the Bible (especially Philippians). She is a confessed Dickens fan and loves curling up with a good book, a hot cup of tea, and a warm woolen blanket and pretending she lives in Victorian England. Marian is delighted to be collaborating with her writing partner and friend, Anita Higman, with whom she has written a series of devotional books.

Scripture Index

Old Testament